S.S.F. PUBLIC LIBRARY
WEST ORANGE AVENUE

SOUTH SAN FRANCISCO LIBRARY

T3-BHD-903

SSF

IMPERIAL SKIRMISHES

Books by the same author:

IN ENGLISH

The Forgotten Colony: A History of the English-Speaking Communities in Argentina
(Literature of Latin America, Buenos Aires, 1999)

Goodbye Buenos Aires
(Shoestring Press, Nottingham, 1999)

Committed Observer: Memoirs of a Journalist
(John Libbey, London, 1995)

Point of Arrival: Observations Made on an Extended Visit
(Pluto Press, London, 1992)

After the Despots: Latin American Views and Interviews
(Bloomsbury, London, 1991)

A State of Fear: Memories of Argentina's Nightmare
(Eland Books, London, 1986)

Small Wars You May Have Missed
(Junction Books, London, 1983)

The Forgotten Colony: A History of the English-Speaking Communities in Argentina
(Hutchinson, London, 1981)

Portrait of an Exile
(Junction Books, London, 1981)

The Press in Argentina, 1973-1978
(Writers & Scholars Educational Trust, London, 1979)

IN SPANISH

Memoria del miedo
(Editorial de Belgrano, Buenos Aires, 1999)

Arthur Koestler, periodismo y política. Apuntes de una vida
(Editorial de Belgrano, Buenos Aires, 1999)

Pequeñas Guerras Británicas en América Latina. Malvina, crónica personal
(Editorial de Belgrano, Buenos Aires,1998)

Goodbye Buenos Aires
(Ediciones de la Flor, Buenos Aires, 1997)

Rosas visto por los ingleses
(reedición)
(Editorial de Belgrano, Buenos Aires, 1997)

En blanco y negro. Represión, censura y olvido en Sudáfrica
(Tempestad, Barcelona, 1992)

De Perón a Videla. Argentina 1955-76
(Legasa, Buenos Aires, 1989)

Retrato de un exilio
(Sudamericana, Buenos Aires, 1985)

Pequeñas guerras británicas en América latina
(Legasa, Buenos Aires, 1985)

Así vieron a Rosas los ingleses, 1829-1852
(Rodolfo Alonso, Buenos Aires, 1980)

La independencia de Venezuela vista por The Times
(Libros de Hoy del Diario de Caracas, 1980)

La censura en el mundo. Antología
(Libros de Hoy del Diario de Caracas, 1980)

Arthur Koestler, del cero al infinito
(Altalena, Madrid, 1978)

Lancelot Holland. Viaje al Plata en 1807
(Eudeba, Buenos Aires, 1976)

Tiempo de violencia. Argentina 1972-73
(Granica, Buenos Aires, 1974)

Tiempo de tragedia. Argentina 1966-71
(La Flor, Buenos Aires, 1972)

POETRY
Se habla spanglés
(Ediciones Lumière. Buenos Aires, 1998)

Day to Day
(Buenos Aires, 1973)

Se habla spanglés
(Ediciones de la Flor, Buenos Aires, 1972)

S.S.F. PUBLIC LIBRARY
WEST ORANGE AVENUE

IMPERIAL SKIRMISHES

War and Gunboat Diplomacy in Latin America

Andrew Graham-Yooll

OLIVE
BRANCH
PRESS

This edition first published in 2002 by

INTERLINK BOOKS
An imprint of Interlink Publishing Group, Inc.
99 Seventh Avenue • Brooklyn, New York 11215 and
46 Crosby Street • Northampton, Massachusetts 01060
www.interlinkbooks.com

© Andrew Graham-Yooll, 1983, 2002
First published in 1983 as *Small Wars You May Have Missed*

All rights reserved. The whole of this work, including all text and illustra-
tions, is protected by copyright. No parts of this work may be loaded,
stored, manipulated, reproduced, or transmitted in any form or by any
means, electronic or mechanical, including photocopying and recording,
or by any information, storage or retrieval system without prior written
permission from the publisher, on behalf of the copyright owner.

Library of Congress Cataloging-in-Publication Data

Graham-Yooll, Andrew.
Imperial skirmishes : war and gunboat diplomacy in Latin America / By
Andrew Graham-Yooll.
p. cm.
Includes bibliographical references and index.
ISBN 1-56656-448-4 (pbk.)
1. British--South America--History. 2. Europeans--South
America--History. 3. Europe--Relations--South America. 4. South
America--Relations--Europe. 5. Great Britain--Military policy.
6. Europe--Military policy. 7. Intervention (International law)
8. South America--History, Military. I. Title.
F2239.B8 G725 2002
980--dc21

2002005099

Cover design: Baseline Arts
Cover image: South American Pictures

Printed and bound in Canada by Webcom

To request our complete 40-page full-color catalog,
please call us toll free at **1-800-238-LINK**, visit our
website at **www.interlinkbooks.com**, or write to
Interlink Publishing
46 Crosby Street, Northampton, MA 01060
e-mail: info@interlinkbooks.com

CONTENTS

FOREWORD

Time passes and small wars fade into the quainter reaches of history. But those who recall the bizarre Argentinian seizure of the Falkland/Malvinas Islands and their recapture by the British in 1982 remember Andrew Graham-Yooll. As editor of the English-language *Buenos Aires Herald*, he had been an unrelenting critic of Argentina's military dictatorship and of General Galtieri's seizure of the islands. Like many brave journalists, he was arrested and driven into exile, where he offered invaluable advice to those of us writing about the war from afar. He understood Argentina and he understood Britain. Not many did both.

As an Anglo-Argentinian, his own story is similar to that which he tells in this book, of a periodic falling out between Britain and South America. The continent is one of which Britons know little, despite their large and continuous contribution to its development in the nineteenth century, both by immigration and by investment and trade. More controversially, Britain together with other North Atlantic states, found itself drawn into one half-hearted imperial incident after another, most of them ending in bloodshed and expense. These form the core of Mr Graham-Yooll's narrative.

Since the end of the period with which the book deals, the West has rediscovered its old taste for such intervention. It has found new clothes in which to dress the old imperialist body, those of humanitarian relief, guarding regional stability, protecting trade and fighting "wars" on drugs, crime and terrorism. To Europeans and Americans these are all wars in the promotion of justice. To those on whose territory they are fought, they can seem nothing but empire reborn. The quest for El Dorado is recreated as the great humanitarian crusade.

Graham-Yooll's history of Western adventurism in one continent is essentially a tale of folly, but it is also a warning. Those who ignore history are condemned to repeat its mistakes.

Simon Jenkins
London

PREFACE

The politics of the twentieth century were marked by small regional conflicts, which in the end perhaps had as much influence on local events as did the great conflagrations that were the First and Second World Wars. This book was written in the wake of one of those small wars which, with hindsight, helped Argentina arrive in the twentieth century when it was almost over.

But the volume was originally devised as an entertainment on events largely belonging in the nineteenth century and which had been long overtaken by much more serious situations in the twentieth. It was largely intended as a look back on colonial policies and practices in the light of a world that had moved on. The research into journalistic and some primary sources had come in part out of a more extended project, which was the history of the British in Argentina—a story that spans three centuries.

When a first edition of the book was published in London in 1983, the brief war between Britain and Argentina over the Falklands/Malvinas Islands was fresh in everybody's minds and, given the academic, military and journalistic study of that conflict, a chapter on it to close a book which offered observations on the lighter side of disputes, seemed out of context and even—given the casualties lists on both sides and Argentina's recent history—in bad taste.

There was a personal reason for avoiding the most recent incident. It had been my professional good fortune to be able to report on the conflict as *The Guardian* (London) correspondent in Buenos Aires, the city in which I had been born and which I had left as an exile in 1976. In 1983, I was still too overcome by the closeness of the conflict, and by domestic events in Argentina which touched me, my generation and many friends too closely. There was no way to make light of it.

There still is none, but given the vastness of the bibliography (included at the end of this volume) it is possible to summarize the conflict in a short chapter in the context of this book, and refer the concerned reader to the wider reading list.

It is also useful to be able to look back on the effects of that small war on Argentina.

For the first time in the twentieth century, from the time of the creation of Argentina's modern army in the early 1920s and since its first coup d'état in September 1930, the armed forces of Argentina had ceased to be valid political interlocutors in the management of the country's business. After years of political instability, in which the threat of one general's disapproval was enough to cause a crisis in government, the armed forces had waged a near civil war against urban terrorists who had not only been defeated before the military came to power in March 1976, but counter-guerrilla action had led to a policy of state terror which had claimed thousands of lives.

The victory over "subversion" might have been assimilated slowly by the population, but economic mismanagement by the military led to financial catastrophe by the late 1970s. Even though it can be said that most families in Argentina had been affected in some way by the so-called "Dirty War", it was the economic crisis that really compounded their distress and hardship. So the military had exaggerated repression and failed in economic management. And then they were humiliatingly defeated in the one chore they were designed for, military action. They were disorganised and badly trained and internally divided when they went to war with Britain. Failure was inevitable.

And after failure, their withdrawal from government was rapid. Today Argentina cannot imagine the armed forces running government. And after Argentina in 1983, other countries went down the path back to constitutional government. Uruguay, Brazil, Chile voted again in the 1980s, in part under pressure from Washington, alarmed at the extent of the failure of the military in government in Argentina. It was time for elections again, especially with the approaching end of the Cold War—in which the beginning of the end came in October 1989 with the demolition of the Berlin Wall.

Thanks to James Ferguson and Signal Books I am offered this new edition, this second chance, to look back on those events and how the continent evolved after 1982. Readers, academics, historians or individuals with an interest in Latin America will draw their own conclusions on the evolution of the continent since then. Whether or not we have learned from the nineteenth and twentieth centuries that war and totalitarian systems do not work in the interests of progress and welfare will have to be seen. For now, we will just have to hope that the failures, and the successes, of those two centuries have taught us a greater degree of tolerance and understanding.

Buenos Aires/London, 2002

INTRODUCTION

It has long been the opinion of the people of the South American republics that the English are a nation of pirates. This is a word suitable for epithets and headlines. It is applied liberally, of course, for no distinction is made between pirates of savage and criminal customs on the Main, corsairs, buccaneers, or privateers—all plunderers of peaceful towns in the interests of personal enrichment or of a remote government's political pursuits. They are lumped together with imperial officials and colonial authorities assuming the role of arbiters of localised conflicts in the name of civilisation; and envoys of the Foreign Office devoting much time to the summons of gunboats for the defence of unfairly treated Britons. Beef and wine and tea and coffee merchants were nicknamed "pirates" for no other reason than that they were British and were thought to have piracy in the blood.

The passage of time has made many of these characters obsolete. But feelings have persistently ascribed to Anglo-Saxons in general the habits of "pirates" and hence the word is also applied to citizens of the United States of America.

The view of the North American "pirate" differs from the image of his English counterpart – with the exception of a short time during which North Americans were known as corsairs because of their frequent application for a "corsair's licence" to operate in the service of the republics which had been recently declared independent after three centuries of Spanish domination.

A nineteenth-century image of the North American pirate was of a portly male dressed in open overcoat, corseted in bulging waistcoat or vest, bearing a top hat, seated in a rocking chair on the verandah of a house in New England, with arm raised and hand pointing in the direction of an area south of the Rio Grande, where he had organised a war that would secure substantial orders for the purchase of guns, barrels of unspecified goods, and cases of liquor of dubious distillation. By this figure's side would lie a club, the symbol later of a policy. Later variations on this character are portrayed as immaculately dressed men who wear dark glasses, bear small black cases, and who introduce themselves as members of the staff of the United States Embassy, of a bank, or of the Republican Party. These characters have entered history only recently and are considered to be pirates of a different kind.

England has always had a strong commercial curiosity about events taking place in Spanish and Portuguese America. The interest dates back to the discovery by Columbus, and to the succeeding voyages commissioned by the Catholic kings of Spain. The tales of wealth unlimited that sprang from the newly-discovered territories flooded

Europe—after Spain failed in an initial attempt at holding them back, to avoid competitive exploration. The legend of the "golden man"—El Dorado—in the upper reaches of the Amazon or in the heights of Colombia fired the imaginations of adventurers. However, more relevant to the needs of countries than the imaginings of travellers and the exploits of conquistadors, were the achievements made possible by war. That is where the pirates and buccaneers, and the gunboats and armies and fleets came in, to blockade, invade, browbeat and seize.

This volume collects a number of tales—all of them the fantasies of men, all recorded history—of those armed incidents, little wars many of them, that took place in the nineteenth century in South America.

England especially, but also the rest of Europe, became involved in them or started them, in several cases. That involvement declined and in more recent times the United States has become pre-eminent.

This collection aims to satisfy readers who may have been unable to read the contemporary press coverage, or missed the news of events which were passed over too soon to be noted in the morning perusal of a newspaper. Not all readers will be double centenarians, so the present volume will help the younger ones to fill that gap in their news. The two newspapers most quoted are *The Times* (founded 1788) and the *(Manchester) Guardian* (founded 1821).

They were available in the early years of the nineteenth century and still are—nearly always. It is thought that this might help readers to associate events of the past with the institutions of the present. The news from those two daily sheets is supplemented with a number of extracts from other papers, and with selected private and official correspondence.

Readers of *The Daily Telegraph* (founded 1855), *Daily Mail* (founded 1885), *Financial Times* (founded 1888), *Daily Express* (founded 1900), and *Daily Mirror* (founded 1903), are requested not to take offence at this partiality and omission of their favourite daily newspapers; these being not available at the beginning, made their inclusion later difficult in such a brief survey. However, it is to be deeply regretted that the newspaper the *Sun* (founded 1969), which gave its readers such an interesting view of hostilities in 1982, was not available to be consulted for its opinion on events in the previous century.

This book is intended to point out some of the misconceptions held by the British, and by most other Europeans, in their view of South America. Principal among these erroneous concepts is that Britain had little to do with South America, because it was more concerned with an Empire that lay elsewhere. Another is that Europe, except Spain, always had a charitable attitude towards the New World.

Some wars are better known than others. Cinematography has acquainted the public with the war between Texas and Mexico, and with the installation of the Archduke Maximilian as Emperor of Mexico, rather better than with many other local conflicts. Events such as the dramatic bombardment of the Venezuelan coast in 1902 by units of the British and German navies, acting with the support of Italian ships, have escaped public attention. However, it is to be regretted that in the wide view of a century and its many events in one vast continent, some will be missed here too.

The nineteenth-century wars to be narrated here are the lesser known and were mostly about property, which put them in a class different to those of the twentieth century, which had a strong ideological content.

This year of 1983, the first anniversary of an armed conflict—with nineteenth-century connotations—over the Falkland Islands, and the 150th of the occupation of those islands by the commander and officers of HMS *Clio*—on the indirect encouragement of a captain and unit of the US Navy—appears to be suitable to bring before the public such a chronicle. Readers will, it is hoped, pardon the intrusion on their attention, at present so pressingly demanded by many bigger wars which cannot be overlooked. It is also hoped that readers will look on these pages as an entertainment and will note how ironical history and its language tend to be.

London/Buenos Aires, 1983

Acknowledgments

My chief debt is to the museums and libraries of London. The British Library newspaper division at Colindale was most helpful with the essential sources for this book and I am indebted to the staff for their guidance. The British Library is, as always, the repository of many treasures on South America in the nineteenth century. Many notes on British operations in South America came from the libraries of the Imperial War Museum and the National Maritime Museum. Equally helpful were the staff of the D.N.S. Watts Library of University College London, keeper of the archives of the Bank of London and South America (Lloyds Bank), and the Public Record Office at Kew.

Special thanks to Ken Murphy, at the *Guardian*, for helping me to trace several articles; to Dr Rodolfo Terragno, for allowing me to read his papers on General San Martín's expedition; to Juan Carlos Herken, for allowing me to read his notes on the war in Paraguay; to the novelist Jorge Edwards, in Chile, for directing me to information; to Dr Daniel Divinsky, in Caracas and Buenos Aires, for information on the blockade of Venezuela; to Dr Félix Luna, in Buenos Aires, for information on the Anglo-French attack on that city; to Ezequiel Gallo, and the Instituto Torcuato Di Tella, in Buenos Aires, for help with the banking crisis in Santa Fe; and to then HBM Ambassador in Bolivia, Stanley Dundan, for directing me to essential bibliography. I must acknowledge special assistance with the speculation in Chapter 9, of Dr Glyn Williams, of the University of North Wales. I should like to express my gratitude to the publishers of *The Army Quarterly and Defence Journal*. I am also indebted to the Guyana High Commission for information on the Essequibo dispute. Thanks also to Daniel de Anchorena, my publisher in Buenos Aires, to Nicholas Tozer, for references on the Falklands/Malvinas war, and Mrs Rosa Amuchástegui.

Chapter One

FROM EMPIRE TO REPUBLICS:
BEFORE 1826

José de San Martín (Museo Histórico Nacional)

Spain had been the subject of envy of the rest of Europe after the 1493 Bull of Pope Alexander VI divided the New World between Portugal and Spain, the latter taking the larger part of the continent, from California to Buenos Aires. While on land the lines were drawn, at sea the supremacy of Spain was soon challenged by English mariners. Privateers operating off the Spanish and Portuguese colonies were a by-product of Spanish conquest; the simple act of reserving vast tracts for the exclusive use of the kings of Castille and their agents made such lands and their wealth a temptation for the adventurous.

However, at first Philip II of Spain saw France as a more dangerous enemy than Britain. The king regarded England as a potential ally even though he had failed in his efforts to make Elizabeth I his wife. British incursions into the Spanish colonies were therefore tolerated, while French settlements near the Castillian possessions in Florida and the Caribbean were raided and destroyed by the Spaniards. As time passed and English attacks on Spanish property became more frequent, Philip II introduced rules to counter the English interlopers and freebooters in the ports of his colonies. The quarrel with England about colonial territory and about the English attacks on the gold and plate routes—from South America to Spain—eventually escalated into a religious conflict. The Spanish king made it his business to try to restore the Pope's authority over the Church of England as the only way to neutralise British designs on the Spanish empire.

In 1564 John Hawkins recorded his own first infringement of Spanish authority in America by delivering slaves to Santo Domingo from the Portuguese colonies in West Africa. Hawkins went further: he proclaimed such trade to be the property of none other than the realm of England and of John Hawkins. Francis Drake joined the Hawkins syndicate of merchants and seamen in November 1566 and from then on the generally peaceful, if at times disturbed, relations between Spain and England degenerated into a conflict lasting, off and on, for three centuries.

Drake's voyages to the Caribbean and to the Spanish colonial Mainland between 1567 and 1569, and during 1572-3, were the beginning of a history of seamanship, looting and naval victory almost without parallel. Drake's first objective was to find the road to the secret Spanish deposit of plate and gold, the "treasure house of the world" at Nombre de Dios, in the Isthmus of Panama. This venture, partly successful, was to be followed by the circumnavigation of the world, under royal patronage and with the financial support of a joint stock company—almost a forerunner of British-South American trade relations. During that expedition Drake plundered and terrorised the South American harbours on the Pacific Ocean.

Another adventurer, Henry Morgan, is remembered to this day in the area for the sacking of Maracaibo in 1669 and of Panama in 1670. Writing of these events a few years later, a Dutchman said that "from hence peradventure will other Nations learn, that the English people are of their Genius more inclinable to act than to write."[1] The Dutchman, John Exquemelin, identified himself as "one of the bucaniers who was present at those tragedes"; he pointed with pleasure to all the piratical achievements of the English and singled them out for special praise.[2]

The golden age of pirates lasted less than a hundred years, up to the end of the seventeenth century. But before it had quite faded away, one medical doctor, Thomas Dover by name, joined a syndicate of Bristol merchants and with Woodes Rogers and

William Dampier, navigators of fame at the time, set out in two frigates fitted for a total cost of £15,000, on what has come to be described as the last of the great privateering voyages.[3] They sailed with a commission by Prince George of Denmark (consort to Queen Anne) and Lord High Admiral of Britain "to cruise on the coasts of Peru and Mexico, in the South Sea, against Her Majesty's enemies, the French and Spaniards."

That voyage was made largely as a result of changes in British maritime policy, which produced a new Prize Act (1708) that gave owners and crew all the prize money. The Crown had previously taken one third. For the government it was an economical form of keeping the fighting going against the Crown's enemies. That voyage also gave the world in general—and Daniel Defoe in particular—the story of Robinson Crusoe, through the accounts of Alexander Selkirk, rescued by Dover and Rogers from the island of Mas a Tierra, in the Juan Fernandes group, where he had been put ashore by a captain with whom he had disagreed.

On Dover's return to England in September 1711, his success in the plunder of the Spanish ports on the Pacific Ocean coast directed attention in Europe to the decline of Spain's control of its colonies. Attention to the volume of riches shared by all who sailed with Rogers and Dover also helped to push a bill through parliament, to create a "Company of Merchants of Great Britain trading to the South Sea and other parts of South America." Thus the South Sea Company was formed with Tory sympathy, to enter into competition with the Whig supported United Company of Merchants of England and the East Indies, or East India Company.

The Asiento contract, signed in Madrid in March 1713 as part of the Peace of Utrecht, gave the South Sea Company the opportunity to establish trading links with South America. Spain was unable to supply its colonies with slaves and this the Company contracted to do. The South Sea Company was granted a lease on the trading posts, or "factories", at Buenos Aires, Vera Cruz and Cartagena, which were to be supplied with four thousand slaves a year. One thousand two hundred were to be shipped to the River Plate—from these, eight hundred were despatched to Buenos Aires and the remaining four hundred to Montevideo and to towns on the Atlantic coast.

The Spanish conspired against the implementation of the agreement from the start, convinced as they were that the English sought access to South America to organise smuggling and spread intrigue in the colonies, and eventually to try to snatch them from Spain. In spite of this suspicion, the slave "factories" made a successful if slow start; trade was largely dependent on the importation of slaves in exchange for hides, metals and other goods in quantities well over the permitted levels. The South Sea Company expanded, by speculation on the stock exchange, until its irregular activities—which included smuggling and widespread corruption—brought about its crash, in 1720, to be known thereafter as the "burst of the South Sea Bubble."

While commercial penetration was attempted in the Spanish colonies, thoughts of a military venture against Spain were still alive in England. In *A Proposal for Humbling Spain* (London, 1711), a tract whose authorship was attributed to "A Person of Distinction", it was suggested that an invasion of the Spanish colonies should begin at Buenos Aires. From there the invaders were to cross the continent to Chile, and march and sail to the north. The whole territory could thus be taken rapidly from Spain. The existence of this pamphlet has been noted by South American historians, who have puzzled over its author beyond the suggestion that it could be John Pullen, Governor of the Bermudas. The invasion proposal and the method by which it should be carried out are important because they recur, in one or other fashion, in plans for expeditions during the next century. What is not in doubt is that Pullen did suggest such an occcupation of the Spanish American territories, even if it is not certain that he penned it in 1711. In 1732, the printers at St Paul's Churchyard, London, published an eighty-page booklet, priced one shilling and six pence, "By the late John Pullen, Esq., Governor of Bermudas." It was the

> Memoirs of the Maritime Affairs of Great Britain especially in relation to our concerns in the West Indies. To which is prefix'd the original letter of the Author, to (and by the Command of) the Earl of Oxford, when High Treasurer of England, in relation to the South Sea Company, and the trade they were designed to carry on; in which consequences of an ill-management in that respect are fully laid open, and the true nature of such a commerce explained.

For anybody who might consider the late functionary's suggestions seriously, he offered the supplement:

> Captain Pain's short view of Spanish America: containing a succinct deduction of navigation, from its original to the discovery of the New World; and an account of the extent, quality, riches, and trade of His Catholick Majesty's dominions there, in a method wholy new, and from authorities never yet known to the publick.

The information thus offered so generously and posthumously was to be of use in an eventual invasion.

Spain was exercising a despotic rule over its colonial subjects. "...The Spaniards of Old Spain, who possess all the posts of power and profit, and lord it insufferably over the Criolio's [*sic*] who, in return for it, hate them mortally and are always ready to do them mischief..." Such a situation "...naturally inspires a spirit of discontent, which may probably one day break forth in an open revolt, or will, at least, leave them in a fit disposition to be wrought on by foreign enemies to join their designs." The late governor went on to say that:

> All understanding men must confess, that Great Britain cannot make a settlement in any place upon the face of the Earth, from whence reasonably it may expect to reap so many advantages, as from one situated upon the River Plate... The Spaniards have not force sufficient either at Buenos Ayres, or the places adjacent, to undertake it [a war].

His advice was thorough and his feelings strong. To attack the fort of Buenos Aires:

> Too great a care cannot be taken in procuring an able engineer. I solemnly protest I know not one in Her Majesty's service that I esteem equal to the undertaking; for I believe no Nation was ever so ill-served in that respect, or entertain'd such ignorant wretches, as we here in England did.

Though the governor had foreseen the necessity of war, his pamphlet was also intended to explain his ideas on how to set up trade in South America. His references to the failure of the South Sea Company were devastating, and if the engineers of his day felt lashed by his pen, so must have the directors of the South Sea Company. He was outraged at the collapse of the venture, furious that England had lost such an opportunity, and convinced that England had entered the Asiento contract too ingenuously, for he was sure that Spain had planned to disregard the slave "factories" clause in the Utrecht treaty. Spain had to be humiliated for such intended treachery. After much remonstrating and outrage at the incompetence of the English, the late governor Pullen had laid out his plan. Once Buenos Aires had been seized, an English fleet should sail round Cape Horn into the Pacific and take the Juan Fernandes Islands as a base. From the islands, one force would have to be disembarked in central Chile, and another in Peru, at Arica. With a foot in Peru, the English forces could advance north with ease, eventually to reach Mexico by sea. The Caribbean could be taken from this mainland base and from the British possession at Jamaica. He wanted the South Sea Company to carry out the operation.

> But if the South Sea Company (for their sins, and because they can have them cheap) send such unlick'd cubs as the East India Company do every year, then, without pretending to any great share of witchcraft, I here foretell them, the first they send will be the last too.

It seems wise to draw attention to Pullen's plan to take Buenos Aires first, and then the western coast of South America. Buenos Aires was the last post in the Spanish empire, on the edge of what English and Spanish maps described as the "uninhabited country of Patagonia." It was little more than a village on the flat bank of the River Plate, whose calm, muddy waters seemed an extension of the great plains roamed by the Pampa indians. It was far from the empire's centres of wealth on the Pacific—which had produced gold and silver for the Castillian coffers—and its trade was restricted by the Crown's monopoly. Imports of goods, including those from Spain, had to be received overland after clearance by the customs of Lima and Córdoba. Spain's forces at Buenos Aires were badly equipped and poorly trained, and certainly not numerous. Hence it was thought that with a toehold at Buenos Aires a well-trained army could easily advance north through the continent.

Pullen's advice, whether dated in 1711 or 1732, caused considerable alarm in the Spanish colonies and during the eighteenth century there were frequent reports of suspected English invasions of the River Plate. *Criollo* inhabitants, those locally born of Spanish settlers, were convinced by the Church's teachings that the English were devils who could only be dealt with by the Inquisitor, heretics whose Protestantism could only be excised at the stake. The Inquisition was never very active in Buenos Aires; but the provincial imagination was easily encouraged. Some colonial inhabitants were inclined to believe that the English and the Germans hid small horns under their hats and long pointed tails down their trouser legs; it was not difficult to inspire in the less-educated some terror at the thought of a boatload of English landing on the shores of the Plate.

In 1740 the Count of Montijo reported to the French that ships carrying seven hundred men had victualled in Portugal and were thought to be on their way to sack South America. In 1746 a number of strongly-armed English naval ships were reported in Rio de Janeiro. None of these reported sailings came to anything and many lesser sightings were being attributed to merchants trying to smuggle goods through Brazil and into the southern Spanish provinces. In 1762 the Governor of Buenos Aires was notified from

Spain that Britain planned a large-scale attack in the South Atlantic. This was to become the first real attempt to take the River Plate ports, with Pullen's text as the blueprint for the operation.

Early in 1762 a Plymouth syndicate bought the 60-gun ship *Lord Clive*, and also fitted the 60-gun frigate *Gloria*, and the 40-gun *Ambuscade*, for a raid on the River Plate. The *Lord Clive* had been built at Hull, in 1697. It had seen action at Gibraltar, Velez and Malaga in 1704, and at Gaspe in 1711. It had been refitted at Portsmouth in 1719 and again at Plymouth in 1740, had seen action once more at Toulon in 1744, and at Menorca in 1756, and had participated in the defeat of the French at the Bay of Quiberon in 1759. It had a record of glory.

John MacNamara, formerly of the East India Company, was put in command of the *Lord Clive*. With the help of the Portuguese at Rio de Janeiro, he added five hundred men to his force in August 1762. He sailed his small fleet into the River Plate in November and after initial scrutiny of the fort of Montevideo, which protected a closed anchorage that did not ensure easy access under fire, MacNamara sailed to the port of Colonia del Sacramento, across the river from Buenos Aires.

On the morning of 6 January 1763 the three ships took up position in front of Colonia. The battle lasted only four hours and ended in tragedy for the British. A series of lucky shots from the small fort at Colonia had set fire to the *Lord Clive*, which was unable to manoeuvre in the shallow waters of the Plate. It did not stop burning till the flames reached the water line. The *Lord Clive* lost 272 men, including her captain. Only four died at the fort. The *Gloria* and *Ambuscade* returned to Rio de Janeiro. The Spanish sank what was left of the *Lord Clive*, which lies in its muddy grave to this day. Sixty-two men were rescued and interned.

The next fright in the colony came not from an expedition but from a book. This was a memoir of forty years in the Spanish colony, by Father Thomas Falkner, one-time ship's doctor with the South Sea Company slavers, who had arrived in Buenos Aires about 1730 and had become a Jesuit after his conversion to Catholicism. He had been well-liked in the colony because of his medical competence and in Europe was held in high regard for his archaeological findings. As a Jesuit he was forced to leave the colonies when Charles III ordered the Society's expulsion in 1767, convinced that it was trying to create an autonomous state within the empire. Father Falkner's book was published in 1774 in London, promising:

> A Description of Patagonia, and the Adjoining parts of South America: containing an account of the soil, produce, animals, vales, mountains, rivers, lakes, etc. of those countries; the religion, government policy, customs, dress, arms and language of the indian inhabitants, and some particulars relating to Falkland's Island.

The book gave the English readers their most comprehensive and competent information to date on the colonies that their government and merchants aspired to own. Falkner recommended that the English authorities should establish a port and settlement on the coast of Patagonia, which was marked by many excellent and well-protected bays. From such a port English mariners could have command of the South Atlantic. The advice so worried the Spaniards that a few years later the town of Carmen de Patagones was founded on the mouth of the river Negro.

Coincidentally, Falkner returned to England in 1771, just as the English dispute with Spain, over possession of the Falkland Islands, was reaching its peak. The eviction of English settlers had been ordered by Spain in 1770 after the sinking, on 13 March 1770, of the sloop HMS *Swift*, at Puerto Deseado. The ship had been based in the Falklands, there to protect the settlers and warn off hostile intruders. After its sinking, the islands remained with little protection from the British.[4] Falkner's book was published in 1774, in May of which year the *Endeavour* evacuated all remaining settlers from the islands, acknowledging Spanish rule—but leaving written claim to the rocks on a plaque. In London, Dr Johnson warned in one of his innumerable pamphlets that it was not worth going to war with Spain over possessions so small and so distant. For the English, Falkner's book marked the beginning of South American travel writing; the French, Germans and Spanish had already published numerous volumes about the area.

Another invasion of sorts was to surprise South America. In August 1797 the *Lady Shore* had sailed from London with, among other cargo, seventy-five prostitutes and forty-four felons bound for the penal colonies of Australia. The ship's French crew mutinied off the southern coasts of Brazil, raised the French flag and sailed into Montevideo. Unable to decide what to do in such an unprecedented situation, the Spanish colonial administration seized the ship and interned the crew and passengers in Buenos Aires. Most of the convicts assumed Latinised names and married. One of the women, however, to be known as Mrs Clarke or "Doña Clara", became well known for the hospitality she was to show to English merchants and seamen. Her house was also to be used as the first English Club of Buenos Aires. But more serious raids were to come.

In 1796 Harry Dundas, Viscount Melville, Secretary for War, was in receipt of a plan which contained "Proposals for an Expedition against Spanish America by the Pacific Ocean."[5] Peace had been signed with Spain and France in 1783; but relations had begun to deteriorate again and under the formidable leadership of William Pitt, English merchants and military were once more taking active interest in the Spanish possessions. The 1796 report had been submitted by Sir John Coxe Hippisley (1748-1825), Member of Parliament, one time East India Company officer, successful diplomat in Rome, and deft political entrepreneur. His plan proposed that regiments could be taken from India for an attack on the River Plate, to be followed by a naval expedition to the west coast of South America.

Contemporaneously, Francisco de Miranda (1750-1816), born in Caracas and having fought on the side of the revolutionaries in France, sought support in London for a rebellion in South America. His plan was to attack Buenos Aires and Caracas, with the invading forces to merge in Peru. He was of the impression that Lima would require the strongest and most numerous arms; but the action would free the continent from Spain.

After the Spanish Governor of Trinidad had surrendered to a British naval force in 1797, the Foreign Office wrote to its new man in Port of Spain and ordered him:

> to promote the measures most suitable to liberate the Spanish colonies and place them in a position to resist the oppressive authority of their government, in the certainty that they could count upon all the resources to be expected from H.B. Majesty, be it with forces, or with arms and ammunition to any extent, with the assurance that the view of H.B. Majesty

goes no further than to secure them their independence, without pretending to any sovereignty over their country or even to interfere in the privileges of the people, either in their political, civil, or religious rights.[6]

Such selfless projects had not applied to Trinidad, or to the mainland Dutch port of Georgetown, seized by the British the year before. However, it was not from the Caribbean that Britain would pursue its policy in South America.

Hippisley had given a copy of his proposals to Major-General Sir Thomas Maitland (1759-1824), a Scots MP who had seen action in India, and also in the Americas, in Saint-Domingue—and had known defeat at the hands of François Toussaint L'Ouverture, the anti-colonialist Haitian former slave and later dictator. Maitland was consulted by Dundas and Hippisley about the plan for an expedition to South America. In his reply early in 1800, Maitland produced an alternative project. He contradicted Miranda.

> An expedition to the Caracas from the West Indies, and a force sent to Buenos Aires, might indeed tend to the emancipation of the Spanish colonists in the eastern possessions, but the effect of such emancipation, though considerable, could never be reckoned upon as in any degree sure in the richer possessions to the westward, and it is to be observed the only utility and principle upon which the Spaniards had attached consequence to their eastern possessions is that, by holding them, they act as a defence to their more valuable possessions to the westward.[7]

Maitland also proposed that the first stage be an attack on Buenos Aires. "Subsequent to the capture of Buenos Ayres... [the] object ought to be to push forward a corps and to take a position at the foot of the eastern side of the Andes, for which purpose the city of Mendoza is undoubtedly best calculated." The next stage:

> The crossing of the Andes from Mendoza into the lower parts of Chili is an operation of some difficulty. Even in summer the cold is intense; but with troops on each side it is hardly to be supposed our soldiers could not follow a route which was long adopted as the most desireable channel for importing negroes into the Kingdom of Chili.

Once the formidable Andes had been crossed, the aim was to "annihilate the government in the Kingdom of Chili" and from there prepare to advance northwards. "Should this plan succeed in its extent, the province of Peru would immediately become exposed to the certainty of capture... We might ultimately extend our operations to the certainty of overthrowing the whole of their colonial force even by force were it necessary." Attacks on the port of Callao, and the city of Lima—the stronghold of the Spanish empire—had to be considered next, "...but this very success, unless it were attended by our being able to maintain ourselves in the Kingdom of Peru, would ultimately end in exciting aversion of the inhabitants against any future connection of any kind with Great Britain." The objective therefore would be to secure the emancipation of Peru.[8]

Rumours of imminent British expeditions spread rapidly in Buenos Aires, Caracas, Santiago de Chile and Lima. The rumours intensified as the awareness grew that Spanish rule was weakening. The colonial metropolis was undermined by severe economic decline and by the threat of Napoleonic expansion. With the rumours came men alleged to be spies. Some of them were colourful characters in a variety of disguises—military, mercantile, scientific. Others appear to have been merchants seeking new commercial outlets, but keeping naval commanders in the area and the Foreign Office informed of local movements, as much to curry favour as to assure themselves of attention to their personal affairs. To the world at large, no British merchant was involved in commerce alone. He was also a government agent.

Britain took over the three Dutch provinces of Essequibo, Demerara and Berbice—later to be known as British Guiana—in 1803. In 1804, Jean-Jacques Dessalines, later proclaimed Emperor Jacques I, declared Haiti independent of France. In 1805 Britain ordered a secret expedition to seize the South African Dutch colony at the Cape of Good Hope. From the Cape a detachment of men under General Beresford sailed the following year for Buenos Aires in ships commanded by Sir Home Riggs Popham.

In the meantime, British attention was still taken by Miranda's preoccupation with ending colonial rule in Venezuela. Miranda, accused of misuse of funds in Cuba, had fled to the United States in 1783. In the US he had met leaders of the revolution but, harassed by Spanish agents, had travelled to London, via France, where William Pitt, anxious to disrupt Spanish authority in the Americas, had given Miranda limited support and protection. In London Miranda organised a type of Masonic lodge, the Gran Reunión Americana, which would attract several of the South American independence leaders—some of whom later started lodges in their own countries. Miranda travelled over Europe looking for more support for an independent empire, ruled by a hereditary Inca royal family, from Mexico to Tierra del Fuego. Miranda thought—probably unwisely—that Venezuela offered the best point of departure for the independence of the Americas, contrary to the opinion of Maitland, and before him of Pullen. With English cash and sympathy—and the blessings of Jeremy Bentham, the economist—and guns bought in the United States, Miranda sailed for Caracas.

The Times, Thursday, 3 July 1806:
The only interesting articles in the American papers which we have received to 27 May, relate to the expedition of General Miranda. The accounts are confused, but we see no reason to doubt the fact of Miranda's success, in which they all appear to agree. Small as his force is, the Spanish government cannot bring into the field anything capable of resisting it. The whole of the troops spread over the *Terra Firma*, including regulars, militia, and irregulars of all kinds, do not amount to fourteen thousand men: of these, the regular force upon which alone any reliance is to be placed, does not amount to one-sixth, and it would require some weeks to bring the whole of it together for active operations. By the time it will have assembled, Miranda will have collected twenty times the number of the native population; and as, we trust, he has been amply supplied with the means of arming and maintaining such a force, there can be little doubt of his having, by this time, obtained, at least, the primary object of his expedition. When he is once established there, we may certainly encourage the expectation that the country will soon change its masters. Nor can we look forward to such an event but with an exulting satisfaction; for, while Spain remains in its present state of subserviency to the will of the Corsican [Napoleon], every diminution of its territory and its resources may be considered as a wound given to the power of France, and a check to the ambition of the tyrant who governs it.

A letter dated in Kingston, Jamaica, 10 May, said that:
the *Echo*... sailed from Aruba in company with the expedition under General Miranda, but

parted from the *Leander*... in a squall... The *Leander* had on board 7,000 stand of arms, and 500 barrels of gunpowder... General Miranda had effected his landing at Puerto Cavello, where the garrison, after discharging a few guns, loaded with sand, opened the gates of the city... He had afterwards proceeded for the Caraccas, where the inhabitants were equally ready to receive him. The *Leander*, after disembarking the general and his staff, with 150 soldiers, returned... The officers belonging to the expedition were dressed in a very splendid manner. They were confident of success... and that powerful engine, the press, had been employed... in printing such papers, both in the Spanish and in the native language of the people, as might best forward the purpose of their new visitants.

There was no doubt at all of *The Times'* favour. Its editorial comment was based on optimistic reports reproduced from the North American papers. One of these, dated 24 May, out of Puerto Rico said:

... General Miranda had effected a landing at Caraccas;... the Spanish government had sent to the city of St Domingo, requesting assistance from General Ferrand, who... would furnish 500 troops...

Captain Hinton, arrived this morning in twenty days from Trinidad, informs us that the English had taken Caraccas, on the Spanish Main. This was probably the expedition under Miranda, and reported as British, from the circumstance of that General being joined by six British frigates, with 6,000 troops, as we learn by an arrival in Philadelphia.

A report dated 26 May said that Miranda's flag "was flying on every fort from Cumana to La Guira [*sic*], and that he had obtained complete possession of the province of Cumana and Caraccas, with little or no opposition." The British frigate *Jason* and the sloop of war *Lilly* had sailed to join him.

On Saturday, 5 July 1806, an editorial in *The Times* remained cautiously optimistic and summarised the reasons for strong British interest in the fate of General Miranda.

The accounts of General Miranda's expedition... mention one circumstance which, if it is true to the extent stated, removes all doubt respecting its success. It is said that the native inhabitants of most of the province of the *Terra Firma* were so well disposed to afford every possible aid to the enterprise that different chieftains had been sent to General Miranda to concert with him the points where he was to make his attack, and to arrange the mode in which they were to co-operate with the force under his command.

The government of the Spaniards has been in this country, as in every other subject to them, peculiarly odious to the natives. The tyrannical exercise of power, the thirst of gain, and the bigotry of religion, have ever combined to render them at once imperious, cruel and oppressive. The prospect, therefore, of being emancipated from such thraldom, will naturally facilitate the operations of General Miranda and at length secure to him the object of his important expedition, in a country whose freedom he has long mediated, and will, we trust, obtain.

In taking a general view of the probable consequences of such an event, we cannot but anticipate the advantages which must result to Great Britain from the vast extension of commerce which will be laid open to it, by the emancipation of that part of the American continent which is the object of Miranda's enterprising spirit. If we were to indulge our imagination in a view of the more remote consequences of his present success, we might look to acquisitions in the vast extent of South America, that would indemnify a great commercial people, for the balance of power obtained against them in Europe.

Within a very short time the good news had changed to bad. On Tuesday, 8 July 1806, *The Times* quoted from newspapers up to 6 June:

We are sorry to find that they bring unfavourable accounts of Miranda's expedition. Reports were prevalent... that the General had been obliged to abandon his design of establishing the independence of his native country; that a Spanish man-of-war brig and schooner, sent from Laguira [*sic*], had obliged him to fly from the coast of Cumana in the *Leander*, and that some of the vessels in company with him had been captured. If this intelligence be authentic, there is little chance that he will ever renew the attempt, except he should meet with more open and powerful support than he has already experienced. His miscarriage in this first instance would have the effect of damping the ardour of his friends, and rendering them extremely cautious of any decisive demonstration in his favour hereafter: but, we trust that the American account is unfounded. The inhabitants of the United States are not in general well-wishers to Miranda, and we perceive that they eagerly catch up and disseminate with extreme industry, and apparent satisfaction, all the reports to his disadvantage. Let us, therefore, hope that this rumour has no better foundation than their wishes. There is also another reason for not attaching implicit credit to the report of his miscarriage. We do not believe there were any Spanish ships of war on that coast. It is too near Jamaica to be made a cruising ground; and though, for certain reasons, Miranda might have received no assistance from the English squadron in that sea, it is by no means probable that it would allow him to be chased and driven off the coast by a Spanish brig and schooner.

The Times, 10 July 1806:

Some accounts say that [General Miranda's] little squadron has been defeated and dispersed; others mention that he effected a landing at Cumana without opposition. It would appear, from the reports of various American captains, that there were two or three French squadrons in different parts of the West Indies.

On 11 July, *The Times* leader said that American papers up to 14 June, reported:

We are reluctantly obliged to attach some share of credit... [to the news]. A New York paper... states, that he intended to effect a landing in the province of Coro, at the extremity of the Gulph of Venezuela... The reports concerning Miranda have been so various and contradictory that truth is scarcely perceptible in the midst of those confused accounts... It is well known that Miranda proceeded from Jacmel to the little island of Aruba... He left it about 16 April, with the *Leander* [a British ship] and his two schooners, and was attempting a landing towards the province of Coro, when his little squadron fell in with two Spanish privateers, one of fourteen and the other of twelve guns, fitted at La Guira, by the government of Caracas. The *Leander*, after attempting to engage the stoutest, suddenly withdrew from the contest, crowded sail, and escaped; the schooners were left to their own fate; and after a trifling resistance struck their colours to the smallest of the Spanish privateers. Two young Spaniards, who were on board of one of the schooners, anticipating the inevitable fate, threw themselves overboard, and were drowned; the remainder were taken and carried into Porto Cavello, where they were lodged in jail; some of the leading men were immediately ordered up to Caracas.

The schooners were entirely laden with ammunition of all kinds, and a considerable number of proclamations in the Spanish language from Miranda's press, conceived in terms well calculated for their object, to inflame the minds of the Spanish colonists.

The fate of the adventurers taken must be lamentable indeed; their criminal rashness will bring many of them to the block, as the Spanish government considers them in no other light than pirates.

The blood, which very likely is already spilt, cannot but fall on the heads of the abettors and promoters of this marauding expedition in this country; it would have been much to be wished for that no suspicions should have appeared against our Government [of the US] in this scandalous affair... No great sagacity is required to anticipate that Spain and France will call upon us for some millions of dollars by way of compensation...

Miranda escaped capture and fled back to London. There, at a house in Grafton Way, off Tottenham Court Road, he was to continue his conspiracy in the company of young officers who were to become the luminaries of South American independence— Simón Bolívar and José de San Martín among them. Miranda eventually returned to Venezuela, with Bolívar. But he bungled the expedition again. Suspected of treachery, he was delivered to the Spaniards. He died in a Spanish prison.

The Times of the period was only four pages long. Given that one of these pages—the front—was taken up entirely by advertising, the amount of space in the rest of the paper devoted to events in South America must be seen as evidence of Britain's desperate need for new trade routes. Napoleon had almost closed Europe completely to English commerce.

The Times, London, Saturday, 13 September 1806, page two, column one. A rather lethargic and routine communication informed readers:

Yesterday we received advices from the River Plate by the *Resolution*, Captain Ham, dated 10 June, at which time no accounts had been received there of the expedition under the command of Sir Home Popham, which sailed some time ago from the Cape of Good Hope.

Britain had snatched the Dutch colony at the Cape the year before after one easy battle.

On the same page, in a later edition, an insertion in column four carried the headline: "Capture of Buenos Ayres":

The Times office, Saturday morning, three o'clock. By an express, which we have just received from Portsmouth, we have to congratulate the Public on one of the most important events of the present war. Buenos Ayres at the moment forms part of the British Empire, and when we consider the consequences to which it leads from its situation, and its commercial capacities, as well as its political influence, we know not how to express ourselves in terms adequate to our ideas of the national advantages which will be derived from the conquest.

The following is the letter to our Correspondent; Portsmouth, Friday Evening. 7 o'clock. I don't delay an instant to inform you, that the *Narcissus* frigate is arrived here, and brings the important account of the capture of Buenos Ayres by the expedition from the Cape of Good Hope, in the latter end of June; I believe on 27 or 28. No further particulars have transpired, but what I have written may satisfy you for the present. An officer whose name I cannot learn, has just set off for town with dispatches for government.

The good news that morning was to coincide with the announcement that Charles James Fox, whom Edmund Burke, his alienated co-religionary, called "the greatest debater the world ever saw", had died after a short illness. Pitt had died in January. Two of the most impressive politicians of England dead in one year alarmed the South American revolutionaries working in London, for from both they had received encouragement and protection. South Americans were left to wonder how much sympathy they could count on. They were not to be short of support. Castlereagh and Canning kept a strong interest in the South American independence movement during the next twenty years. However, it would appear that the two men were not enthusiastic about Popham's expedition to Buenos Aires, even if they were inevitably carried away by the rejoicing at the initial success of the adventure, which represented such a moral blow to France.

The Times, 15 September 1806:

It is with great pleasure that we lay before our readers the *Gazette Extraordinary* of Saturday last, which announces the surrender of Buenos Ayres to the British arms. This conquest is highly important from its intrinsic value, but still more so from the circumstances which attended it, and from the very critical time in which it is made known to the British public and to Europe. There can be hardly a doubt that the whole colony of La Plata will share the same fate as Buenos Ayres; and from the flattering hopes held out to the inhabitants in the proclamation of General Beresford, they will see that it is their true interest to become a colony of the British empire.

The circumstances which attended this success are in the highest degree honourable to the British name, and to the character of our brave army. Here, as at the Cape of Good Hope, the enemy abandoned their excellent positions when they perceived the British troops advancing resolutely to the charge.

The capture of the Cape of Good Hope, however, was effected by an expedition evidently adequate to the object. The capture of Buenos Ayres, on the other hand, was made by a very inferior force, relying merely on its courage. The whole body of British troops, marines, and sailors landed, did not amount to 1,700 men. The Spaniards, to the number of 2,000, according to General Beresford (or 4,000, as magnified by Sir Home Popham) were strongly posted on heights, and the only mode of approaching them was through a morass. The enemy also had, as in the battle of Maida, a full knowledge of the inferiority of the force that was attacking them. General Beresford states "that the enemy, from his position, could have counted every man we had." Notwithstanding all those advantages, they would not venture to await the attack of the British troops, and abandoned the important city of Buenos Ayres to an inferior army.[9]

The country stands now on a much prouder footing than it has done since the negotiation with France commenced. In Calabria, the excellence and superiority of the British troops have been shewn to the enemy and to all Europe. By our success in La Plata, where a small British detachment has taken one of the greatest and richest of the Spanish colonies, Buonaparte must be convinced that nothing but a speedy peace can prevent the whole of Spanish America from being wrested from his influence, and placed for ever under the protection of the British Empire. What region of the habitable world could he then look to for "ships, colonies, and commerce"? There is another circumstance attending this success, which distinguishes our army as much for its generosity, as for its superior bravery and discipline. While the French armies plunder and ruin every country (hostile, friendly, or neutral) which they set their feet upon, the British army gives up, even to its enemies, that wealth which the laws of war had made its own. All private property was respected in a city which could make no resistance. Such an unexplained generosity and moderation will doubtless make the inhabitants of the Spanish colonies wish to be connected with Great Britain. By such an union we should have a never failing market for our commodities, and our enemies would be for ever deprived of the power of adding the resources of these rich countries to their other means of annoying us.

The reports of the taking of Buenos Aires, by William Carr Beresford, major general and lieutenant governor, occupied nearly a page and a half of that Monday's edition of *The Times*. Sir Home Riggs Popham's accounts, written aboard the *Narcissus*, filled a column, and exulted at the success. It was only right that he should be overjoyed; it had been his idea to attack Buenos Aires and he who had convinced Major General Sir David Baird at the Cape of Good Hope to release troops to that effect, as well as to order that reinforcements be taken on at St Helena's island. Popham it was, though, who, after the attack on Buenos Aires, seemed concerned more with the loot left behind by the fleeing viceroy, Sobremonte, than with the acquisition of the colony. In Portsmouth, on 17 September, the treasure filled six wagons.

> The procession was followed by vast numbers of seafaring persons in this port; the population of the town turned out to witness it, rending the air with their patriotic acclamations in honour of the bravery of their countrymen and of the triumph and treasure they have gained from the foe.[10]

Reports on the benefits to be derived from the new colony continued to arrive at *The Times'* offices. There was the excitement of a continent acquired as a colony. South America had at last been taken. A huge expedition was organised to keep the land that had long been lusted for. France and Spain had to be taught a lesson. On 3 October the paper said preparations were being made at Portsmouth to send four thousand men, led by General Craufurd, with orders to capture Chile.

Craufurd was to establish an uninterrupted communication with General Beresford, "by a chain of posts, or any other means"—over a distance of nine hundred miles, between Santiago and Buenos Aires, another reminder of the Pullen and Maitland plans. Brigadier Sir Samuel Auchmuty was given another 4,000 men and ordered to reinforce General Beresford. And yet more help was sent from the Cape of Good Hope under the command of Lt Colonel Backhouse, of the 47th Regiment (later 1st Bn. The Loyal Regiment) and also in command of the 38th Regiment (later 1st Bn. The South Staffordshire Regiment). They would all, however, arrive too late to help Beresford's 71st Regiment.

On 24 October, *The Times* said that "the *Discovery* and all the old men of war at Sheerness and in Queensborough Swale" had been examined and if proved seaworthy would take stores out to Buenos Aires. A task force was being organised. On 4 December, an item reproduced from a paper at St Helena said that "the citizens of Buenos Ayres are daily coming forward to swear allegiance to His Britannic Majesty; our officers and soldiers are treated with greatest hospitality, and, from every appearance, the inhabitants seem rejoiced at their change." All that had been true, for a time.

News, however, took nearly four months to reach London from Buenos Aires. Not a line of it was true any longer. The population of Buenos Aires had failed to appreciate the advantages of British rule. On 12 August, before that first celebratory report in *The Times*, the Spaniards had recaptured Buenos Aires. Santiago de Liniers, the town's captain general in the absence of the viceroy Sobremonte, had organised a counterattack by gathering the ill-trained and badly-equipped troops who had surrendered so rapidly to the British in June, and by enlisting reinforcements from Montevideo, as well as a militia of civilian riders and *gauchos*. Beresford's small force had been overpowered by the enemy troops and also by a civilian uprising. The British soldiers in the streets of the town had been treated to a torrent of scalding water and boiling fat, stones and sticks, which poured from behind the parapets of the flat roofs of the town's single and two-storey buildings. Beresford had surrendered. Many of his troops were disarmed and then given the freedom of the town. They lodged with families in the town; in general they had been well received by the middle and upper classes of the town while the British were masters.

Beresford and his officers were interned near Buenos Aires. Then, fearing a second attack, the Buenos Aires government ordered the prisoners' removal to remote provinces. Beresford and his cousin, Lt Colonel Denis Pack, fled with the help of a *criollo* said to have links with the South American masonic lodge in London. The two men were later accused by the Spaniards of a breach of honour for breaking parole. Beresford argued that Liniers had been the first to break the capitulation agreement by imprisoning him and his staff and later by ordering transportation and internment, rather than letting them return to Europe. The argument between the English and Spaniards about the right of the action was to continue for some time. Pack remained on a ship in the River Plate to take part in a second attack on Buenos Aires, while Beresford returned to England and went on to fight against Spain.

On 23 December 1806 *The Times* said that it had received reports of the recapture of Buenos Aires, in correspondence from Lord Strangford, obtained through Madrid and Lisbon. "We do not consider them [the reports] entitled to the least credit." However, confirmation of the rumours was published on 17 January. It had been a bad year and the new one started badly too. On 8 December *The Times* had announced, from the Hamburg papers, Napoleon's decree declaring the British isles in a state of blockade. And on 10 December the peace treaty between Prussia and France had been reproduced in London.

The *Fly*, the fastest brig in the navy, was ordered to catch General Craufurd and reroute him to the River Plate instead of Chile. Colonel Backhouse who had been sent from the Cape of Good Hope to reinforce Beresford was the first to arrive in the River Plate and found no senior officer to report to. He proceeded to capture a number of small settlements on the coast of what is today Uruguay and put the troops ashore to rest. He was joined in January by Sir Samuel Auchmuty, who captured Montevideo in swift and brilliant action on 3 February 1807. With Auchmuty was Admiral Sterling who arrived to relieve Sir Home Popham, by then no longer a celebrity in the imperial cause. Popham had been ordered to return to London to face court martial on charges of deserting his post at the Cape. He got off lightly, with a reprimand.

Craufurd was next to arrive in the River Plate, followed by General John Whitelocke, ordered to capture Buenos Aires. Whitelocke's rank was that of Governor General of South America, with an income of £12,000 per annum. Whitelocke reported that:

> upwards of 170 men have gone over to the enemy previous to my arrival, and some since. The more the soldiers become acquainted with the plenty of the country offers and the easy means of acquiring it, the greater will be the evil, as the temptation is irresistible to the common mind, beyond the calculation of those acquainted with the locality.

Such a survey seemed to convince Whitelocke that the operation was not worth his pursuit; the land was corrupting, the people unfriendly, and even if there were no insurmountable geographical difficulties, these two factors were unbeatable. Whitelocke bungled the operation. His chief of staff, General Leveson Gower, proved equally incompetent.

On 28 June 1807 they went ashore at Ensenada, south of Buenos Aires. In spite of information from Colonel Denis Pack, who had escaped captivity in Buenos Aires and taken part in the capture of Colonia del Sacramento, and was available to Whitelocke for consultation, progress was slow and hampered by natural difficulties. The same swamp that Beresford had negotiated with some trouble, but without loss of cannon or stores, bogged down Whitelocke. Men sank to their waists in the cold winter mud. Rations were lost; the troops were hurried, harassed, ill-fed; and orders were not given in proper time. Whitelocke was harsh with his officers and tried to win the friendship of his men by using barrack-room slang, which rather than gain him favour lost him respect everywhere.

There was little communication between the columns of Gower and Whitelocke. When Gower, finding the river to the south of Buenos Aires unfordable, circled the town to the west, away from Whitelocke's force in the east, they lost touch completely. Lt Colonel Bonege, the quartermaster general, when asked later about the administrative arrangements for the march, replied, "I never heard of any calculation or arrangement whatever about this subject; I was totally ignorant of the plan of operations which the general intended to pursue."

On the day of the attack, Whitelocke lost contact with all his staff. The time for attack was set at noon. But as the hour grew closer, the officers did not report to collect their orders. They drifted up to the house of the Santa Coloma family, where Whitelocke established his headquarters, near the edge of the River Plate, at mid-morning. Auchmuty, when reprimanded for arriving so late, protested that "midday is, in my opinion, an improper time to march through the streets of a populous town." The time of attack was altered to 6.30 a.m. the next day. The officers had a siesta while the men tried to make themselves comfortable and warm in that coldest month of the winter.

The orders solved nothing. At times they were incomprehensible; some of the paragraphs made riddles for military students. For example:

The cannonade in the centre to be the signal for the whole to rush forward.
Two corporals, with tools, to be attached to the head of each column.
The whole to be unloaded, and no firing to be allowed on any account.
Each officer commanding a division of the left-wing, which is from the 88th to 87th inclusively, to take care that he does not incline to his right those of the right-wing, that is, light brigade and 45th regiment.

There was no mention of where Whitelocke could be found. The last paragraph quoted above was omitted from some of the copies of the confirmatory written orders, presumably because it was unintelligible to the staff officer making out the copies.[11]

The British army entered the city with unloaded rifles to the most bitter civilian reaction English troops had known. The entire population opposed them. When he reached the centre of the city, Whitelocke had lost two thousand men, wounded, dead, and prisoners. But he still had a reserve, in Montevideo and on the ships at anchor in the

River Plate, of six thousand able men.

Santiago de Liniers, by then promoted to viceroy, asked Whitelocke to surrender. To everybody's surprise, he did. He also surrendered Montevideo and agreed to withdraw from the Plate. He was of the opinion that Britain could never rule such a hostile place. His officers were bewildered, his troops furious with frustration and grief. On the night of 7 July 1807, walls in Buenos Aires were witnesses to a rare mixture of graffiti. Spanish and Creole revellers scrawled their rejoicing at the victory against the British and repudiated the terms of the surrender offered to Whitelocke. English soldiers wrote obscenities against Whitelocke. The feeling among the officers and men was summed up by one officer, Lieutenant Colonel Lancelot Holland—who had as his task to transcribe Whitelocke's confused orders—in the entry for that day in his own diary.

We were ordered to march out without arms. It was a bitter task, everyone felt it; the men were all in tears. We were marched through the town to the Fort. Nothing could be more mortifying than our passage through the streets amidst the rabble who had conquered us. They were very dark-skinned people, short and ill-made, covered with rags, armed with long muskets and some a sword. There was neither order nor uniformity among them.[12]

The souls of their dead would have no rest. For a long time after the battle the residents on the south side of the town, where the invaders had arrived, said their nights were disturbed by ghosts who spoke English. This caused difficulties for the priest at the church of San Pedro Telmo: he had no interpreter to help with his attempts to conduct a service of exorcism. Whitelocke was later to be accused of surrendering Montevideo without cause, for the position was not in danger. According to a contemporary account, one of the military leaders of Buenos Aires, Alzaga, is quoted as telling Liniers:

"Put in that he shall also evacuate Montevideo." Said the Viceroy: "That is out of the question; it would spoil the whole matter." Alzaga insisted, "Let us put it down; it can be easily taken out." It was put down and it was not objected to.[13]

On this occasion *The Times* appeared wary of committing the mistake of over-optimism of the year before. On Thursday, 27 August 1807, the paper said:

From the proclamation issued by General Whitelocke it appears that an early attack on Buenos Ayres was in contemplation, and a pretty confident hope seemed to be entertained that the enterprise would prove successful. Whatever difference of opinion may exist with respect to the value of the object which we are solicitous to recover, there can be but one sentiment in regard to the issue of the attempt to regain possession of this settlement.

However, there were many second thoughts this time.

The commercial advantages to be derived from the Vice-Royalty of Buenos Ayres should, perhaps, be regarded as of far less comparative importance. The inhabitants have hitherto manifested no disposition cordially to embrace an English interest. To retain possession of it would always require a very considerable force, and these are not the times when this country with any sort of prudence or foresight, can thus strip itself of a garrison requisite for its own defence.

By then the news of defeat was on its way to London.

The attack upon Buenos Ayres has failed and, long before this, there is not a single British soldier in the Spanish port of South America. The details of this disaster, perhaps the greatest which has been felt by this country since the commencement of the revolutionary war, were published yesterday in an *Extraordinary Gazette*.[14]

The next day the paper carried a furious criticism of the armistice and evacuation terms. A few days later, on 22 September, Sir Home Popham was found by *The Times* to be the person responsible for the South American failure. On Wednesday 30 September, the paper told its readers in contained fury:

It being clearly understood that the late disastrous affair at Buenos Ayres is to be thoroughly investigated, and the conduct of the commanders to be judicially scrutinised, the purpose for which we so zealously called the attention of our countrymen to their apparent mismanagement is now fully answered, they are to be put upon defence and we shall therefore say not one word more of General Whitelocke, till that defence is before the public.

The same edition contained a letter in defence of Lt Colonel Denis Pack and General Beresford. It denied that they had broken their parole at Buenos Aires on the grounds that Viceroy Liniers had not kept to the agreement of surrender. *The Times* had reproduced translations of severe attacks on both officers, first published in *El Publicista*, Buenos Aires, and *La Gaceta de Madrid*.[15]

There was a wave of anger among merchants who just a few months before had been led to believe that, in spite of Napoleon's efforts to cripple English trade, a great new market had been opened in South America. Now, suddenly, it had been closed. A plan for a third expedition to Buenos Aires, this time to be led by Sir Arthur Wellesley, Duke of Wellington, was discussed as a possibility to salvage a few scraps of national honour; but developments in the Peninsular war demanded his presence in Europe.

A profusion of purportedly knowledgeable literature about the Spanish American colonies and, later, about the trial of General Whitelocke, was in circulation. The many and varied editions on Buenos Aires and the inland provinces became best-sellers. *The Times* and *Morning Chronicle* reports provided the material for many of the books. An example of the texts used appeared in *The Times* on Friday, 13 November, under the title:

South America: Letter from a merchant in Buenos Ayres, containing a true account of the proceedings of the forces of His Catholic Majesty, under the command of Don Sr Jago Liniers and Bremont, Viceroy, Governor and Captain General of the provinces of the river La Plata, and those of the forces of His Britannic Majesty under the command of Lieutenant General John Whitelocke, from the period of their disembarkation to attack the said capital, until their surrender on 7 July 1807.

Popham became the target of much abuse. Satirical poems were aimed at him, the language of some being extremely harsh. Although a motion against Popham in the Court of Common Council was defeated,[16] his claim for a share of the property taken at Buenos Aires was rejected. *The Times* remarked with some sarcasm:

A British jury determined that he is not entitled to such share... The conduct of this gentleman is to undergo a further investigation during the ensuing session of Parliament, in relation to the bargain respecting the division of this very plunder, which bargain was made at the Cape with Sir David Baird, before Sir Home heaved an anchor on his patriotic expedition to South America. [17]

The chief justice felt that the division of plunder established a bad precedent in the navy. Eventually, Popham would get a share, though not all he wanted.

Whitelocke was the subject of many cutting cartoons.[18] He went on trial early in the year after his surrender. His correspondence with Liniers containing the terms of the British intimation and later capitulation was reproduced in all its embarrassing detail.[19] General Beresford meanwhile[20] was the subject of praise for action in the Peninsular war.[21]

The four charges against Whitelocke, for dereliction of duty, occupied most of a newspaper column on 27 January 1808. The trial opened the next day. As *The Times* began its coverage of the trial, though the proceedings were restricted, on 30 January, the paper also reported out of Charleston, South Carolina, that the Buenos Aires authorities had banned all non-Spanish ships from the River Plate. Four British naval ships that remained in the estuary had given assurance that they would not interfere with local trade on the river "as the Spaniards have supplied them [the British] with everything they wanted."

Nineteen officers, all lieutenant generals, formed the court that tried General Whitelocke. The trial itself attracted wide interest and comment. It may have been of some comfort to Whitelocke to learn, during his trial, that Viceroy Liniers had been replaced and put under arrest in Buenos Aires at the investigation of the more conservative Spaniards in the Cabildo—the town's council and main authority. Liniers was charged with trying to seduce Ana Perichon, the wife of an Anglo-Irish merchant, Thomas O'Gorman, and worse, with trying to introduce her to local society.[22] In fact, the seduction was a *fait accompli*—the publicity surrounding it merely reflected the envy felt for Liniers, a Frenchman, by the Spaniards. His affair with Ana Perichon, a Mauritius-born woman of French ancestry, predated Beresford's invasion. Local gossips had observed Miss Perichon regularly entering and leaving Liniers' rooms in the Fort. At the height of his success against the English, and of his promotion to Viceroy, the Spaniards had been unable to dislodge Liniers. Now Ana Perichon provided the instrument of his downfall.

The proceedings of Whitelocke's own trial, the presentation of evidence and the defence, took up most of the editions and their supplements of *The Times* of Wednesday, 16 March, and of Thursday, 17 March. Sentence was read at Horse Guards on 24 March and its text published on 26 March. He was cashiered.

Just before Whitelocke went for trial, General Miranda published a request for renewed support for another venture to the north of South America. He asked for seven thousand men. "There was a time when such a plan had a most captivating aspect; at present it seems to be embarrassed with various difficulties. We must either force the South Americans to avow their own independence, or we must persuade them." It was Saturday, 9 January 1808. *The Times* suggested that one way to win the trust of South America and restore confidence in England would be to return the spoils taken from Buenos Aires in 1806. The paper said that Miranda was casting wider in Europe because he had lost confidence in England. "If Miranda has no reason to trust England, England has no reason to trust him, as both have been defeated in South America..." And yet, Miranda's ideas were attractive still: "Buonaparte has got the continent of Europe in his hand; squeezes it at pleasure..."

Not all was to be defeat in South America. Great consolation would be found in the successful transfer of the court of the Bragança royal family from Lisbon to Brazil. Dom Joao, the Portuguese regent, his family and his entire court, around two thousand people, sailed out of the Tagus on 29 November 1807, under the protection of the British fleet. As military victories go, it may not have been much. But it was a remarkable moral triumph: a whole court moved. Napoleon Bonaparte had lured King Ferdinand of Spain into captivity and by so doing would precipitate momentous events—independence—in the Spanish colonies of America. His attempt to do the same in Portugal failed. The rule of the Bragança family was near bankruptcy at home. Their administration of the Portuguese provinces of Brazil had weakened to near collapse—and it was threatened with revolt, even though the only uprising, in 1788, led by *Tiradentes* "Tooth-puller", a dentist, had been quelled. The removal to Rio de Janeiro was to give the Portuguese court a new lease of life, rather than the ignominy of exile. In South America it would bring about a historic change just as impressive as in the Spanish possessions.[23]

Napoleon's press, though regretful that the success achieved with the Spanish court had not been attained in Portugal, found comfort in the departure. One week before, the British minister in Lisbon, Lord Strangford, who left for Rio with the Portuguese court, had described the desperation in the capital at the proximity of the French, and the swiftness of the French advance.

Le Moniteur, in Paris, wrote on 5 December:

> The House of Bragança has lost Portugal; it experiences the fate of all the Powers who have put their confidence in England. It is a very important success for France to have deprived the English of the excellent ports of Lisbon and Oporto. A new portion of the ancient Continent will be purged of the English influence. If the independence of the United States has been useful to France, the new establishment of the House of Bragança in another part of the New Continent also promises her great advantages. The relations of the Court of the Brazils with Portugal, the commercial connections which it will be obliged to form with Europe, will turn to the profit of France and her Allies.
>
> What do the Brazils produce? Cotton, and other articles similar to those which are received from the colonies. Other markets must be found for them; for England already overflows with colonial produce. These markets will be looked for upon the Continent. They will be found in France, for the supply of our manufactures and for our consumption. And these operations, in place of being effected by the intervention of Lisbon, will be done with France. And by these means will ensure to us, besides so many advantages, the profits of a direct trade.

Such unabashed gloating offended *The Times*:

> It is somewhat extraordinary, that it [Le Moniteur] should endeavour to prove the occurrence [emigration of the royal family of Portugal] highly beneficial to France, on account of the connection that must continue to subsist between the government of the Brazils, and that of Portugal in its present state of vassalage to Buonaparte. It never occurs to the writer of this article, that any irritation can exist in the mind of the Prince Regent against the oppressor of his country; nor does he seem to perceive that the only intercourse between Europe and the new Court of South America must be through the medium of England.[24]

The French view of events proved short-sighted. Britain did gain from the protection given to the Bragança family. The establishment of the emigrated court, however, led Britain to believe that it could patronise the Portuguese court with impunity and intimidate Brazil whenever a decision at Rio de Janeiro did not meet with English agreement.

Early in January Londoners were told that "further particulars respecting the departure of the Court of Portugal gradually transpire."[25] The Prince Regent had taken with him forty-two chests of plate; he had been accompanied by approximately two thousand members of his civil service—including their families—and before departure he had ordered that some of the guns of the Fort of Lisbon be spiked to protect the British fleet. This last order was not fully obeyed by Portuguese officers, who thought that if they annulled all their guns, they would wipe out their chances of resistance against the French if that were ever possible. The Prince arrived in Brazil on 8 January "after a remarkably fine passage."[26]

Only a few weeks after the Regent's departure, rebellion against the French erupted in Lisbon, on New Year's Eve.[27] The uprising was crushed and General Junot, the French commander in Lisbon, dissolved the Regency of the Bragança family and annexed Portugal to France.[28]

On Monday, 18 January 1808, Londoners read of one of the first benefits to be derived from the Prince Regent's emigration to Brazil. English goods were to be admitted to Brazil on payment of the same duties that they had previously paid on import to Portugal. Alongside such good news was an "Ode for the New Year, 1808", by Henry James Pye, poet laureate. While Dom Joao's emigration to Rio de Janeiro was to cause an upheaval in Brazil, by the simple fact of the installation of an imperial seat, and a part of its civil service, in a town where the port had previously been a provincial landing stage, it was also to be the factor that would ensure Brazilian unity.

While Britain appeared most vehemently determined to remove Spanish influence from South America, some of its forces in the Caribbean, encouraged by British merchants, helped to restore Spanish rule in Santo Domingo in 1808. British merchants first helped Henry Christophe—later the Haitian Emperor Henry I—to win the civil war in Haiti in 1808. But then the British merchants wrested from Christophe, for Spain, the eastern two thirds of the island of Hispaniola, Santo Domingo, which had been a Spanish possession since the first European landing by Columbus—although it had been under Haitian black rule since the island had been declared independent.

South American Independence
England's political encouragement of the independence movements in South America was to be rewarded as her military adventures never had been. Ironically, it was the stumbling steps toward republicanism in the former New England colonies that most inspired South Americans. And Britain encouraged imitation of the model, suggesting that the independent North American states should be an inspiration, while South American leaders were divided about whether to establish republics or constitutional monarchies.

In the captaincy general of Venezuela, where Miranda had failed so dismally a few years before, revolution against Spanish rule was declared. *The Times*, on Monday 2 July 1810, announced:

Revolution in the Caraccas: The revolution in the Caraccas first broke out in the city of Venezuela, on 19 April. The soldiers having gone over to the insurgents in a body, the change of government was effected without bloodshed. The administration of affairs, until the suffrages of several districts of the Provinces could be regularly collected, was *ad interim* committed to a body of twenty-three of the most distinguished inhabitants of Venezuela, under the appellation of the Supreme Junta, at the head of which was the Marquis de Casa León; and under them were appointed four secretaries for the respective departments of Foreign Affairs, Justice, Finance, Marine and War. On the 20th the New Government issued a manifesto in justification of their proceedings. This document contains a summary of the events which succeeded the forcing the defiles of Sierra Morena by the French army, describes the hopeless situation of affairs in Spain, and declares that the object of their revolution is—to protect themselves against the pretensions of the other nations of Europe, the seduction of the French cabinet, and even against any designs which the late Spanish representatives may entertain upon their country; to maintain themselves in their political dignity; to support as far as possible the legitimate dynasty of Spain; to render more tolerable the condition of the unfortunate Ferdinand VII, should he be released from captivity; and to support the glory of the Spanish name, by preserving the remains of that noble and generous nation, and offering to their brethren of the mother country a secure asylum, not only from French oppression, but also against all attempts on the part of the other nations of Europe.

There were several political reasons for the moderation of the terms in which the revolutionaries of Venezuela couched the statement of their coup d'état: Spain, for example, might shake off the ignominy of French domination, and attempt to recover her colonies. Certainly, after 1814 Ferdinand VII did his utmost to recover the South American possessions, without a care for diplomacy. Alternatively, France might support a Spanish raid on the wayward colonies or try to retain the territories for herself. The Venezuelans were also concerned not to offend either England or the United States.

A proclamation dated 19 April and published in the *Caracas Gazette* said, on 27 April, that the "day of 19 April bore throughout the stamp of beneficence and generosity, and in the streets, not a single voice was heard but in favour of submissive petitions, just claims, well-merited rewards, together with *vivas* acclamations." Among the decrees passed on 20 April, "they exempted the Indians from the tribute hitherto exacted of them, in order that the primitive inhabitants of our soil should be among the first to enjoy the advantages of our civil regeneration."

As if to underline those advantages, just one month later the much coveted colony of Buenos Aires announced its autonomy from Spain. *The Times*, Tuesday, 7 August 1810:

> On 22 May the Cabildo of Buenos Ayres with the consent of the Viceroy, held a general meeting of the inhabitants to deliberate upon the proceedings to be adopted in consequence of the melancholy accounts just received from the mother country. The result of their deliberations was, that the superior government of the province, previously exercised by his Excellency Don Baltasar Hidalgo de Cisneros, should be transferred to the Cabildo, until the appointment of a provisional Superior Junta, which latter body should carry on the government according to law and in the name of Ferdinand VII, until a general Congress could be convoked of deputies from all the provinces in the Viceroyalty, for the establishment of such form of government as might be deemed most convenient.

On the 24th the Cabildo issued a proclamation constituting... a superior junta and notifying their appointment to the people. A considerable body of the most respectable of the inhabitants, including the commandant and officers of the Volunteer Corps, expressed themselves dissatisfied with the election made by the Cabildo. The consequence was that the proclamation of the 24th was revoked, and a general meeting of the inhabitants was held on the 25th in front of the Town House, to receive a fresh list of members. The Cabildo, after some deliberation, made their appearance in the balcony of the Town House and proposed to the people the provisional superior junta... The people, upon proposition of the Cabildo, agreed... In addition, it was understood between the Cabildo and the people, that the Junta should have in readiness, within a fortnight, a force of 500 men to proceed into the interior; the expense of the levy and expedition to be defrayed by the salaries of [Viceroy] Don Baltasar Hidalgo de Cisneros, and such public boards as the Junta might think fit to reduce, care however being had, at the express desire of the people, that none of the said officers should be wholly unprovided for.

They were all honourable revolutions. The South American provinces, some of them at least, wanted to be independent of Spain; but after nearly three centuries of colonialism it was not a simple matter to break old bonds. Not many empires or colonial masters—with the exception of eight centuries of Arab dominion in Spain—had lasted as long and had been as successful. The colonies preferred to call for autonomy first. Independence was too large a prospect.

In view of the events of the previous years, the English establishment was cautious.

Accounts were received yesterday by ministers from the river Plate, communicating the important information that the inhabitants of Buenos Ayres after the example of those of the Caraccas, had deposed the viceroy and established a provisional government. We are enabled to lay before our readers some interesting documents concerning this event. It will be seen from these that there is nothing of a revolutionary spirit, no intention of casting off their allegiance to the parent state and assuming independence in the proceedings of these colonists; on the contrary, they profess unalterable fidelity to Ferdinand VII, or any government lawfully representing him. It is evident, however, from the military measures they have adopted, that they are determined to assert their independence, should the state of the mother country, or any other circumstances, render it necessary and advisable.

In consequence of this change in the government, some regulations favourable to commerce were established. The duties on the export of hides were reduced about nineteen per cent, as were those on tallow twelve per cent. The duties on other articles are proportionally reduced, but the scale was not settled when the vessel, the *Mutine*, that brought the dispatches, came away.

The viceroyalty became the United Provinces of the River Plate. They were not united, but that was no impediment to the imposition of an ambitious and well-intentioned title.

HMS *Mutine* had lain at anchor outside Buenos Aires for some time. Its captain had been instrumental in applications to Viceroy Cisneros on behalf of about fifty English and Scottish merchants in the town—most of the British community residents there—to prevent the Spanish authorities from enforcing the colonial laws that allowed non-Spaniards only forty days' residence in the colonies. The Britons had remained since the capitulation of 1807, anxious to sell off their stocks and those of their principals in Europe at the best possible profit, and had avoided expulsion by a series of successful petitions to the authorities. Finally, in May 1810, all the British had been ordered to leave. Days before the deadline for their expulsion, the revolution had taken place in Buenos Aires and the Britons resident there had been reprieved by the Junta.[29] Although there were suspicions that the British, led by a Scot named Alexander Mackinnon, had actively conspired to remove the viceroy, no proof could be found to support such indications.[30] "The inhabitants of Monte Video had resolved to adhere to the proceedings of the inhabitants of Buenos Ayres. The latest accounts from that settlement are of 25 May, at which time the utmost tranquillity prevailed there." This last phrase was speculative and rather premature.

The announcement of autonomy, in Caracas and Buenos Aires, and later in Asunción (Paraguay), provoked unrest throughout the continent. The turmoil was to last nearly two decades. Caracas was rapidly recaptured by Spain, beginning a war for independence which would last twelve years. Some years later, revolutions in Chile and Peru followed events in Caracas and Buenos Aires, and would have to await a combination of events and personalities which made South American independence possible. All had strong links with Britain.

José de San Martín, a fastidious captain born in the north-eastern reaches of the viceroyalty of the River Plate, educated from an early age in Spain, inspired in England, and only just returning to the country of his birth as a mature officer, was, with Simón Bolívar, the most notable of these personalities.

> He was tall, well-made, very broad across the shoulders and upright in his carriage; his complexion was sallow, and he possessed a remarkably sharp and penetrating eye; his hair was dark, and he had large whiskers. His address was quick and lively; his manners affable and polite... What more particularly excited my attention [in his private study] was a large miniature likeness of himself, hung between prints of Napoleon Buonaparte and Lord Wellington, all three being framed in a corresponding manner.[31]

San Martín's vision of South American liberation had been in part acquired, in part evolved by himself, by contact with British officers he had met during the Peninsular war. He set out to try to accomplish a latter-day version of the Pullen and Maitland plans to wrest the continent from Spain. San Martín wanted a monarchical establishment for South America, in opposition to the younger Bolívar's ambition for a federation of republics.

Bolívar was an immensely romantic figure. At one point he had inspired Lord Byron to go to Venezuela; failing that, Byron named a boat *Bolívar* instead. Women adored Bolívar. His romantic conquests were many; his pleasure in parties, whoring, and a wild existence won him as much admiration from his followers as did his campaigns— and as much hatred and slander from his enemies as were prompted by his military achievements.

> In the time of his military campaigns, when his headquarters were in a city, town or village, dances were arranged nearly every night, and his pleasure was to dance and valse, then vanish from the room to dictate some orders and dispatches, and again dance, and work again. In this way his ideas became clearer and stronger, and his style more eloquent... When the bad weather prevents our going out, His Excellency gets his own back by lying on the hammock and rocking fast, or walking along corridors of the house sometimes singing, some-

times reciting verse, or conversing with others who walk with him.[32]

San Martín arrived in Buenos Aires early in 1812 and had to organise a regiment of grenadiers with which to proceed to Chile and thence to Peru. He also had to defend Buenos Aires, so recently declared autonomous, from the Spanish stronghold at Montevideo and to protect the revolutionaries against themselves, for they were by then involved in much bickering about policy. At the battle of San Lorenzo, ninety miles north of Buenos Aires, in February 1813, San Martín's newly-created grenadier regiment underwent a trial by fire, defeating a contingent of Spanish marines who had landed to prepare an attack on Buenos Aires. The most impressive witness of that day was a Scot, John Parish Robertson, who, with his brother, had been in the River Plate since the British expeditions. Robertson was on his way to visit property in Corrientes province when he ran into a party of San Martín's troops who were about to occupy the San Lorenzo convent, on the banks of the river Paraná, to ambush the arriving Spaniards.

> Surely, you are... San Martín, I said, and if it be so, behold here is your friend Mr Robertson. I had no difficulty in persuading [him] to allow me to accompany him to the convent. Only mind, said he, that it is neither your duty nor your business to fight... I rode by the side of San Martín as he moved onward at the head of his men in dark and silent phalanx... When in an instant, and at full speed, the two squadrons of horse debouched from behind the convennt, and flanking the enemy on each wing, commenced with their glittering sabres a slaughter which was instantaneous and frightful... I was very glad to quit the still reeking field of actionn. I begged San Martín, therefore, to take my wine and provisions for the benefit of the wounded men of both parties, and bidding him a hearty adieu, I quitted the scenne of action, with regret for the slaughter, but admiration of his coolness and intrepidity.[33]

San Martín took his grenadier regiment over Argentina to Mendoza. There, while holding the post of Governor of the Cuyo provinces for three years, he silently, almost secretly, organised a mighty army to cross the Andes and invade Chile in 1817. He left behind, guarding Mendoza, a small unit of British veterans who had deserted the invading army of 1806-7.

It took San Martín, in combination with the Irish-Chilean officer Bernardo O'Higgins, one year to rout the Spanish army in Chile. From Chile he had to advance north against the vice-regal stronghold in Peru. For this he had the support at sea of Lord Cochrane. The Scottish nobleman had sought in South America a new career when his own as a naval officer, member of parliament, and city entrepreneur lay in ruins. In London, Cochrane had been accused of attempting to swindle the Stock Exchange—a charge never fully substantiated. Under contract to the new Chilean government, Cochrane seized dominion of the sea from the Spanish fleet, which was based at Callao, Peru.

In the memoirs of one of the more famous of the British volunteers to serve with San Martín, General William Miller, the sense of excitement and adventure that invaded Chile at that time was intense and widespread. The fighting men and the population regarded themselves as participants in the creation of a new republic, carved out of an ageing empire. Chile's main port, Valparaíso, according to General Miller, offered "an imposing exciting spectacle to behold, [the] bay crowded with shipping." Men marched to the shore "with music playing, through cheering multitudes. The population of Santiago and of the country had poured into Valparaíso, and every avenue was crowded with spectators."[34]

But Peruvian Creoles and the Spanish landowners were in no hurry for independence. They had to be convinced of its desirability and, in the delays caused while trying to do this, San Martín fell out with Cochrane—who believed in a rapid, successful attack. San Martín argued that a military victory was temporary and, without political changes, would only be followed by the restoration of Spanish rule. Cochrane and the Argentine general were never on good terms. The Scot accused San Martín of arrogance, meanness—for not paying his seamen the wages promised—and treachery—for abandoning Chile to become, for a short time, Protector of Peru, following a declaration of independence on 28 July 1821. After a meeting with Bolívar at Guayaquil in July 1822, for reasons that have remained secret to this day, San Martín left his post and South America. He went into exile in France. Bolívar, who had already annexed Ecuador to Colombia, remained to fight on for full Peruvian independence. San Martín had spent little more than a decade of his adult life in South America.

British Involvement

Among the first of the many British personalities of the independence wars to reach the continent was William Brown, an Irishman born in Foxford, County Mayo, a merchant seaman who had arrived in the River Plate in 1810. His arrival was in quest of a commercial life but, after suffering losses to the Portuguese in the Banda Oriental (Uruguay)—then in an uneasy truce with the Spaniards at Montevideo—he took action to make good his losses by seizing a Portuguese prize. As this seemed easy, he took some more enemy ships. In the two years that followed he was plied with gifts and honours to win his services for the revolutionary cause. He at first argued that his wife, Eliza Chitty, was pregnant and later with young children and needed his company; but he was eventually won over by the junta of Buenos Aires and from merchant master he became an admiral and founder of the Argentine navy. In a series of encounters with the Spanish fleet at Montevideo, Brown, demonstrating brilliant seamanship, was the victor.

Another helpful Briton was John Thomond O'Brien, of County Wicklow, who took part in the liberation of Chile and Peru as an officer with San Martín.[35] And Daniel Florence O'Leary was aide-de-camp to Bolívar, as well as his leading biographer and historian. There were a host of others. The Venezuelan liberator, Bolívar, had recruited in England and Ireland a motley army of malcontent regulars, as well as frustrated officers whose European careers had not been satisfactory or had been prematurely thwarted. They were the men made redundant by the end of the Napoleonic wars and they readily joined Bolívar's army of independence, where the prospects of battle, promotion, and romance were attractive. As many as five thousand went to Venezuela from the British isles; their efforts, marches, battles and sacrifices have given them, the men of the British Legion, a prominent place in the history of Colombia and Venezuela. In reality, they all rushed to join a fantasy; they were recruited sometimes by earnest men, sometimes by scoundrels. The uniforms which they had made for their expedition were lavish in their regimental colours and quite inappropriate in the tropics—even though they fitted the military and social ideas of Europe. Some subscribed their savings towards a stock of port and good meats, but their money was embezzled by a crooked agent. Britain tried to stop them with the Foreign Enlistment Act of 1819; but that was seen as a feeble attempt at demonstrating concern for non-intervention.

In 1816 the United Provinces of the River Plate confirmed their autonomy, declared in 1810, and proclaimed themselves independent. A Briton was the first to send the news to Europe. Robert Ponsonby Staples had been in Buenos Aires since the invasions, trying to secure a position as diplomatic envoy for Britain. But he was ignored by the Foreign Office and officially rejected by Buenos Aires. So he became diplomat *de facto*.

... Mr P. Staples signs himself as Consul of His Britannic Majesty. This circumstance occasioned much speculation on change as the merchants trading to Buenos Ayres knew of no person there who has of late officiated in that character. They therefore suppose that some change may have taken place in the principles and conduct of the government to induce this gentleman to so announce himself.[36]

The news the merchants really wanted was the recognition of the former colonies as independent republics. But it was too early for this, as *The Times* explained in October 1816:

Some time ago Mr Staples was sent out to Buenos Ayres in the character of British consul, but not being able, consistently with the amicable relations and friendship which subsisted between the Spanish and the British governments, to recognise the insurgent governments, he obtained his passport and returned home.[37]

More trouble loomed for England in the Americas. The two countries that attracted most attention in Britain, Brazil and the United Provinces of the River Plate, in 1816 threatened to go to war for possession of the province (Uruguay) known in Buenos Aires as Banda Oriental, and in Brazil as Cisplatina. The Portuguese claimed they were acting in support of Spain, where Ferdinand VII had returned to the throne after the defeat of Napoleon. By crushing Buenos Aires, Spain hoped to recover her former colony there even if it meant losing Montevideo to Brazil.

The Times, Tuesday, 1 October 1816:

It has been reported that a Portuguese force intended an invasion of Buenos Ayres, by virtue of a treaty with Ferdinand of Spain. The republican general, Artigas, is waiting for them on the frontiers with 30,000 men. All the population are under arms, even women. We are positively informed that there are whole companies of women, furious and enthusiastic, who have volunteered on the occasion. The invaders may be the invaded.

Which information supported the wishful thinking in a preceding paragraph in the same report, announcing the installation of an independent national congress of the provinces of the Rio de la Plata in the city of Tucuman: "Now that the best harmony prevails amongst the republican governments of that part of South America, the most brilliant results for the cause of freedom will be the consequence."[38]

The following day, a letter from the Lloyds agent at Buenos Aires said:

We had accounts from Rio de Janeiro that the expedition destined against Montevideo sailed on 12 June, and would touch in at St Catherine's where it is expected they were to remain during the winter, although the inhabitants of that city are placing it in a state of defence. The Portuguese will have little difficulty in obtaining possession of it, but we doubt much of their succeeding on the Bank Oriental [Uruguay]. The people here [Buenos Aires] have an idea that the views of the Portuguese government are directed against this place [Buenos Aires]; but we presume they will permit us to remain quiet, at least until they obtain a firm footing on the other side [Montevideo].[39]

Brazil invaded Montevideo the following year, but not Buenos Aires. However, Creoles and Europeans in Uruguay remained in constant rebellion against the Portuguese.

With the exception of Brazil, under an autocratic but nevertheless fairly moderate imperial rule, South America entered the third decade of the nineteenth century in turmoil. What had been the provinces of New Granada (now Colombia, Venezuela and Ecuador) tried to remain united as Gran Colombia; but rivalries and jealousies broke into the open and eventually three separate countries would be proclaimed. Peru was trying to complete its independence from Spain; Chile was nearly bankrupt; Buenos Aires was on the verge of civil war.

In London, and in the manufacturing towns of the north, pressure grew on Westminster to recognise the new republics as the United States had begun to do in 1822. The US had enunciated the Monroe Doctrine against European intervention in the Americas in December 1823. Traders were of the opinion that Britain could appear as a protector of the new nations and therefore reap the benefit of the commerce which such a move would elicit. The government, however, was now reluctant to offend Spain. Nevertheless, Canning, the Foreign Secretary, soon arranged with the United States that they would work together in South America to end Spanish rule and keep France out.

The Times, Saturday, 31 January 1824:

It is now more than fourteen years since the war first sprung up between Spain and her colonies; and so long as the contest continued, we, though solicited by both parties, most religiously abstained from assisting either. The disposition of the people of this country being favourable to the South Americans, our governments, in order to check that disposition, to invalidate and render it useless, passed the Foreign Enlistment Bill, by which it became illegal even for individuals to engage in the service of the revolted provinces: so that neutrality more severely rigid than that observed by England during the continuance of the contest between the European and the American Spaniards cannot be conceived.[40] But the affair has now long been decided, the South American have prevailed by their native strength; peace is practically established between the contending parties, the independences of the South American states has been acknowledged by Foreign Powers—of whom, be it observed, we were not the first.

Once again it was not quite as simple as that. Within a month Ferdinand VII demonstrated his anxiety to regain the South American colonies: "I have ordained the abolition of the regime called 'constitutional', and published regulations for trading between Europe and South America."[41]

However, in England the campaign to impress upon the government the need to recognise the new republics was under way. As a demonstration of the plans for independence, *The Times* reproduced the draft constitution of Brazil—which was in the process of converting its imperial house into a constitutional monarchy—on 23 February; the Mexican constitution was printed in the 1 March 1824 edition.

On 6 March, the paper was again regretting, editorially, the absence of diplomatic recognition.

> We claim and enjoy free commerce with the trans-Atlantic provinces. We are willing to allow Old Spain the grace and advantage of being the first to acknowledge their independent sovereignty; but should she hesitate, our recognition in no case can be delayed long...

On 16 March the paper reported the defeat of a motion in Parliament to recognise the former colonies. On 17 March, an editorial said: "We trade with them, we station consuls in their ports, and, at the moment that we publicly attest the inability of the mother country to recover her ancient possession of them, we declare that we shall not suffer a third power to interfere." On 17 May: "The question of recognising as independent the late Spanish possessions in the Americas, or at least such parts of them as are no longer torn by civil conflict, assumes a shape which every day forces itself more upon the attention of ministers... As respects the interest of British commerce, a decided course becomes the immediate duty of this government..." On 18 May: "...has brought the unqualified refusal of the Spanish government to entertain, in any shape whatever, the question of a recognition of the independence of South America... It had the effect of depressing most of the South American securities yesterday." On 27 May: "The Spaniards, in order to suspend what we hope we may call the imminent recognition of the independence of the South American states by this government, put forth at intervals wild reports of the armaments which they are going to send out for their subjugation..." On 7 June: "Proceedings of a meeting of traders in Liverpool in favour of the independence of the new states of America" [over two columns of print]. On 8 June: The meeting was "an event of much importance." On 16 June: "Proceedings in the House of Commons last night with respect to the recognition of the independence of the South American states was less interesting than might have been expected... Mr Canning indicated that no change had taken place..." On 19 June: "Meeting in Manchester in favour of the independence of the new states of South America." On 21 June: The Manchester meeting... "we presume that it is a point of official form only, which delays a moment longer this recognition on the part of the King's government..." On 22 June: "HMS *Cambridge* left the anchorage of [Montevideo] having landed Mr Hood, the consul for this place; Mr Woodbine Parish, consul general for Buenos Ayres, and Mr Rowcroft, consul general for Peru..." On 1 July: In spite of news of the recapture of Callao by the Spaniards "drawing after it the re-occupation of Peru", the paper reports on a meeting in Leeds in favour of recognition, "If Mr Canning be sincere in his declarations he cannot now plead the indifference of the people of England." On 6 July, in a report from *El Argos*, in Buenos Aires, *The Times* noted that the British consul there had held a first official meeting with the minister of foreign affairs. On 7 July: Mr Canning's credential at Buenos Aires was addressed to "His Excellency Rivadavia, secretary of the government, at Buenos Ayres. Of the Spanish government? No; but of the Republican government, to the exclusion of the Spanish..." The same edition regretted the loss of Peru to the Spaniards; but recorded the establishment of friendly relations with Colombia. And that same day (7 July) the paper started quoting, under Foreign Funds, prices for Buenos Aires which had recently floated a large bond issue on the London market through Baring Brothers. Quotations for Chilean,

Colombian and Mexican bonds had been given since the beginning of the year, and for Peru since March.

The *Times'* vigorous campaign could not fail. On 29 July it quoted the opening message of the new session of the Buenos Aires legislature, which gave account of the accreditation of plenipotentiaries of the United States and England. But the crowning success was still to come. As General Sucre defeated Spanish rule in South America at Ayacucho on 9 December 1824, the imminence of a treaty of friendship between Britain and Buenos Aires was announced. On what was to become a memorable Saint Andrew's Day in 1824, the British minister, Woodbine Parish, told diners at Faunch's Restaurant in Buenos Aires that he had been charged with opening talks for such a pact. He later wrote to London:

> We were a very numerous party, upwards of seventy, and I must say I never saw such a scene in my life as took place after what I told them (of my powers to treat with the government)—they appeared all mad and I expected that the tables and chairs would have followed all the bottles and glasses out of the windows, in true Spanish style. Some of the Buenos Ayreans who were desirous to drink Mr Canning's health, threw away their glasses and insisted upon having bottles of wine instead of glasses to drink it in... and yet they were sober.[42]

The Treaty of Friendship, Navigation and Commerce was signed in February 1825.[43] The treaty's results in trade would lead to Argentina being described as one of the pillars of the British economy for almost a century.[44] In that year, Lord Cochrane returned to England, to find that he had become a household name of immense popularity after his destruction of the Spanish and Portuguese fleets in Chilean, Peruvian and Brazilian waters. The British government refrained from invoking the Foreign Enlistment Act against him.[45]

A new age was near; but it was difficult to adjust to the end of colonialism. Colombia was in the throes of disintegration, a sad footnote to more than a dozen years of war waged by Bolívar. The Liberator had dragged the country screaming into independence, but perhaps too fast; and it had not adjusted to its new status. The failure to live within the boundaries of a constitution had forced Bolívar to assume dictatorial powers, although this he regarded as a failure.

The Times, Thursday, 6 March 1828:

> Extract from a letter from Bogotá, dated November 1827: This country is on the very brink of ruin. Nothing but a military government can save it. Their boast of Republicanism is a true mockery of common sense. The laws are openly eluded, and set at defiance by the authorities, employers, and individuals of every description. The grossest immorality reigns through all the classes. A people who call an honest man a *pendejo* [fool], and an infamous cheat *un hombre vivo* [clever], can only be ruled by a rod of iron. Bolívar has many enemies because he is persuaded of this truth, and is not a thief like the infamous hypocrite Santander.[46] A civil war, great as the calamity is, must take place before the country be regenerated—if it not be already past redemption. Either Bolívar, or his intimate friend Urdaneta—ought to be appointed Dictator. Bolívar suffers under a pulmonary affection. Without the greatest care he cannot live long. The sources of justice are polluted, venality is paramount, the public coffer empty. An Englishman in the Colombian service poisoned himself three or four nights since, because he could no longer endure his state of utter mis-

ery and destitution.

The authoritarian solution was one favoured by expatriate Britons; but the years ahead would provide ample evidence that civil war solved nothing. Bolívar died on 17 December 1830, aged 47, in Colombia, damning his countrymen's corruption and their ingratitude. The Times' obituary, on 19 February 1831, scoffed at the great man's final expostulations.

Looking back, there is reason to wonder at the contrast between the relative speed of the independence process and the painful length of the post independence civil wars. The Spanish empire had relied on an extended triangle of three ports, Cartagena, Callao and Montevideo, for the defence of South America. There was not enough money to finance armies on land, so the security and policing of the provinces was left to a weak mixture of "old Spaniards" or colonial expatriates, and local recruits. This made it quite easy later for rebellious chieftains to raise armies against the Spanish authorities. And the fragile and extended triangle of ports was rapidly defeated by enemy navies. And after independence, with small, untrained navies, but with strong rebellious land forces, the dispute for power was concentrated on the land. The fight for property spread through most of the century.

NOTES:

1. John or A. O. Exquemelin (Esquemeling), *Bucaniers of America: or, a true account of the most remarkable assaults committed of late years upon the coasts of the West Indies, by Bucaniers of Jamaica and Tortuga, both English and French, wherein are contained more especially the unparalleled exploits of Sir Henry Morgan, our English Jamaican hero, who sacked Puerto Velo, burnt Panama, & Co.* (London, 1684).
2. Peter Kemp, and C. Lloyd, *The Brethren of the Coast*. (Heinemann, London, 1960).
3. Kenneth Dewhurst, and Rex Doublet, "Thomas Dover and the South Sea Company", *Medical History*, vol. 18. no. 2, April 1974.
4. See Peter Johnson, "The Saga and Salvage of HMS *Swift*", *Buenos Aires Herald Magazine*, 4 March 2000.
5. Rodolfo H. Terragno, "A Plan Conceived in Britain in 1800 anticipated the Campaign of San Martín" (unpublished investigation, London, 1982). See the *Observer*, 27 February 1983; *Clarín*, Buenos Aires, 21 March 1983. *Maitland & San Martín*. Rodolfo H. Terragno, Universidad Nacional de Quilmes, Buenos Aires, 1998.
6. George Pendle, *A History of Latin America*. (Penguin, London, 1981), p. 80. Quoted from Ricardo Levene, *A History of Argentina*. (University of North Carolina, 1937), p. 193.
7. Terragno, "A Plan".
8. Terragno, "A Plan".
9. Battle of Maida, 4 July 1806. British troops deterred a French invasion of Sicily.
10. *The Times*, Friday, 19 September 1806.
11. E. R. B. Hudson, "The English Invasion of the River Plate", *The Army Quarterly and Defence Journal*, vol. 71. no. 2, January 1956, pp. 238-44.
12. Lancelot Holland, *Viaje al Plata en 1807*. (EUDEBA, Buenos Aires, 1976).
13. J. P. and W. P. Roberton, *Letters on South America*, vol. 1, p. 128.

14. *The Times*, Monday, 14 September 1807.

15. *The Times*, 28 September 1807. *La Gaceta de Madrid*, 25 August 1807. The incident might seem trifling at this distance, but it was a matter of much controversy at the time. Beresford was still being accused of a breach of military honour in Buenos Aires in the twentieth century. See Carlos A. Pueyrredón, "Un inculpado de alta traición, la fuga de Beresford", *La Nación*, Buenos Aires, July 1930.

16. *The Times*, 4 and 5 December 1807.

17. *The Times*, 19 January 1808.

18. Carlos Roberts, *Las invasiones inglesas del Río de la Plata, 1806-1807, y la influencia y organización de las provincias del Río de la Plata*. (Peuser, Buenos Aires, 1938). An essential reference book on the invasions; contains a good selection of contemporary cartoons.

19. *The Times*, 4 January 1808.

20. Castlereagh to Ansley, 19 January 1808, *The Times*, 20 January 1808.

21. *The Times*, 14 January 1808. See also Alexander Gillespie, *Gleanings and remarks collected during many months' residence at Buenos Ayres and within the upper country*. (Leeds, 1819). Gillespie was one of the officers transported to Catamarca.

22. *The Times*, 27 February 1808.

23. Pendle, *Latin America*, p. 120.

24. *The Times*, 20 January 1808.

25. *The Times*, 6 January 1808.

26. *The Times*, 12 April 1808.

27. *The Times*, 16 January 1808.

28. *The Times*, 8 March 1808.

29. Andrew Graham-Yooll, *The Forgotten Colony*. (Hutchinson, London, 1981), p. 56.

30. Ernesto Fitte, "Los comerciantes ingleses en vísperas de la revolución de mayo", *Investigaciones y Ensayos*, Academia Nacional de la Historia, Jan.-June 1967 (Buenos Aires), pp. 69-139.

31. John Miers, *Travels in Chile and La Plata*. (London, 1826), vol. 1, p. 158.

32. Quoted in Pendle, *Latin America*, p. 105.

33. J. P. and W. P. Robertson, *Letters on South America*. (Murray, London, 1843), vol. II, pp. 9-15.

34. John Miller, *Memoirs of General Miller*. (Longman, London 1829), vol. I, p. 278. Quoted in Pendle, *Latin America*, p. 105.

35. In 1837 O'Brien was arrested in Buenos Aires while carrying a letter from General Santa Cruz, in Bolivia, to General Rosas, Governor of Buenos Aires. The Irishman was trying to buy ships for war against Chile (FO 6/63, Mandeville to Palmerston, 1 and 3 March 1838).

36. Graham-Yooll, *The Forgotten Colony*, p. 65. Erneto Fitte, "Crónica de un cónsul oficioso británico", *Boletín de la Academia Nacional de Historia*, no. 34 (Buenos Aires), p. 719.

37. *The Times*, Friday, 11 October 1816.

38. *The Times*, Tuesday, 1 October 1816.

39. *The Times*, 2 October 1816.

40. The Foreign Enlistment Act was introduced in May 1819. It barred British subjects from entering foreign armies. It was never enforced and appeared to be a sop to Spain. In 1818, Colonel English had recruited 1,200 men at £50 each to serve in Venezuela and "General" Devereux had recruited another 2,000 from a Dublin hotel for Simón Bolívar's army.

41. *The Times*, 21 February 1824.

42. Quoted in H. S. Ferns, *Britain and Argentina in the Nineteenth Century*. (Oxford University Press, 1960).

43. *The Times*, 6 May 1825.

44. Ferns, *Britain and Argentina.*
45. *The Times,* on 2 November 1860, published the obituary of Lord Dundonald, Admiral Cochrane, who had died on 30 October. "One of the great characters of a past generation has just departed... No soldier or sailor of modern times ever displayed a more extraordinary capacity than the man who now lies dead..."
46. Late in 1828, Santander conspired against Bolívar.

Chapter Two

BUENOS AIRES, BRAZIL AND THE BANDA ORIENTAL, 1826

Admiral William Brown (Edmond Lebeaud)

The province of the Banda Oriental (Uruguay), which Brazil called the Cisplatine, on the eastern margin of the River Plate, had been the cause of a continuous dispute between the Spaniards and the Portuguese. The Portuguese had used the fort of Montevideo, and the western town of Colonia del Sacramento, as a base for smuggling their products into the Spanish colony at Buenos Aires. The Spaniards had founded Montevideo, the city, in 1724, but only managed to expel the Portuguese from the Banda Oriental at the end of the eighteenth century. The disagreement over possession of the territory had been inherited by the independent government of Buenos Aires and the Emperor of Brazil. In 1816 Brazil had tried to occupy what it considered its own province, ostensibly in support of Ferdinand VII in his efforts to regain control of Buenos Aires. Spain, and the Portuguese in Brazil, were defeated by an army of *criollo* patriots with the help of the fleet of Admiral Brown of Buenos Aires. But Brazil did not relinquish its claim.

Dom Joao, Emperor of Brazil, left Rio de Janeiro in 1821 to restore the Bragança court in Lisbon. He had been King John VI of Portugal since 1816. His son, Dom Pedro, remained as regent of Brazil, encouraged by his father—and Pedro's wife, Leopoldina—to seek the leadership of the dissidents who desired independence from Portugal. Dom Joao saw the manoeuvre as the only way to secure the unity of both countries and retain the power of the Braganças. Dom Pedro declared the independence of Brazil at Ipiranga, in Sao Paulo, in September 1822, and in December he was crowned Pedro I, Emperor of Brazil. He had little enthusiasm for democratic ideals, but in 1824 accepted a constitution drafted by his liberal Portuguese entourage, to the detriment of the more liberal text of the creoles. Europe praised the new charter.[1]

Dom Pedro's popularity—or rather, that which his father had afforded the regency because of its special circumstances in the South American colonies—declined rapidly. The young emperor, aged twenty-four at the time of his coronation, knew few of the niceties of European courts, and his rule lost much of the appeal Joao had given the court. The public eye was more attracted by the neighbouring republics, which seemed to offer a more modern political system.

At the beginning of November 1825, Buenos Aires announced the annexation of the Banda Oriental. It was a decision taken with the sympathy of the autonomist leaders in the province, who preferred this to control by Brazil, as they understood independence of the province could be declared soon after. However, to Dom Pedro the annexation represented another blow to his image, and to his popularity. He threatened to go to war with Buenos Aires.

The idea of empire inspired visions of opulence and excess, of great buildings and contemporary progress. That was the European view of imperial status. In Imperial Brazil the excess was there but it was different. Brazil offered attractions for the merchant, the diplomat and the adventurer, variously seeking wealth and new experiences. The novelty was occasionally unexpected. "As we landed, we were assailed by a smell of fried sardinhas (a sort of small herring) and of pork from innumerable little stalls, kept by men and women of every colour under the sun..." wrote John Parish Robertson.[2] There were:

... streets so narrow that it was with the greatest difficulty one carriage could pass another in them. The houses were from two to four stories high. Not a pane of glass was to be seen in any of them. Instead of this, the openings in the house for light and air were shrouded by balustrades of latticed wood-work... The few carriages I saw were drawn by two mules... Every here and there two athletic blacks were to be observed carrying a large palanquin, the female inmate of which was sacredly guarded from public gaze.

Robertson was particularly interested in the condition of women in the towns he visited, as his frequent remarks about them suggest. He seldom saw women at parties and the parties themselves were too short.

As to society among the Brazilians at Rio de Janeiro, it may be said there is none, for I cannot call that society from which females are excluded. Generally speaking, the husband of a Brazilian wife is not so much her companion as her keeper.

The manners were many and varied:

The number of persons I met in full dress—black coats, black satin breeches, silk stockings, gold knee and shoe-buckles, opera hats, gold headed canes, and ponderous gold seals—led me to think there must be a great many dinner parties going forward. I was mistaken; for as I went into a shop to buy a pair of gloves, the man milliner who served me was precisely thus attired.

At Rio de Janeiro I contemplated despotism in some of its worst forms; unrestrained vice in many of its debasing effects, and appalling slavery under some of its most odious aspects... I heard the flogging of a slave and my heart failed me, and sickened on listening to the unheeded appeal of his piteous cries of mercy...

I saw a King with pompous ministers, ruling by caprice; I saw men enervated by climate, and relaxed by vicious indulgence... A jingling, old, uncouth looking vehicle, drawn by six mules in rusty harness, and bestridden by antiquated-looking coachmen (not postilions) approached me. Two swarthy and diminutive hussars, mounted on horses like rats, preceded, in the capacity of out-riders, the cumbrous machine. It was followed by about a dozen of the same kind of household troops, and proved to be one of the royal carriages, containing the portly personage of Don Joao, the king... People on horseback dismounted as the royal cortege approached, some foot-passengers of the lower order kneeled, all took off their hats and came to a stand.

By contrast with the restrictions on women in the capital, the country seemed reasonably liberalised. Daniel Kidder, a nineteenth-century traveller, visited a plantation outside Sao Paulo, owned by a woman.

Our social entertainments at Jaragua were of no ordinary grade. Any person looking in upon the throng of human beings that filled the house when we were all gathered together, would have been at a loss to appreciate the force of a common remark of Brazilians respecting their country, viz that its greatest misfortune is a want of population... It is a pleasure to say, that I observed none of that seclusion and excessive restraint which some writers have set down as characteristic of Brazilian females. True, the younger members of the company seldom ventured beyond the utterance of *Sim Senhor, Não Senhor*, and the like; but ample amends for their bashfulness were made by the extreme sociability of Donna Gertrudes. She voluntarily detailed to me an account of her vast business concerns, showed me in person her agricultural and mineral treasures, and seemed to take the greatest satisfaction in imparting the results of her experience on all subjects.[3]

In November 1825 Brazil signed a treaty of friendship with England similar to those already signed by Britain with several of the other new republics. The treaty contained a provision by which Brazil agreed to the suppression of the slave trade. It was a first step towards abolition. Britain and, later, abolitionists in the rest of Europe, considered by now that the commerce in human life had to be ended as a mark of civilisation and cultural advancement and was vehement in urging other countries to end the trade. Although Brazil agreed, it would only terminate the slave trade more than half a century later.[4]

Though it was no more than a fortified riverside village, Montevideo was the warehouse of traders from Europe and North America operating in the River Plate, Chile and southern Brazil. It was quiet and poor and had little to offer; its people's diet was largely beef, and little else. The cultural level was unimpressive. The chaplain aboard HMS *Cambridge*, which took the British consuls Hood and Parish to the River Plate, said that "Montevideo is well furnished with French silks and Birmingham hardware", but there was "not a bookseller's shop in the place". A lady, when handed a book "took it, and, after holding it some time upside down, returned it, saying she had never seen it before."[5]

Robertson had noted that there was no hostility between the natives of the Banda Oriental and the English, which he found surprising in view of the numerous British attacks on the coast, including the occupation of the town in 1807. He enjoyed the town as best he could, while searching for trade and storage space for his goods before shipment to Buenos Aires. The principal families of the town held *tertulias*.

> I was invited to many of these evening parties, and found them an entertaining melange of music, coffee-drinking, card-playing, laughter, and conversation... Every lady that I saw in Montevideo waltzed and moved through the intricate yet elegant mazes of the country dance with a grace immutable... The only drawback upon the delightful way in which I now spent my evenings was the necessity of returning home through long narrow streets so infested with voracious rats as to make it perilous sometimes to face them... If I attempted to pass those formidable banditti, or to interrupt their meals or orgies, they gnashed their teeth upon me like so many evening wolves. [6]

Bones and flesh of slaughtered bovines lay in the muddy streets, the houses were low and dark, the stench from within them was as bad as that without. Amid the preoccupation of walking safely in the uneven streets the pedestrian had to be wary in all places of his manners. "It is an offence not to greet people in the street or to pick one's teeth in their presence."[7]

Until 1820 General Artigas had been the leading political personality in the Banda Oriental. A rough *criollo* landowner with a private army, he had first established his strong-arm rule in the western half of the Banda Oriental, before trying to take land in eastern Argentina from other *caudillos*—semi-feudal chieftains with large land holdings and strong political influence. Eventually, defeated by Buenos Aires, he was forced into exile in Paraguay. Since his departure, the political leadership of the Banda Oriental had been in constant upheaval.

Buenos Aires and the surrounding provinces had stumbled from one dispute to another in a disagreement about the form of government they wanted: whether federal or centralised administration. But the direction of foreign affairs, under Bernardino Rivadavia, and the treasury, headed by Manuel García, had been sufficiently progressive and efficient to impress Europe. Buenos Aires had a bank, whose strongest shareholders were English and Scottish, and which, with the help of the Robertsons, had negotiated a bond issue on the London market, through Baring Brothers. Buenos Aires wanted one million pounds sterling from the bond issue, to build a port—for which plans estimated works lasting eight years, to construct a waterworks system for the capital, and to establish several trading posts on the borders.

Buenos Aires was a small town built on a grid with very few paved streets, most of which reached only a hundred metres from the main building, the Fort. The rest were mud. Wrote one visitor to the town:

> Of the public buildings the Fort is the seat of government; it is situated near the river, with residences inside. Though surrounded by a ditch, with cannon mounted on the ramparts, draw-bridges, etc., it could make but little defence against a serious attack. One would suppose that those who chose the spot on which the city is built had in view the prevention of attack by hostile fleets, the shallowness of the water being a defence against any danger of this kind. [8]

Another observer found much to interest him in the city: "The most splendid *tertulias* were given by madame; and I saw congregated night after night at her house, such specimens of female beauty and vivacity as would have excited envy or commanded admiration in an English ballroom," wrote that inveterate admirer of the local women, John Parish Robertson.[9] However, while he flattered their beauty, he found them lacking in education. But other things mattered more: "music is much cultivated in Buenos Ayres. There is always one lady in every house who can furnish a good performance of all the tunes required for the minuet, the waltz, and the country dance." Of the people in the country, Robertson said that the *estancieros* or ranchers were rustic "in manners and rude in scholarship and address." They made little money and lost at least half in gambling.

> A good substantial, roughly furnished home in town, with very little furniture in it, a large sleek, fat horse, on which to ride—a *poncho* or loose amplitude of camlet stuff, with one hole in the centre of it for his head, and falling from his shoulders over the body—large silver spurs, and the head piece of his bridle heavily overlaid with the same metal—a coarse hat fastened with black leather under his chin; a tinderbox, steel, and flint, with which to light his cigar—a knife in his girdle, and a swarthy page behind him, with the unroasted ribs of a fat cow, for provision, under his saddle—constituted the most solid comfort, and met the most luxurious aspirations of the *estanciero* or Buenos Aires country gentleman.

The small-holder or *chacarero*:

> is generally brave, frank, and hospitable. His spouse and daughter are fond of gaudy finery, and he himself, on the *Día de Fiesta* or holiday decks out his horse and person (they being more "one flesh" than he and his wife) in rich trappings and gay apparel. Nothing can be more picturesque or pleasing than to see him mounted on his charger.[10]

Buenos Aires, the Banda Oriental and Brazil prepared for war at the end of 1825. The annoyance they had caused one another bubbled over. In January 1826, the *Manchester Guardian* announced:

> The papers... to 11 November, afford us intelligence which we were prepared to receive— the active preparations of both the governments for the war, which we conceive inevitable. A privateer of ten guns sailed on 9 November from Buenos Ayres to cruise against the Brazil

flag; she had on board 120 seamen, the greater proportion Americans. Several others were fitting out—their destination is reported to be the East Indies, a very valuable trade being carried on, particularly with Macao, under the Brazil flag. The intelligence from that city is also interesting, as it throws light upon the late state paper, and leads to a belief that active assistance had been promised by Bolivar before the Buenos Ayres government formally annexed the Banda Oriental to the United Provinces of La Plata. Colonel [Daniel] O'Leary, of the Colombian service, with despatches from Bolivar arrived at Buenos Ayres on the evening of the 4th. The state paper, incorporating the Banda Oriental with the United Provinces, was issued by next day. The same officer (who is of the staff of Bolivar) immediately departed for Rio de Janeiro with despatches for the emperor, in the handwriting of the Liberator, stated to be of the highest importance. On the other hand the court of Brazil are making active preparations to reinforce the army in the Banda Oriental; one vessel has sailed from Rio de Janeiro... The Brazilian government has not acted towards the Banda Oriental either with wisdom or justice; it will now see that its attempt to retain that district is so unjust, so useless if successful, so hopeless of accomplishment, and fraught with so much danger from the opportunities it may afford to the discontented party in its own territories, that the war will not be of long duration.[11]

The *Manchester Guardian* forecast that "to all appearance this war will be prosecuted with the greatest vigour; trade is therefore at a standstill... The Brazilian government, we are inclined to believe, will ere long repent of this determination... Two Englishmen are stated to have been murdered by the natives." A first attempt at mediation between the belligerents, by the British minister, Sir Charles Stuart, had failed dismally and "he set off in a great huff." Brazil had embarked 1,500 men and issued a "flaming proclamation".[12]

Just a few days later, on 25 February, the *Manchester Guardian* announced that Brazil had declared war on Buenos Aires.

The British residents were alarmed for their property on account of the measure anticipated on the part of the Buenos Ayres armies, of declaring the slaves free as soon as they arrived on the banks of the river... which had been formally threatened.

Such a threat terrified the British, for, though they demanded the abolition of slavery, they still feared a rampage by freed slaves, if the blacks were given emancipation suddenly. Buenos Aires had abolished the slave trade in 1813, and though blacks were still offered in the sales columns of the local newspapers, their children were born free and the import of slave labour was forbidden.

The letters from well-informed English merchants express the belief that the Buenos Ayres government would not have issued the state paper of 5 November, annexing the Banda Oriental to their territory (which was in fact a declaration of war), without the assurance of the co-operation of Bolivar. The accounts state that the Brazilian government has a large fleet and will undoubtedly preserve their superiority at sea. On the other hand, all the letters agree in the opinion that if the liberating army march to the assistance of Buenos Ayres forces, the issue of the campaign cannot be doubtful, and that though the march upon the capital, Rio de Janeiro, may be slow, on account of the difficulties of the country, yet the enemy will meet with little resistance in placing the republican flag on the towers of the Brazilian capital. The English merchants were taking the precaution of putting their valuables on board ship to be transmitted to England.

Events were not quite as the *Manchester Guardian* speculated; but who was to stop a correspondent from indulging in a little exciting speculation? Brazil did have a superior fleet and its seamen were experienced at sea, but not in a wide and shallow river. Simón Bolívar's forces never came to rescue Buenos Aires and the Banda Oriental, largely because Bolívar had his own political difficulties in Colombia and Venezuela, including a report from Spain that a powerful invasion of the Main was planned from the island of Cuba. Although the size of the squadron and number of men was vastly exaggerated, Ferdinand VII was still aggressively determined to recover his old colonies.[13] Bolívar could spare emissaries of peace, but no troops. An invasion of Brazil was unrealistic and neither Buenos Aires nor the Banda Oriental could have mustered the necessary strength. Buenos Aires had too many domestic quarrels to plan a huge overland expedition such as the invasion of Brazil would require.

Troops from the Banda Oriental advanced into southern Brazil and stayed there. Buenos Aires fought a largely defensive war in the River Plate. Admiral Brown made only a few incursions up the Brazilian coast.

Brazil blockaded the River Plate. This had several results. It produced an alarming growth in privateering. North American gunrunners offered their services to the government and obtained a "corsair's licence". Although Buenos Aires spent its Baring Brothers bond issue on the war effort, its internal trade was relatively unharmed. Brazil prevented exports and imports; but an active domestic commerce was the result. English and Scottish merchants in Buenos Aires and Montevideo suffered the absence of shipping for their goods, but managed to remit some currency. The stocks they could not ship they stored to be sold at good profit at the end of the war.

In any case, the English market was saturated with raw materials and produce from the colonies and the new republics as a result of speculative buying. "The spirit of adventure—the spirit of gambling and speculation—was last year [1825] pushed to an extent never exceeded at any period of the history of this country since the South Sea project," was the alarmed description given of the market by the Earl of Liverpool, in a bill to reform banking regulations.[14]

The Times caught up with the news on Wednesday, 1 March. It reported that:

> a strong squadron sailed on the 22nd [December] to blockade Buenos Ayres, on instructions received at Rio de Janeiro. The declaration of war by the Imperial Government had reached Montevideo, but no formal declaration had been issued on the part of Buenos Ayres... The Brazilian naval force anchored in Uruguay is stated to have acted with great violence towards the English steam packet, the *Druid*, belonging to Mr William Parish Robertson, which left Buenos Ayres... under British colours... Mr Robertson strongly remonstrated with the commander in chief who, after some discussion, ordered the packet and the passengers to be set at liberty, and offered the assistance of his men to get the packet from the sand bank [where it had run aground].

The *Druid* was new to the River Plate and very much the pride of the Robertson brothers. Admiral Brown had written in his diary on 15 November 1825, that:

> the *Druid* steamboat made her first trip to San Isidro on Sunday, with forty passengers on board, at five dollars a head... Mr Robertson, to whom the boat belongs, gave a party to twenty of the first English residents in Buenos Aires on board... Notwithstanding the whole

party were English, Mrs Sheridan tells me that not more than six had ever been in a steamboat before, having left Britain before these kind of vessels were much known or used...

It is not clear why it was only on Wednesday, 29 March 1826 that *The Times* reported that "by letters from Montevideo, we learn that the Emperor of Brazil has declared war against the republic of the United Provinces." However, it was the formal announcement of the initiation of hostilities. A few days later, on 12 April, the paper said that:

the Emperor of Brazil has contrived not only to place himself in the wrong by advancing projects of ambition which he cannot defend on any plausible pretext of justice or necessity, but he has exasperated his adversaries by petty aggressions and needless insults. Instead of acting at first on the defensive, and endeavouring only to guard the territory which he acquired by trick and retains by usurpation, he sends his puny squadron to interrupt the commerce and to menace the capital of the republic.

It was the interruption of commerce that eventually gave Britain an active and a decisive part in the conflict. The need to intervene became more evident as more and more English ships, or others carrying goods destined for British customers, were captured by the Brazilians and declared prizes.[15] At one point the Brazilians were holding ten British ships, and one each from Germany, the United States and Holland, pending a prize court decision.[16] Lord Ponsonby was sent by Britain to Brazil to arrange the terms of peace, as the traders became increasingly alarmed at the fate of their wares. At the time, Mexico had banned the shipment of silver to Europe by merchants or agents owing duties, thus causing "several cases of severe hardship" among English representatives who were "indebted to the government for duties; the dollars were detained till the amount should be discharged."[17] British trade with Spanish America had been too severely disrupted and order had to be restored.

Ponsonby was selected for the task in South America at the King's request. He had fallen into disfavour with George IV. The rumours of the lord's amorous excesses caused displeasure in Court. Ponsonby hated his mission and loathed the people with whom he had to negotiate. He found them uncultured and uncouth, and very much removed from the joys of English society. At his first stop, in Brazil, he did not propose but imposed the peace terms necessary to British interests, in demonstration of his contempt for the imperial court. The *Manchester Guardian* caught up with him in South America.

Rio de Janeiro, 28 June—Lord Ponsonby proceeds to Buenos Ayres in the *Doris*... Accounts from the river Plate [state that] the imperial [Brazilian] squadron, consisting of the *Netherby* frigate, Captain Norton, mounting 38 guns, two twenty-two corvettes, several eighteengun brigs, schooners and gun-boats, have got a confounded hammering. The frigate and two brigs were taken by the Buenos Ayrean squadron, which was composed of only two small ships and three brigs! Several of the Brazilian vessels made a bolt after the first broadside. The wreck of the blockading squadron have returned to Monte Video quite crest-fallen. The Buenos Ayrean vessels are manned entirely with English and Yankees, who were all very hearty in the cause. Most of the Brazilians, though officered by English, have a very mixed crew, and mostly impressed men.[18]

Englishmen (and many Scots, Irish, Welsh and North Americans) fought other

Britons, while an English nobleman tried to mediate.[19] The war moved, in the manner of war, between skirmishes and inactivity. Buenos Aires, still with a fleet smaller than that of Brazil, applied to buy the Chilean fleet, left behind by Lord Cochrane. Admiral Brown became a folk hero. Crowds gathered at the edge of the River Plate or rowed out into the river in small boats to catch a glimpse of his actions against the Brazilians. He used small ships to lure larger vessels into shallow water and there ran them aground; he often challenged much larger craft than his own to the bewilderment of the Brazilians. He taught his native crews to sing Irish songs, and his English officers to sing with them. Ashore he was feted constantly. *The British Packet and Argentine News*, on 12 August 1826, announced English theatre performances to raise funds for Brown's fleet: "After the play of The Mountaineers a recitation is to be delivered in the manner of Mr Mathews, and the representation will end with the burlesque tragedy of *Bombastes Furioso!"* [20] Proceeds were to:

> afford relief to the widows of those killed and for the wounded of the national squadron. The audience was numerous... Admiral Brown and his family occupied a box near the stage. The gallant chieftain seemed to court privacy and sat at the back part of the box all evening. A number of his hardy men dispersed in different parts of the house...

People hung pictures of Brown in their homes and pinned up newspaper cuttings about his battles; his portrait appeared next to those of saints and statesmen in offices and shops as well as in private houses. For Brown it was as much a time of triumph as of tragedy. His future son-in-law, Francis Drummond, a 24-year-old seaman from Dundee who had first served in the Brazilian navy and then moved to command one of Brown's ships, *Independencia*, was killed. Drummond's 16-year-old bride-to-be, Brown's daughter Eliza, on hearing the news, dressed in her bridal gown, walked into the River Plate and drowned.

Manchester Guardian, 14 April 1827:

> Buenos Ayres, 7 January: Admiral Brown has been on the coast of Brazil, with the *Sarandí* and *Chacabuco*, where he had taken many prizes and destroyed a number of vessels. An extraordinary fellow this! On the 26th, hearing that twenty-one sail of Brazilian schooners and gunboats had gone up the river Uruguay, he started after them with the brig *Balcarce*, schooners *Maldonado, Sarandí, Union, Uruguay, Guanaco, Pepa*, and six gunboats. As yet he has not attacked them... I believe he intends to starve them out. People speak in the highest terms of the army's effective state... There is no prospect of an amicable adjustment taking place for some time with the Brazilians, and active operations for the war appear but just beginning. The ships purchased of the Chileans are a total loss to the government, and the greater disappointment to Admiral Brown, who felt confident with such a force. Trade is represented as very bad... The next packet will no doubt bring intelligence of the entry of the Buenos Ayrean army into the Brazilian territory. Great destruction of property is expected to be the consequence of the invasion, and no doubt is entertained but the war will be in favour of Buenos Ayres, whose army is in every respect superior to that of Brazil.

The army, however, played a minor role in the war, which was fought mostly at sea. Only the Banda Oriental army, allied to Buenos Aires, had a fairly active part, and that was on Uruguay's northern border and in the southern states of Brazil. In view of succeeding events, the news may be read as an attempt at misinformation by the Buenos

Aires war ministry, or wishful thinking by the *Manchester Guardian's* correspondent.

The Brazilians were giving as hard as they got. On 3 May it was reported that His Majesty, on returning from a visit to Rio Grande:

> whither he had gone to exert himself to put an end to the war, said "This war will continue till the Cisplatine province, which is ours, shall be free from such invaders, and till Buenos Ayres recognises an independence of the Empire of Brazil, with the incorporation of the Cisplatine, which freely and spontaneously desired to make a part of this empire."[21]

Yet on 1 August 1827 the *Manchester Guardian* said progress had been made in Lord Ponsonby's efforts to secure a peace agreement, and the Buenos Aires minister had travelled to Rio de Janeiro for negotiations.

> In the meantime, as if by agreement, both armies remain inactive. At sea, however, the captures by the Buenos Ayres privateers are of great importance, both as to numbers and to value. One vessel is reported to have captured 14 merchantmen, and accounts are received of two English ships being taken. It is fair to state that many of these merchantmen, particularly from this country, have been carrying warlike stores to the Brazils, in which case they become lawful prizes; but accounts had reached the English admiral on the station that the privateers had commenced plundering immediately on capture, without waiting for condemnation by any lawful authorities. The *Thetis* frigate had been detached in consequence, to capture the privateers offending. Admiral Brown sailed from Buenos Ayres on 9 June, with eleven ships of war... The mercantile news is rather more favourable from the Brazils...

On 25 August the *Manchester Guardian* announced that a preliminary peace treaty had been signed at Rio de Janeiro. Britain had prevailed upon the two main rivals—Buenos Aires and Brazil—to part with the Banda Oriental and permit the creation of an entirely new republic (Uruguay). But it was only a preliminary agreement; the war continued.

While Buenos Aires had fought well and made some diplomatic gains, its domestic politics were in upheaval, and its image in tatters. Buenos Aires had tried to rise to the level of imperial Brazil, and had installed Rivadavia as president, thus attempting to offer an appearance of coherent administration. But Rivadavia's work was hampered by pressure from the provincial leaders who opposed his inept and over-centralised rule. In June 1827, President Rivadavia offered his resignation as a challenge to his detractors. He was shocked to find that it was immediately accepted by the legislature, where his provincial opponents were dominant.

No sooner was the dispute with Brazil at an end than the rival parties in Buenos Aires were to start their own armed conflict. On 2 February 1828, the *Manchester Guardian* announced that a revolution in Buenos Aires had begun. In a rebellion led by General Juan Galo Lavalle, the commander of the ground forces against Brazil, General Carlos María de Alvear, had been arrested, together with the Governor of Buenos Aires—who had succeeded Rivadavia, but no longer in the office of president.

In Brazil, too, conspiracy was reported in the north; and in the south, the commander of the Banda Oriental army, Juan Antonio Lavalleja, had invaded large sections of the province of Rio Grande, independently of events in Buenos Aires. Lavalleja announced that he was able to continue the war indefinitely or until Brazil conceded independence to the Banda Oriental.

At that time, Dom Pedro I, who had been destined to become King Pedro IV of Portugal on the death of his father, abdicated the throne of Lisbon in favour of his daughter, María, in a renewed effort to win sympathy in Brazil. He wished to show that he was wholly concerned with the fate of the new country rather than with the remote European court. But the reverses suffered by his army in the south and losses suffered by his navy in the River Plate continued to test his popularity.[22] Pedro ordered his brother, Miguel, to organise the orderly succession of the crown of Portugal, but found that, instead, Miguel usurped the throne. With difficulties threatening the war effort in Rio de Janeiro, Lisbon and Buenos Aires, peace had to be signed.

In August 1828, the *Manchester Guardian* announced that a treaty had been concluded.

> The independence of the Banda Oriental is established, under the guarantee of Great Britain, during a period of 15 years, and the whole of that province, together with Montevideo, is to be delivered up by the Emperor of Brazil within four months from the ratification of the treaty... Lord Ponsonby, who had recently arrived at Rio from Buenos Ayres, is said to have signed the treaty on the part of England. The conclusion of the treaty of peace between Brazil and Buenos Ayres seems to have been accelerated by the news from Portugal. The emperor had full information then of Miguel's usurpation.[23]

To some complaint by the new Governor of Buenos Aires, Manuel Dorrego, against British interference in River Plate affairs, Lord Ponsonby wrote on 8 August 1828, with his usual contempt, from aboard HMS *Thetis.*

> Your Excellency cannot have any respect for the doctrine set up by some crude theorists "that America ought to have a political existence separate from the political existence of Europe". Commerce and common interest of individuals have formed ties between Europe and America which no governments nor perhaps any power possessed by man can now unloose, and whilst they exist Europe will have the right and certainly will not want the means, nor the will to interfere with the policy of America, at least so far as shall be necessary for the security of European interests.[24]

It was a coarse summary—but it would remain the most accurate description of British and European policy towards South America for a century.

On signature of the treaty, Britons loaded fifteen ships with goods for Buenos Aires. In London, throughout the year, Lord Strangford had expressed concern for the damage to British trade interests that the blockade of the River Plate had caused. Earl Dudley, in the House of Lords, had argued that if others could break the blockade, British ships should do so too, and that privateers had to be persecuted and punished.[25] On 30 September 1828, Brazil lifted the blockade of Buenos Aires, and the peace treaty was ratified in Montevideo on 4 October.[26] *The Times,* on 20 December, had some reservations.

> We cannot but observe that, though on both sides all right to the possession of the disputed territory of Monte Video is renounced, yet that both retain just so much power of interference in the concerns, as may ultimately embroil them with it, and with each other. The seventh and tenth articles executed, as they must necessarily be by bodies of imperialists and republicans—differing from each other on politics and "lawful government"—contain about as much good materials for a misunderstanding or a quarrel as could reasonably be

desired in any amicable adjustment. In making this remark we do not mean to insinuate that the difficulties of the case could have been otherwise obviated, or that, in the circumstances and dispositions of the contracted parties, there is much danger of a fresh rupture. Having both more territory than they can well govern, attempts at new conquests would evince insanity; and neither having acquired glory while they sacrificed interest during the struggle, their appetite for fighting may be expected to be allayed for some years to come.

That appetite would take fifteen years to reawaken, and Britain would again be involved. In the meantime, revolutionaries in Buenos Aires, again led by General Lavalle, executed General Dorrego, and the rebels were in turn defeated by General Rosas, who became governor.

Before Lord Ponsonby left Rio de Janeiro for England, he advised the Brazilian government:

> that if an immediate settlement of the claims for spoliations of English commerce was not made, on the 6th of May he would order the English admiral to make reprisals on all Brazilian ships. The private accounts state that notification had exceedingly irritated and annoyed Dom Pedro. The sum in dispute is said to be about £400,000.[27]

After initial protest, Brazil entered into negotiations with the agents.

NOTES:

1. *Manchester Guardian*, 8 July 1826.
2. J. Robertson, *Letters on South America*, vol. I, pp. 141-52.
3. Quoted in E. Bradford Burns, *Latin America, a Concise Interpretive History*. (Prentice-Hall, New Jersey, 1972), pp. 106-7.
4. *Manchester Guardian*, 28 January 1826. *The Times*, 11 and 25 June 1870. Slavery was abolished in May 1888.
5. Rev. Hugh Salvin, *Journal Written on Board of His Majesty's Ship Cambridge*. (Newcastle, 1829), pp. 18-19. Quoted in Pendle, *Latin America*, p. 112.
6. Robertson, *Letters*, vol. I, pp. 104-5.
7. Robertson, *Letters*, vol. II. p. 323.
8. Anonymous, *Cinco años en Buenos Aires, 1820-1825*. (Solar, Buenos Aires, 1970). The author signs himself only as "an Englishman". Authorship has been attributed to Thomas George Love, founder of *The British Packet and Argentine News* in 1826.
9. Robertson, *Letters*, vol. I. pp. 176-99.
10. Robertson, *Letters*, vol. I, pp. 55-9.
11. *Manchester Guardian*, 28 January 1826.
12. *Manchester Guardian*, 4 February 1826.
13. *Manchester Guardian*, 10 June 1826.
14. *Manchester Guardian*, 25 February 1826.
15. *Manchester Guardian*, 26 August 1826.
16. *Manchester Guardian*, 15 September 1827.
17. *Manchester Guardian*, 16 September 1826.
18. *Manchester Guardian*, 16 September 1826.
19. Andrew Graham-Yooll, *The Forgotten Colony*. (Hutchinson, 1981) p. 87.

20.   With this play, a verse burlesque written by William Barnes Rhodes in 1810, the company later known as the Cambridge Footlights first came to public attention in February 1883.

21.   *Manchester Guardian*, 14 July 1827.

22.   *Manchester Guardian*, 17 May 1828, 13 September 1828.

23.   *Manchester Guardian*, 1 November 1828.

24.   Quoted in H.S. Ferns, *Britain and Argentina in the Nineteenth Century*. (Oxford University Press, 1960)

25.   *The Times*, 21 March 1828.

26.   *Manchester Guardian*, 10 January 1829.

27.   *Manchester Guardian*, 11 July 1829.

Chapter Three
THE FALKLAND/MALVINAS
ISLANDS, 1833

Gaucho soldier (A. D'Hastrel)

In the nineteenth century the Falkland Islands were of only passing interest to either the British government or the general public. There was to be no war over the islands until late in the twentieth century. But in 1833, events marked a change in a long and occasionally acrimonious dispute over ownership of the islands. That year Britain took formal possession of the islands as a result of a quarrel between Buenos Aires and the United States. The British action aroused a certain envy in the French, whose interest in South America was rekindled and pursued with vigour elsewhere in the continent.

The French, under contract to Spain, had colonised the East Falkland in 1764. Spain had then paid France to abandon all claims to the islands. Spain then demanded that Britain withdraw its settlers from the West Falkland, which order was obeyed in 1774. The British left a plaque on the islands, establishing that they were a possession of George III, but this was ripped out in 1776—during an inventory of the islands' installations by a Spanish official—and taken to Buenos Aires. There it would be recovered by General Beresford in 1806.

Britain maintained the claim on the precedent of settlement and, less precisely, on the grounds of discovery. A Spanish community grew at Port Egmont, on the western island, and, in spite of the evacuation, British and North American seamen installed themselves *de facto* in the East Falkland. Spanish ships' masters registered as Spaniards the few babies born on the western island; and British captains recorded as British the births to a handful of women on the eastern mass, on the other side of Falkland Sound. The menfolk were mostly the crew of sealing and whaling ships. Spain, under Napoleonic rule and with rebellious colonies, was in no condition to give much attention to the small windswept possession. The settlers lived without laws other than their own rules of coexistence and acknowledged no authority apart from that of the senior officers of the ships that called there.

In January 1820, the government of Buenos Aires sent David Jewett, a North American with the rank of "army colonel in the Buenos Ayres navy", to the islands, "commissioned by the Supreme Government of the United Provinces of South America to take possession" of them, which he did on 6 November. He found fifty ships there, registered at places such as Liverpool, Leith, London, New York and Stonington, sheltering in the islands' coves. Jewett was unable to establish his authority over this hard-living crowd and he returned to Buenos Aires. In June 1828, a decree published in Buenos Aires named a political and military commander for the islands, Jorge Pacheco. He was awarded the appointment in part payment of government debts. He subcontracted one of his own creditors, a Franco-German immigrant named Louis Vernet, to establish a settlement at Port Louis—named after Louis Antoine de Bougainville, who had founded a French settlement there in 1764—on the eastern island. Vernet travelled there in 1829 with his brother, and his brother-in-law, eighteen black men on a ten-year contract, twelve black women, seven single German males, four English families, six English bachelors, and eight other families of varied nationalities as well as some *gauchos*, indians, and transported felons. Apart from the shipping usually anchored there, the new colonists were told that at Port Louis, on the eastern island, there were seventy settlers, mostly English, who claimed to own about twenty thousand head of cattle, though these were mostly wild. Vernet immediately put his men to work rounding up the cattle and taming the wild horses. He was respected and his orders were obeyed, even if the pay he offered was low and in the form of paper vouchers.

The Buenos Aires government also empowered Vernet to exact duties from foreign ships using the islands or hunting for seal on the coast. Vernet therefore tried to extend his authority to the surrounding seas. He wanted to stop some of the wanton killing and waste which was endangering much of the wildlife with early extinction and threatening his future income. To secure payment from men who were accustomed to using the islands as they wished, without any rules to obey, was not an easy task. Vernet contracted an English seaman, Matthew Brisbane, of the schooner *Elbe*, to patrol the coast, collect taxes, and act as Argentine superintendent of the islands, in exchange for a share in the profits of the colony.

Captain Brisbane's difficulties arose almost immediately when he tried to collect payment on catches by three North American schooners—*Harriet*, Captain Gilbert Davinson; *Breakwater*, Captain Don Carew, both of Stonington, Connecticut, and the *Superior*, Captain Stephen Congar, of New York. Captain Congar, of the *Superior*, made a prompt settlement with Vernet and left one thousand skins as a guarantee. From Port Louis, however, the *Superior* sailed to Buenos Aires where Congar reported Vernet's action as piracy. The United States consul took an interest. Captain Carew organised the *Breakwater*'s breakaway. Though Vernet had seized all the ship's papers and put a five-man guard on board, Carew and three men overpowered the sentries and, after putting them ashore, sailed for Stonington. For his part, Captain Davinson of the *Harriet* refused to make any payment to Vernet but, after some indecision, agreed to take the islands' commander to Buenos Aires and there submit their argument to the local courts. Brisbane remained behind in the islands, in charge of the workforce, who were assured by Vernet that he would shortly return to pay wage arrears.

The *Harriet*'s arrival in Buenos Aires was reported by *La Gaceta Mercantil* on 22 November 1831; the account of the *Breakwater*'s arrival at Stonington, and Carew's description of Vernet's act of piracy, appeared in the 2 December issue of *The British Packet and Argentine News*. The *Harriet*'s captain also reported Vernet to the US consul for piracy.

George Slacum, the US consul in Buenos Aires, had already lodged a protest with the minister of foreign affairs and had written to US President Jackson's secretary of state, Edward Livingston. A copy of his report to Washington reached Captain Benjamin Cooper, commander of the US fleet in the South Atlantic at Rio de Janeiro. He ordered Captain Silas Duncan, of the USS *Lexington*, to sail to the River Plate, enquire into the truth of consul Slacum's reports and, if necessary, offer protection to the United States shipping in the area. After calling at Buenos Aires—where Captain Duncan unsuccessfully demanded the arrest of Vernet and the return of the *Harriet*—the *Lexington* sailed on 9 December to the Argentine settlement in the Falkland Islands, known as Malvinas. There, according to the settlers, Duncan ordered his crew to destroy as much as they could of Vernet's installations. Duncan took as prisoners a number of colonists—many fled inland—arrested Brisbane, and sailed back to Buenos Aires.[1] He did not record in his log any mention of the damage caused.

La Gaceta Mercantil reported on 8 February 1832 the return of the *Lexington* to

Buenos Aires and said that the ship was carrying a group of islanders as hostages in reprisal for the capture of the *Harriet*. They were put ashore and the ship sailed without publicity.[2] In response to official Argentine protests, Captain Duncan had declared that the islands were uninhabited because the settlers had been removed. He had stated also that Argentine sovereignty over the islands could not be acknowledged while Britain had an unresolved claim to them. The US State Department sent a lawyer to Buenos Aires, but from the time of his arrival in June 1832 he demanded the arrest of Vernet on charges of piracy. This lost him the sympathy of the authorities who had hoped that he would help to find an honourable solution. Relations between the United States and Buenos Aires were virtually severed for the next eleven years.[3]

Vernet remained in Buenos Aires, trying to press his case in the courts. The British consul, Woodbine Parish, who in December 1829 had celebrated the arrival in office of General Rosas,[4] now warned the governor that the establishment of a settlement on the islands was an unfriendly act. Similar cautions would be issued by the diplomat's successors, Henry Fox and Philip Gore.

The Buenos Aires government was preoccupied with the domestic outbursts of rival parties, so it was only some months later, in October 1832, that it appointed a sergeant, José Francisco Mestivier, as Governor of the Malvinas. He travelled on the ship *Sarandí*, commanded by José María Pinedo, who was to take charge of guarding the islands' coasts as Brisbane had done before. Mestivier arrived some months after the *Lexington* had left its trail of destruction; the settlement had not recovered from the devastation caused by Duncan's crew. The new governor had to try to make the colony habitable again and at the same time had to face unrest in his small army—criminals, tramps, and deported felons—which was in upheaval over pay. Within a few weeks the unrest became mutiny and Mestivier was murdered.

Pinedo, the coast guard, took over the government and with a detachment of his crew captured the mutinied troops. As he completed his task, Pinedo was informed, on 20 December 1832, of the presence of the HMS *Clio* in the waters off Port Louis. Pinedo was under the impression that he would receive help to arrange the transportation of the mutinied men and made the *Clio*'s commander, Captain J. F. Onslow, welcome ashore. It was at their first meeting, on 2 January 1833, that Onslow informed Pinedo that he was there to claim the islands for the British Crown. Pinedo made a symbolic delegation of the islands' government in the person of his foreman, Juan Simón who, however, showed no interest in the post.

It is not clear why Pinedo made no effort to resist the British intrusion. His failure to do so was to become a source of acute embarrassment to Buenos Aires, but he may have thought that what was left of his mutinous force had little chance of imposing Argentine rule. Pinedo was ordered to board the *Sarandí* with his prisoners and a number of settlers. The Argentine flag from Port Louis was delivered to him on board the next day. A British ship, the *Rapid*, escorted him to Buenos Aires. The *Sarandí* arrived in Buenos Aires on 15 January and seven of the ten prisoners accused of taking part in the murder of Mestivier were immediately executed.

Meanwhile, Captain Onslow gave the storekeeper at Port Louis, William Dickson, a Union Jack and ordered him to fly it whenever a ship anchored off the colony and on Sundays. But, more important, Onslow gathered Vernet's labourers and farm workers and asked them to try to work as they had under Vernet for another four or five months. Then, if nobody had returned to pay their wages, they should take their value in wild cattle and either stay on the islands or make their way to the mainland. It was an informal arrangement and almost an invitation to cattle rustling. The labourers must have been attracted by the idea of collecting in cattle rather than paper vouchers.[5] Onslow's orders were only to claim the islands; he had not been told to establish an administration there. He was apparently indifferent to what might happen in the islands when he had gone. His offer was generous but irresponsible.

By mid-January, just fifteen days after his arrival, Onslow sailed away from the Falklands, and in his wake sailed the *Tyne*, another British ship which had accompanied the *Clio* in the seizure of Port Louis. The islands became a kind of no man's land. Brisbane returned to them in March 1833 in the hope of restarting the business. Later, Captain Fitz Roy's HMS *Beagle*—with Charles Darwin aboard—called for a few days and departed again. Dickson, the storekeeper, and Brisbane, the Argentine superintendent, paid the farm workers with vouchers in lieu of wages. They could only apologise for the continued absence of Vernet. However, Vernet had resigned as commander of the islands that month, while in Buenos Aires. He wanted to avoid antagonising the British whose help he needed to claim damages from the North Americans.

Autumn in the islands was appalling. The workmen grumbled that their debts for stores were growing and that the vouchers they received were insufficient. They had agreed to receive pay per head of cattle or horse penned, but the bad weather prevented them from rounding up any animals.

May arrived. It was the fifth month since Onslow had made the outrageously generous offer. The labourers could take possession of the cattle now in lieu of wages. Brisbane and Dickson prevented them from taking such action, though no alternative was offered.

The settlement was now reduced to twenty-one men and three women—one of them pregnant with the child of one of Vernet's *gauchos*. Most of them were Argentines. There were also nine British seamen attached to one Captain Low, formerly of the sealing vessel *Unicorn*, which had been sold to Captain Fitz Roy of the *Beagle*. The nine awaited repatriation. In the minds of those remaining on the islands the future must have looked uncertain. The recent past was not much comfort. The *Lexington* attack, Vernet's departure, Mestivier's murder and Pinedo's capitulation did not offer much hope.

In Buenos Aires the islands were of low priority. Political rivalries and shooting affrays in the streets required more immediate attention. A correspondent wrote to *The Times* on 1 June 1833: "Little is now said of the Falkland Islands affair, but all are anxiously awaiting news from England upon the subject. The Americans are delighted that they have got out of this scrape, and that the odium now rests on John Bull." A few days later, on 17 June, Manuel Moreno, the Argentine minister in London, presented a formal protest against the British occupation of the Malvinas islands.

The mood at Port Louis itself was deteriorating. Eight men, the most conspicuous of the malcontents, prepared to take what they had been offered as their due. They were convinced that they could not act without using force, because Brisbane was still in control and was determined to protect Vernet's property. The eight began to boast about their planned uprising. They were led by Antonio Rivero, aged 26, of Buenos Aires. He had spent six years in the islands and he was owed a substantial sum by Vernet. He had with him two other *gauchos* and five indians.

Early on 26 August 1833, Low—known as "the captain" and therefore the embodiment of authority—and four of his men sailed out of Berkeley Sound on a short seal hunt. No sooner had he left, than the eight rebels struck. They shot and killed Brisbane, Vernet's agent; they used their swords to kill Simón, who had been named Pinedo's representative; they cut up Dickson, the storekeeper, who had been charged by Onslow to fly the Union Jack; they killed a German, named Wagner; and one indian used his *bolas* to catch another man, Ventura Pasos, who was stabbed to death by Rivero for being witness to the other killings. The dozen or so men, three women and two children—most of them Argentines—in the settlement of Port Louis fled to a cave on a near-by island, while Rivero and his gang looted every house in the colony and drove the cattle inland.

The settlers were only rescued and assisted on 23 October—nearly two months later—when a British survey ship, the *Hopeful*, arrived in Port Louis. The captain was unable to chase inland after the rustlers; but by a ship sailing north he sent a message about the events to Captain Michael Seymour, commander in the South Atlantic at Rio de Janeiro. In January 1834, HMS *Challenger* put ashore six Royal Marines under Lieutenant Henry Smith—whom Captain Seymour appointed Officer Commander of the Eastern Falkland Island, effectively the first British governor on the islands—with orders to capture Rivero and his gang. An American missionary was among the first to make contact with Rivero. The Reverend Titus Coan was aboard the North American ship *Antarctic*, whose master tried to buy from Rivero a fat cow and six steers. When consulted, Lt Smith forbade the transaction but was glad of the information on Rivero's whereabouts. Rivero eventually betrayed his friends in the hope of leniency and surrendered. Lieutenant Smith reported recovering fifty-three horses.

In March 1834, Charles Darwin, the naturalist, returned to the islands aboard the *Beagle*. With some sarcasm he wrote from there to a friend in Buenos Aires, Mr Lumb—an Englishman at whose home he had stayed, and whose wife served teas that reminded Darwin of England—wondering in his correspondence if the Buenos Aires authorities would call Rivero's action a justified rebellion against the tyranny of England.[6]

Rivero and five of his men were taken in chains, first to Rio de Janeiro and then to England. But a court in London failed to admit his trial because it was not clear under what laws and jurisdiction he could be tried. With some discretion—Britain wanted to avoid a protest by Buenos Aires of abuse of human rights in the person of Rivero—he and his men were shipped to Montevideo and quietly put ashore in the middle of 1835.[7]

Mandeville, the British minister at Buenos Aires, wrote to Lord Palmerston on 3 January 1838, with reference to the opening message of a new session of the Buenos Aires House of Representatives:

> It then adverts to the worn out question of the Falkland Islands, and declaims as usual upon the injustice of its occupation by Great Britain—without, I believe, receiving much sympathy or support from the public, except the very few persons who have speculated on an

establishment there. It will make an annual paragraph in the message until the subject dies of exhaustion, unless some unworthy motive should induce the government to reproduce it and take shelter under its cover to screen themselves from the stigma of injustice by not complying or of delaying to comply with any well grounded reclamation that Great Britain has or may have to make to them.[8]

In 1841 Britain formalised possession of the Falkland Islands as part of its overseas colonies. In 1842, the government of Buenos Aires enquired whether Britain might not agree to cancel the 1826 Baring loan, on which Argentina had defaulted, in exchange for recognition of British possession of the islands. The Foreign Office said the islands were not worth that much and, in any case, the loan was a private arrangement between the Buenos Aires government and the investors. On 25 July 1848, Sir William Molesworth, MP for Southwark, and the representative in Parliament of the "philosophical Radicals", as well as proprietor of the group's magazine, the *Westminster Review*, brought to the notice of the honourable members the fact that the expense of keeping a territory such as the Falkland Islands was not warranted by their limited usefulness and suggested that they should be returned to the United Provinces.

The suggestion was rejected. The timing was wrong.[9]

NOTES:

1. Ernesto Fitte, *La Agresión Norteamericana a las Islas Malvinas*. (Emecé, Buenos Aires, 1966).
2. The *Harriet* was auctioned in Buenos Aires in September 1833 and sailed for some years with the name *Choele-Choel*.
3. US Secretary of State Thomas Bayard advised the Argentine Minister in Washington Víctor Quesada, on 8 March 1886, that no reparation could be considered by the US while Britain had a claim to the islands.
4. Parish to Aberdeen, 12 December 1829.
5. Ernesto Fitte, "El Sangriento episodio de agosto de 1833 en Malvinas", *Papiro*, año VII no. 22, Enero-Junio 1982.
   Academia Nacional de la Historia: Actuación de Antonio Rivero en Malvinas. Ricardo Caillet-Bois, Humberto F. Burzio (Buenos Aires, 1966).
6. It was not seen in that way. The report of the Academia Nacional de la Historia, Buenos Aires, 1966, describes Rivero as a criminal without any political motive. Some political circles, however, have tried to give Rivero a sense of nationalist rebellion.
7. PRO CO 78/2. See also Fitte, "El Sangriento" (Public Record Office, Colonial Office).
8. PRO FO 6/63. (Public Record Office, Foreign Office).
9. See Chapter 6.

Chapter Four
CHILE, BOLIVIA AND PERU
1836-1839

Ball in Santiago, Chile, 1841 (C. Gay)

Two decades after their independence, Chile and Peru went to war. The immediate cause of the conflict was Chile's fear that the union of Peru and Bolivia would pose a serious threat to Chilean territorial integrity. But there was an older cause for war: the economic situation of the rivals and their mining interests in their border territory. And Peru had failed to repay a loan to Chile. The row had its origins in 1822, before Peru was independent.

In 1822 the government of Chile, led by the hero of the campaign that had ended Spanish domination, General Bernardo O'Higgins, was informed that it had been awarded a loan of one million pounds sterling—the equivalent of three and a half million pesos—which Chile did not want and could not afford. The fact that it was unwanted appears to have been irrelevant to the Chilean minister plenipotentiary in London, Antonio José de Irisarri. He was an ambitious diplomat and writer, born in Guatemala, then in his mid-thirties. He had been interim Supreme Director of Chile for a few days in 1814, and later Governor of Santiago. In 1818, the Chilean government posted him to London with orders to raise a loan with which to finance the liberating expedition to Peru. Two years later, Irisarri needed the loan more than Chile.

Chile had needed the money to finance Lord Cochrane and General San Martín. Irisarri had been asked to:

> negotiate, either with the governments of European countries or with private persons, loans for a sum sufficient to cover the cost of our (military) operations, this government approving in advance the privileges that must be conceded to obtain the said loan and the interest agreed upon.[1]

San Martín had given him another delicate task: that of looking for a member of an European royal family who might be an acceptable monarchic figure-head to rule over a constitutional union of South American republics. The houses of Brunswick, Orange, and Bragança were the most favoured as being able to adjust to the leadership of South America.

From his residence at Portland Square, Irisarri wrote home to Santiago to report his difficulties in the banking world; but he always sprinkled his correspondence with the names of nobles and the wealthy. The Guatemalan who acted as Chilean representative was soon running up large bills for domestic requirements, clothing and social engagements. His social whirl made the whoring, feasting and spending of other South Americans in Paris and London before him look austere. All to no avail: no government in Europe could be found to lend Chile the money, and no banker thought that the interest rates offered were high enough. The envoy found some prominent names who agreed to subscribe to a fund; but no group of bankers prepared to subscribe the full sum for Chile.

Time passed and Irisarri was ordered by Chile to abandon the search for a loan in England. The government in Santiago had decided it could not afford such a luxury. Letters crossed, but there appears to be no doubt that Irisarri refused to abandon the project in spite of being in receipt of orders to that effect. He was too involved in negotiations, and to stop them would have been embarrassing; he was too deep in debt to consider not borrowing the money. In May 1822, Irisarri entered formal agreement with

Hullett Brothers & Co., London, to raise a loan for one million pounds. Not only were the interest rates demanded high, but Irisarri also offered all comers good business opportunities in Chile. Of the one million pounds, Chile received only £665,000; the rest went in advance interest payments, agents' commission, and a share for Irisarri, in addition to a sum of £17,000 reserved by the diplomat to cover wage arrears and his expenses.

Chile was suddenly in possession of money—and debts—that nearly doubled its normal annual revenue: two million pesos in 1817. Moreover, the original purpose of the loan, financing the expedition to Peru, had long since been covered by patriotic fund-raising in Buenos Aires, Mendoza and Santiago. This was the normal way in which states had covered their debts until then. Subscriptions were usually organised among local merchants and landowners until the necessary sum was collected. John Miers, merchant and traveller, said that "British merchants came forward with loans of money" which greatly relieved the authorities. The loans were normally paid for by governments with certificates which were accepted in payment of duties at the customs house.[2]

Out of a strong sense of national pride Chile assumed responsibility for the Irisarri loan, even if the results of such a debt were devastating. O'Higgins was forced to leave government the following year, accused of ignoring the Senate's decision to cancel the loan application while Irisarri had still been negotiating it. For the sake of a sense of prestige O'Higgins had decided to accept Irisarri's efforts rather than reject them as the Senate had ordered.

In 1824 the Chilean government expropriated church property, confident that it could be sold to raise the cash to pay off the debt. But the sale failed, and in the end much of the land had to be returned to the monasteries. Although every effort was made to administer the money carefully, much of it went towards personal loans, to pay military wages, and to buy armaments, among other items. Irisarri also bought an unwanted ship for Chile and loaded it with unneeded stores. All of this merely confirmed his affluence to the English, but caused distress in the Chilean treasury. When the interest on the Chilean bonds began to fall in London, only a few months after the loan had been awarded—as the market reacted to Chile's difficulties—Chile planned to buy back some of the depreciated certificates. But this step was never taken. Had Chile tried such a recovery, prices would in any event have risen immediately.

Irisarri removed himself to Paris. On 23 July 1825, the *Morning Chronicle* published what purported to be a ferocious letter to the editor. There was no doubt that the scribe's target was the Chilean representative, even if he was not mentioned.

> Without being in want of money, nor even asking for it, this London agent [Hullett Brothers & Co.] saddles Chile with a debt of one million pounds sterling out of English pockets, for the benefit, in reality, of himself and the Creole Spaniard [Irisarri] who acted the part of Plenipotentiary to the Stock Exchange in that drama—the latter worthy lost no time in transferring himself together with two hundred thousand pounds sterling of John Bull's money to Paris, where he now out-tops Princes in his style of living.

In December of that same year the *Morning Chronicle* was ordered to pay Irisarri £400 in damages. The court considered that the complaint of libel brought by the Chilean diplomat was justified.

Between 1823 and 1824 Chile managed to award a loan of 1.5 million pesos to

Peru, which was awaiting a loan of its own for £450,000 from England. The Chilean government hoped that the interest and payments from Peru would go some way towards alleviating its own burden. But when the first repayments fell due, Peru refused to pay on the grounds that the terms of the loan from Chile had not been ratified.

Peru's refusal to repay the loan became one more source of friction between the two countries. The other causes of distrust concerned the two countries' boundaries with Bolivia—which also involved ownership of guano deposits and a lingering dislike of the still monarchic minded Peruvians by the staunchly republican Chileans. To these would be added the alliance of Bolivia and Peru into one federation, which Chile feared was formed for aggressive purposes.

Revolution had improved the South Americans, wrote one traveller.

> They have gained, too, as a consequence of it in their trade and pecuniary transactions with England; for, to say nothing of the large sums received by them in loans, for working of mines, & co. for which little or nothing has yet been returned, we very much question whether the merchandise sent to South America has, on the whole, produced to the shippers much profit...[3]

That is how many British trading houses came to think of South America in the 1820s. At the same time, many South Americans saw Britain and Europe as usurers. But still the partnership grew, and strengthened:

> English tailors, shoemakers, saddlers, and inn-keepers hang out their signs in every street; and the preponderance of the English language would make one fancy Valparaiso a coast town in Britain. The North Americans greatly assist in this, their goods consisting of common furniture, flour, biscuit, and naval stores... The number of pianofortes brought from England is astonishing. There is scarcely a house without one.

Thus wrote Maria Graham in her *Journal of a Residence in Chile* of a country she had gone to with her husband, where she had been widowed, and which excited her and vexed her.[4] Britain and Chile would always be close. In the next fifty years, Chilean imports from England would equal the combined total of those from France, Germany and the US.

There was, obviously, a local contrast to this Englishness, which was described by John Parish Robertson.

> There is another class of inhabitants not to be found in Buenos Ayres, but abundant in Chile and Peru, descended from the early settlers, and who had lofty pretensions to birth. Many of them were furnished with titles of nobility. This class, however, had no better claims either to manners or education than their neighbours. A long course of living *à son gré*, of indulging in all the loose habits such a climate very often generates, and of falling into a disregard of such outward decorum and family observances as involved the slightest personal inconvenience, caused the dignity of the nobleman to yield to the ease of the plebeian... We have had the honour of dining with some of these noblemen; and we have seen them sit down to dinner with their shirt sleeves rolled up to their elbows, their shirt collars arranged purely for the convenience of free breathing; the females of the house attired in their morning *déshabillé* and the party attended by black slaves, clothed with the same happy and unceremonious reference to ease and comfort... Two female slaves, towels over their shoulders, carried large silver basins round the table after dinner, for the necessary purpose of ablution. The luxury of finger-glasses had not yet superseded... this more primitive

mode, at once of washing hands, and evincing family concord. After this, taking from a glass a small wooden toothpick, with elbows on the table, and in all familiarity of chit-chat, listless, a little, and monotonous, the party began to pick their teeth.[5]

The *Manchester Guardian* wrote on 21 February 1829:

We are sorry to find that the affairs of most of the new governments in America are in a state of considerable disorder. The revolution in Buenos Ayres we mentioned... was highly satisfactory to the mercantile community, and indeed to all the most respectable classes of the population, and was effected without any disorder or violence whatever; but we believe some apprehensions are still entertained, lest the partisans of the late ruling parties should be able to raise forces in the interior of the country, and thus, for a time at least, disturb public tranquility...

The recent serious conspiracy in Colombia against Bolivar, at the head of which was General [Francisco de Paula] Santander, was an evidence of the unsettled state of feeling in that republic; and renders it but too probable that the date is yet remote when the inhabitants are destined to enjoy the advantages of a settled government...

The situation of Peru and Chili is likewise far from satisfactory; one just about to be plunged into war with a neighbouring state; and both already unable to fulfil the obligations they have contracted.

Things are even worse in Mexico. There a violent revolution has just taken place, attended by a pillage, for several days, of the capital city itself... Under such circumstances of violence it is satisfactory to learn that the establishments of the foreign merchants, particularly the English, appear to have been respected...

The new continent, which was to redress the failings of the old world, in the words of George Canning, was disintegrating already—only a few years after its component provinces had started life as independent nations.

Where war threatened, on the Pacific, the British feared a decline into anarchy. *The Times* reported on 4 April 1836 that:

letters dated Callao, 9 November, give a most distressing account of the present state and future prospects of Peru. The country has been in a state of revolution since 23 February 1835. [Andrés] Santa Cruz, President of Bolivia, entered Peru in May, and his army and that of General Salaverry were approaching each other in November last. British and other foreign merchants are great sufferers; the road between Lima and Callao, its port, is infested with banditti, who even enter the city, as there are no troops there. The great body of Old Spaniards have been driven out, taking great wealth with them, and though the resources of the country under a quiet and honest government might easily pay off their debts and make it prosperous, it is expected that in thirty years it will fall again into the hands of the indians, who compose the main strength of the army.

In 1836, General Andrés Santa Cruz completed his conquest of Peru and created the Peruvian-Bolivian Confederation, splitting Peru into two provinces, one in the north and the other in the south, and joining them to Bolivia. He named one president for each of the three areas he had created in the confederation, and proclaimed himself Protector—which he made a lifetime and hereditary office. Such a post might appear to be excessive and outrageous, but the idea of a confederation of autonomous provinces was still in the mind of some generals and liberators of America. Miranda had died—with his dream of an Incan empire—twenty years before in a Spanish prison; Bolívar was only recently dead, the union he had envisaged never achieved; and San Martín—who had wanted a monarch—regretted his failure in lonely exile in France.

Britain, France and the United States welcomed Santa Cruz's confederation. For them it made trading and diplomacy easier—one interlocutor instead of two or three. And Santa Cruz was regarded as a shrewd politician and good administrator. Chile and Argentina watched Santa Cruz with distrust; but their objections were not strong enough to prevent Britain from making a treaty of commerce with the new confederation.

"Treaty with the Peru-Bolivian Confederation", announced the expansion-minded *Manchester Guardian* with some pleasure.

> By documents with which we have been politely favoured by a gentleman recently returned from Lima, our commercial readers will be gratified to learn that the treaty concluded by Her Majesty's consul general, Belford Hinton Wilson, with his excellency General Santa Cruz, has given universal satisfaction to all the British subjects resident in that country, and we have no doubt it will be duly appreciated and ratified by Her Majesty's secretary of foreign affairs. The documents consist of a letter addressed by the British residents in Lima, and the consul's answer... 6

Meanwhile, Chile accused Peru-Bolivia of harbouring the former president of Chile, General Ramón Freire, at the head of a group of exiles, who were conspiring to return to Santiago. Chile also complained that the commercial regulations introduced in Peru by General Santa Cruz did not take into account Peru's obligations to Chile. To give strength to its protests, Chile attacked Peruvian shipping and took several prizes, but was prevented from taking any further action by the captain of the British ship *Talbot*, at Callao. The British officer arranged an agreement between both states for a four months' truce. When that time was up Chile refused to ratify the agreement and instead sent eight vessels under the command of Admiral Blanco who, on 29 November 1836, blockaded the Peruvian ports.

At this point, Chilean plans were thrown into disarray by the murder of the Chilean president, Diego José Víctor Portales, in June 1837. Portales, a civil servant of some note and member of a wealthy family, had acquired a fabulous fortune when granted the monopoly of the tobacco, tea and liquor trade—known as the *estanco*—the course chosen by the government to secure a steady, if reduced, source of revenue with which to pay its debts. Using his wealth, Portales had entered government in 1830 first as a minister, later becoming president. He was noted for his disdain for democracy, but he also showed a strong concern for economic order. Before his murder he had imposed in Chile an element of financial and political stability which was to last for more than a century. With Portales dead—at the age of forty—and with the apparent favour of Europe, General Santa Cruz was convinced that he could impose his ways in defiance of Chile.7 *The Times*, 22 August 1837:

> Declaration of war by Buenos Ayres against Peru. By the ship *Brutus*, Captain Adams, we have Buenos Ayres papers to 27 May. *The British Packet* of that date contains a declaration of war by the Republic of Buenos Ayres against Peru, now under the protection of General Santa Cruz, who is also President of Bolivia. Chili declared war against Peru some time ago. So there are two against two: Chili and Buenos Ayres against Bolivia and Peru. All the republics of South America are thus mingled in the strife, except the Banda Oriental and

the old Republic of Colombia, now divided into three Republics of Ecuador, New Granada, and Venezuela. It will be difficult for these to avoid being drawn into the vortex, particularly Ecuador, which from its local position is most exposed. The declaration of war is accompanied in the Buenos Ayres papers with a very long manifesto, setting forth the causes which in the opinion of the government render the step necessary. The Banda Oriental is also in arms—not against Peru, but against itself. General Fructuoso Rivera, former president of the Republic, and who only a few months since was defeated in an insurrectionary attempt against the government, is again in motion, having collected a force on the frontiers of Brazil, with which he intends to march to Montevideo if he can. Preparations are making to give him a warm reception. The Brazilian brig *Eloisa* has been seized at Buenos Ayres and confiscated, in consequence of being about to depart from that port ostensibly for the Cape of Good Hope but really for the West coast of Africa, to engage in the slave trade.

Chile was favoured by a rebellion in northern Peru against the protectoral system of Santa Cruz. The *Manchester Guardian* of 31 October 1838 told its readers:

> We are sorry to inform you that Peru is again in a lamentable state of revolution... all the north of Peru, which includes the departments of Libertad, Janin, Huayles, and Pierra, had declared against the confederation [in July]. Generals Nela and Sierra had marched on Lima with 2,500 men, and had arrived at Chancay, about four leagues from Lima, where they were joined by General Obregoso, the President of Peru, with six hundred cavalry from Lima, to complete the combination, and declared the revolution against... Santa Cruz. There are two battalions of Bolivian troops stationed in Lima, and General Miller, Governor of Callao, and General Moran, who has commanded the naval forces, have been considered staunch friends of Santa Cruz... General Santa Cruz is in Bolivia and had a considerable force there; and, should no revolution be made against him there, he will not give up the ship without trying his strength. The expedition from Chili, consisting of thirty-three transport with 5,000 men, including soldiers and sailors, sailed from Valparaiso...

On 5 March 1838, *The Times* reproduced extracts from a private letter dated in Lima the previous October.

> The Chilian expedition destined for the invasion of Peru... sailed on 15 September. It arrived off Arica on the 24th... a party of 200 men landed without opposition, the Peruvian forces being at the time at Tacna. The party took possession of the custom-house stores, but had not long been in charge thereof when it was discovered that British property, to the amount of upward of $3,000 had been plundered; but on representations being made by the English consul and Captain Eden, of HMS *Rover* (which vessel had accompanied the expedition from Valparaiso), Admiral Blanco immediately made good the loss, and shot the captain in command of the party at the door of the custom-house. The Chilian squadron sailed from Arica on the 26th. ult...
>
> It is generally supposed that they will occupy Arequipa, as the Peruvian troops had been withdrawn from that town, and all the government employés, as well as the bishop and other persons of consequence, had emigrated... Santa Cruz was at La Paz...

The newspaper's correspondent remained convinced that Chile could not defeat the confederation. The paper forecast the failure of the rebellion against Santa Cruz, the disruption of the alliance of Buenos Ayres and Chile—because the northern Argentine provinces of Salta, Tucumán and Jujuy had declared in favour of Bolivia—and mainly, it would seem, because the correspondent was confident in Santa Cruz's ability to win.

... a stronger and more united feeling to resist an invasion, a more determined detestation of the parties concerned in such invasion never existed in these countries. The abhorrence felt towards the Chilians has been greatly augmented by the scandalous fact of their having landed at Cobija (the only port of Bolivia) a party of robbers and murderers, about one hundred in number, who have been thus let loose from the Chilian prisons to commit fresh crimes in Bolivia. They have been entitled the "innocents"...

The Chilean invading force entered Arequipa in mid-October and continued its northern advance. As they gained ground, Chile rejected a peace agreement offered by General Santa Cruz. Chile became incensed at the apparent continued sympathy shown by Britain towards the Peruvian-Bolivian confederation, a sympathy principally reflected in the assistance given to Dr José Joaquín Mora, private secretary to General Santa Cruz, to travel to London, with the post of consul general, to drum up support for Santa Cruz. Mora sailed to London on a British ship via the Chilean port of Valparaíso

In April 1838, Chilean ships blockaded Lima's main port at Callao, and other ports to the north and south. General Santa Cruz countered in August by announcing that he would blockade Valparaíso, although he lacked the naval strength to do so. In London, it was Dr Mora's difficult task to try to restore European confidence in South America. The Money Market and City Intelligence section of *The Times* of 24 October 1838 reported that an:

attempt is about to be made by the new government of Peru to redeem their lost credit in Europe, by originating some measures for the relief of the English bondholders under the loans raised here in 1824. Their case is as strong, or perhaps stronger, than that of any other sufferers in the same way, since those loans which were brought forward in the very height of the prosperity fever of that time fetched the highest prices of any of those negotiated for the trans-Atlantic states. The shares in the second loan were sold at a sort of auction of public bidding in the Royal Exchange, and the scene which then took place through the eagerness of the numerous competitors for it, was probably without any parallel since the days of the South Sea Bubble... The current price obtained was about 90 per cent; the same stock has subsequently been as low as nine, or it may rather be said has become utterly unsaleable; the dividends upon it are unpaid since 1825

The bonds had rarely been quoted since then and even the announcement of Peru's intentions to regain its credit caused no excitement: "the public mind is very much sobered down from that state of excitement which such announcements as these used formerly to bring on."

There was another reason why Peru could no longer raise any strong interest in its economic development. The only resource that Peru could now offer was guano, in the south. The precious metals that had made it the seat of power in the Spanish empire had been exhausted. The power of the cities on the Pacific had vanished. Europe now looked to the eastern South American countries, Brazil and Argentina, for wealth. Peru meant little more than revolutions and commercial instability.

Chilean troops occupied Lima, and though the Peruvian governor retained control of the fort of Callao and Santa Cruz brought up an army of about nine thousand men to within twenty miles of Lima, Chile's invading force commanded most of the coastline south of the capital. The English papers continued to give accounts of the imminent defeat of Chile and their correspondents explained at length why General Santa Cruz, the mighty man of the Pacific, could not lose. On 24 December 1838, a reporter for the *Manchester Guardian* wrote from Peru that:

> we have just received information from General Morán, that the army under his command had completely routed the Chilians, taken all their baggage and made a considerable number of prisoners. The Protector (Santa Cruz) will leave this evening for his army. Two privateers, that were fitted out here a short time since, have taken one of the Chilian men of war, and brought her into Callao, and burned two of the Chilian transports. The war may be considered over. [8]

It was, almost, but with almost the opposite effect. Chile continued to land troops north of Lima and on 20 January 1839 the invading army defeated the forces of the Confederation at Yungay, in the department of Ancash, north of Lima. Santa Cruz fled into exile and a few weeks later the Confederation was at an end. Peru tried and failed to reverse roles and subject Bolivia. The Chilean army withdrew to its frontiers when Peru acknowledged its debts to Chile. By an agreement signed on 12 September 1848,[9] the debt was finally cancelled.

NOTES:

1. Claudio Veliz, "The Irisarri Loan", *Boletín de Estudios Latinoamericanos y del Caribe*, no. 23, December 1977 (Amsterdam). This is an excellent and well-documented account of the story abridged here.
2. Miers, *Travels in Chile and La Plata.* Quoted in Veliz, "The Irisarri Loan".
3. J. Robertson, *Letters on South America*, vol I, p. 17.
4. Maria Graham, *Journal of a Residence in Chile.* (Longman, London, 1824), p. 131.
5. Robertson, *Letters*, vol I, p. 43.
6. *Manchester Guardian*, 23 November 1837. The treaty was signed on 5 June 1837.
7. It seems advisable at this stage to distract the reader from attention to the conflict between the republic of Chile and the Peru-Bolivian Confederation—because the war did not have much fighting and because the digression fits in here chronologically—to note a trifling issue in Colombia. This bears no relation with incidents in the Pacific but, as stated, it is contemporary.

   Early in 1837, there arose a misunderstanding between Great Britain and the Colombian state of New Granada. The event "attracted towards that feeble republic all the thunders of British diplomacy", which is a remark from the Annual Register for 1837 (p.381).

   It was stated that in circumstances that were not quite clear, on the night of 20 November 1836, Mr Russell, the English vice-consul in Panama, was involved in what could be described as a street brawl with a man whose name was Paredes. The native gentleman came out of the fight rather badly and reported having sustained a wound. "A crowd collected and Mr Russell was, it was alleged, unceremoniously knocked down, disarmed, hurried off to prison, and all his official papers seized."

   The fight gave rise to correspondence between the Minister for Foreign Affairs of New Granada, Mr Pombo, and Mr Turner, the English Consul in Panama. Mr Turner demanded the release of Mr Russell, the punishment of those who had imprisoned him, the return of his papers at a public ceremony, and a monetary compensation to the detained official.

   New Granada's authorities regretted that the British government had reacted so firmly with knowledge of only one side of the dispute and also regretted that the diplomat had not awaited the outcome of the judicial investigation. General Santander, the president, issued a proclamation that contained an appeal to the honour of his countrymen and summoned their resistance against British pressure. However, the argument was soon closed with the appearance outside Cartagena of a squadron led by Commodore Peyton. Mr Russell was freed, the charges were annulled, and he was paid £1,000 compensation for injuries received. President Santander retired in March 1837 and in his farewell message expressed his surprise that "the orders of a government, so enlightened as that of the great English nation, should be accompanied by threats of resorting to force, and that the information, which discussion supplies in international disputes, should have been rejected."

8. *Manchester Guardian*, 24 April 1839.
9. Veliz, "The Irisarri Loan".

Chapter Five

FRENCH BLOCKADES, 1838

Juan Manuel de Rosas (private collection)

General Juan Manuel de Rosas, Governor of Buenos Aires, was a *caudillo* who had gained his political power and military influence in the 1820s as a supporter of a federalised system. He was an opponent of centralised government at Buenos Aires and its advocates in the Unitarian movement—an educated elite who looked on the provinces as backward and feudal[1]—although his own government was itself centralised at Buenos Aires.

"General Rosas was unanimously chosen, and forthwith sworn in, amidst the acclamation of the populace, who were loud in their expressions of rejoicing," the British minister Woodbine Parish had written on 12 December 1829; "he has justly deserved such a mark of the public gratitude and confidence. The only obstacles were his own modesty and great reluctance to be placed in so ostensible and responsible a situation..." Modest he was not; cunning was perhaps a more appropriate term. Rosas was a wealthy landowner of patrician lineage; a leader of men, he used flattery and barbaric discipline, and was a charmer in society. He owed his popularity largely to the fact that he was prepared to ride with the half-castes, indians and *gauchos* whom he led, rather than issue them orders from a position of removed authority. He was utterly brutal with insubordination and intolerant of the mildest opposition.

Rosas served three years in office and, having defeated rebellions and anarchy, required of the legislature that he be re-elected to office with absolute powers. The legislature refused; Rosas left, and organised a campaign against the native indians in the southern reaches of Buenos Aires, on the frontier with Patagonia—where Charles Darwin met him and said of him that he was most dangerous when he laughed. The public demonstrations by Rosas' supporters, who called him the "Restorer of the Laws", eventually persuaded the legislature to surrender its powers and grant those demanded by Rosas. The British minister, then one Mr Hamilton Hamilton, wrote of the governor on 14 April 1835:

> Thus, after a long and disastrous interregnum this unfortunate country has received a government—a government given to it apparently at the call of a considerable portion of its inhabitants, but a portion which is unquestionably far from being either the most considerable or the most respectable; a government which has in fact been thrust upon it, at a moment of deep panic and alarm, by the bigoted and besotted remnant of the Old Spanish dominion, and by the half civilised retainers of the individual who has been selected to preside over it...[2]

One month later, the same minister reported on "the disquietude generally prevalent here... and the insults to which have been exposed many foreign residents who are unwilling to assume the distinguishing badge of the Federal Party, a term synonymous with the party of General Rosas." The "distinguishing badge" was a red ribbon, to be worn on sleeves, lapels and bonnets, its use enforced by roving bands of the governor's supporters. Hamilton himself had been refused entry to the Fort of Buenos Aires when on official business because he had not worn such a ribbon. He apologised to Wellington for recounting the incident in such detail, but he nevertheless explained his concern.

> There has been of late abroad a spirit of so much umbrage, of so much animosity, of so much disrespect towards foreigners, and more particularly towards foreign agents—a spir-

it, however, which I incline to believe not natural to the country, but of which the propagation and development is encouraged by some few leading individuals... that some little wholesome reproof, some little salutary counsel, seemed to be indispensable.[3]

Hamilton was eventually replaced as British minister in Buenos Aires by John Henry Mandeville. Almost immediately, Rosas established a strange link with Mandeville. Sometimes he appeared to be friendly—the governor encouraged Mandeville in his flirtations with his daughter, Manuelita Rosas—but Rosas also ridiculed the minister in public, or poured scorn on him on the grounds that Mandeville spread malicious gossip about the governor's household. Rosas spread equally malicious gossip about the British minister and the female company he kept. Mandeville, it was true, seemed out of his depth at times. But he was of the opinion, as was Palmerston, that ungovernable countries needed rulers like Rosas, for the sake of stability, and so tried to humour the despot. This distressed Rosas' enemies, though the British community generally understood such a stance as necessary.

Meanwhile, the French residents in Buenos Aires—who were among Rosas' strongest foreign critics—protested frequently about the ill-treatment they received compared with the kindly attentions given the resident Britons. The French wanted the abolition of national service for their residents, an exemption granted to the British, and the release of men who had been forcibly drafted into the Argentine army or had been detained for resisting conscription. The French also wanted Buenos Aires to recognise the right to "claim indemnities in favour of Frenchmen who have suffered unjustly in their persons or in their properties."

A French commander, Admiral Leblanc, recently arrived in the River Plate, demanded that Rosas give better treatment to his countrymen, under the threat of blockading the town. He sent an aide to meet General Rosas to demand that the law of the Argentine republic towards foreigners should no longer apply to the French and that their property should be treated "as are treated the persons and properties of the most favoured nation [meaning the British] until the intervention of a treaty" in the style of the "friendship and commerce agreements" which Britain and other European governments demanded of the young republics.[4]

Mandeville was immediately called to the foreign ministry and informed of the French ultimatum.[5] It was normal for Rosas to inform Britain of events first; he admired British liberalism and envied Britain's status in the world. On 24 March 1838, Mandeville wrote to Lord Palmerston to say that a French blockade was imminent. Rosas dealt rapidly with some of the French complaints, replying to Admiral Leblanc that the release of an imprisoned French national, Peter Lavie, had been ordered; and on the matter of forcible conscription he stated that no such action had taken place. Leblanc accepted the two explanations and pressed the two remaining demands: for treatment equal to that given the British—who had a treaty to protect them—and for the right to claim compensation from the government by the French nationals who had suffered unfairly. These Rosas said he could not grant until a treaty had been negotiated. The letters exchanged by the two men read like a parody of conflict in a theatrical representation. The translations perhaps do not do justice to the originals.[6]

From aboard the frigate *Minerve*, at anchor in Montevideo, Rear Admiral

Leblanc wrote on 12 April (on the treatment of Frenchmen and their property).

> Your Excellency cannot but perceive that this demand is a mere temporary guarantee in favour of my fellow-countrymen; that it does not attack your principles; that it does not even refute them; that, *in fine*, it does not derogate from your laws; that it merely offers my fellow countrymen a simple guarantee against a will in opposition to the completely favourable one you at present manifest with respect to them...

And on the demand for payment of indemnities:

> ... What is there more just or more moderate than this demand? And how could it be pretended to refuse it? Can it be said that its object is to impose on the Argentine government exorbitant and arbitrary pretensions? Undoubtedly not, in such case there would be error or bad faith... If, on the contrary, they were unjust and arbitrary, and you refuse to indemnify the person who might have suffered by them, would not this refusal be unworthy of your generous sentiments, and would not your Excellency be the first to acknowledge their injustice? And if you refuse to admit this demand, might not your denial be interpreted as caused by the fear that you would experience of not being able to justify the legality of your acts? Your Excellency cannot imagine, as you have done me the honour to state, that I have presented myself before Buenos Ayres at the head of a squadron to impose upon the Argentine government by a display of force. I have never conceived of the idea of threatening any one; threats have always appeared to me useless and unworthy of a man of honour... If your Excellency is willing to accede to these two demands... the blockade will immediately be raised.

Rosas was not willing and said so. He asserted that the French government had no injury to regret and in turn complained that his own explanations were being rejected. According to Rosas, France was asking for too much in the demand for guarantees for hypothetical incidents that might take place in the future. On 26 April Rosas stated that the demands:

> no longer regard injuries done to Frenchmen, or violations of any real right of France, but only relate to pretensions which being necessarily the object of a treaty, the Argentine government can discuss with the same liberty as any other government, in the manner most agreeable to its interests, and without its refusal being a just motive for carrying on hostilities.

Leblanc abandoned his cajoling manner and in more forcible language insisted that there had been abuses by Buenos Aires. He suggested that reparations and future commitments were perfectly in order. In this letter, dated 5 May, he threatened that until Buenos Aires offered security it would remain under a tight blockade. The admiral then travelled to Rio de Janeiro to purchase "small craft to maintain a more rigorous blockade". Sporadic reports reached the British press from then on of the closure of the western ports of the River Plate; no shots were fired.[7]

However, it was not a full blockade and this the *Manchester Guardian* was pleased to note on 31 October, when it carried a report out of Montevideo, dated 15 August.

> ... the blockade of Buenos Ayres is continuing, all vessels arrived have been obliged to remain at this port as before, but, notwithstanding, prices of imports have been sustained better than could have been expected. This maybe partly attributed to the continual running of small craft between this and Buenos Ayres, and other ports of these provinces owing

to the moderation thus far exercised on the part of the French; but, should they become more severe, and make prizes of all they capture in this traffic, it will reduce it very much, and the lessened demand thereby will be sensibly felt in our market.

It had by then become obvious to the French that a blockade of the river ports would never have much more than a partial effect on the province's economy. The closure of the port distressed foreign merchants who had to ship currency to Europe, but there was still the longer, overland route to southern Brazil, which was not greatly favoured because of the presence of bandits and dissident chieftains bent on raising funds for personal comfort and political ventures. Yet the route could be used with a well-armed guard or by negotiating overland passage beforehand with the agents of the local landowners. In Buenos Aires there was a decline in the exchange, but in the provinces the small manufacturing business and trade carried on as usual. The events that took place in the ports could be obviated in the provinces.

The European powers were inclined to use the blockade as a simple weapon of pressure. In South America, however, the blockade was only understood as an act of war—not a means of settling a minor dispute. In South American eyes, the declaration of a blockade was a military offence, not an economic one. Cities and ports could live, while blockaded, on the supplies of their countryside.

While the French blockaded Buenos Aires, Rosas' troops were at war with the remnants of General Lavalle's army in the north of Argentina. And in Uruguay, Rosas was trying to support a friendly government against a common enemy which had harboured exiles from Buenos Aires. Of fighting in the Banda Oriental, the *Manchester Guardian* said, at the end of October:

> The civil war here appeared lately to be approaching a crisis, from the reverses which the government partly met with, and we had hoped to have seen peace shortly restored. We think this, however, very doubtful now, and that it may still be of some duration. Meantime, the opposing party are so near as to threaten the city itself with a siege.

Yet Rosas soon sought more active British intervention to end the blockade, aware that the English merchants in the town were increasingly annoyed by its continuation. Mandeville wrote to Palmerston to advise him that:

> General Rosas refers to the Treaty with Great Britain as the origin of the war... the cause of the French Blockade is the British treaty, and he infers that the confederation will be always exposed to quarrels with Foreign Powers as long as it is observed.[8]

In mid-December the *Manchester Guardian* announced that the French had delivered yet another ultimatum to Buenos Aires on 28 September:

> the blockade having on that day been in existence just six months. On the 30th, General Rosas sent his reply, which was said to amount to no more than a passage of compliments, expressive of his desire to see the dispute accommodated... The British corvette *Calliope* had sailed, as we conjectured, at the request of Rosas to the commander, in order that he might confer with M. Roger, the late French consul at Buenos Ayres, with a view to induce him to return and re-open negotiations for an adjustment of the differences...

But Admiral Leblanc suspected that Rosas planned to try to play one off against the other and forbade Roger's return.

The people were busy fortifying the coasts of Buenos Ayres. The French had ten vessels of war of different descriptions in the river Plata, and had armed several small craft taken as prizes. More ships were still expected from Europe. The blockade was very strictly maintained...

Although shots were fired the following year, there were few casualties and most of them were recorded as damage to small craft. Little changed in the next twelve months, except the intensity of British indignation.

Official British inactivity in the face of the French action caused vociferous reaction from merchants. In December 1839 an editorial comment in the *United Services Gazette* stated:

The French have extended their blockade of the great La Plata in the invasion of the territory. They now garrison at Monte Video... Their object, under the disguise of seeking reparation for wrongs, is the seizure of territory and this for the double purpose of obtaining the manufacturing supply of South America and excluding the English. A million sterling in English goods is thus shut up in the blockaded ports... The existence of the British Empire depends on its revenues, its revenues depend on its commerce, its commerce depends on its manufactures, and the great and almost the only vent for its manufactures is in its own colonies, and in North and South America. In Europe that vent, always obstructed by the jealousy of the continental manufacturers, is now nearly closed. England sells more to Brazil alone than to the whole continent. The object of the French is to cut off this source of our national strength, not by fair competition but by fraud...

A correspondent to *The Times* opened the new year with fury. On 3 January, one letter signed "An Observer" asked:

Sir, to what amount of insult, to what extent of impoverishment or ruin will the most imbecile set of men which England was ever governed by, lead us? What are Lords Melbourne and Palmerston and their coadjutors about, Sir? They care not how their country is degraded, they care not for the merchants or manufacturers, or for their country's prosperity, so long as they can bask in the sunshine of a court.

The problems lay in that existing customs duties in France were high. In turn, French manufacturers were complaining that they could not obtain many raw materials "without paying for them in hard cash". As a result, France was searching for sources of cheaper raw materials in the new republics, and in doing so had awoken the suspicion of British traders. France, in turn, was alarmed by the prices asked for raw materials in the British colonies and was worried that many "merchants in Bordeaux, and several at Havre are remitting large sums to the Indian colonies of England and Holland," according to the *Journal de Paris*.[9]

Blockades were intended to be boring and this one, like all, stagnated. The results sought were not achieved as soon as expected. Under pressure from the commercial community, Britain made representations to France, and later actively entered negotiations in the River Plate to bring an end to the French action. In the peace terms Rosas gave no more than he had ever offered: a long-term treaty of friendship with France. He did accede to give it his special and immediate attention, which wording satisfied the French.[10] The conclusion of the French blockade which would facilitate the resumption of trade was announced in November 1840. Mandeville was able to advise Palmerston:

of a letter which His Excellency the governor and captain general of the province addressed to me upon the conclusion of the peace with France, in which His Excellency manifests his deep and sincere gratitude to Her Majesty's government for its good offices and for the interest it has shown towards this republic in its long and heavy struggle with France.[11]

The "Pastry War"

New Spain, or Mexico, had become independent of Old Spain by the Treaty of Córdoba in August 1821. It was to be known as the Mexican Empire. Military groups and congress agreed to make the imperial throne hereditary, but by the end of its first year Emperor Agustín (I) Iturbide was losing power and his image as a military hero of the war against Spain was tarnished by incompetence and an inability to end conspiracy. He dissolved congress, and in doing so gave his military opponents the excuse to intensify conspiracy against the empire. Among the leaders of his opponents was General Antonio López de Santa Ana, whom Agustín had at first encouraged and promoted, and then dismissed. Santa Ana proclaimed a republic at Vera Cruz in December 1823 and Agustín I fled into exile. On his return the following year he was shot.

Early in 1824 the Mexican republic adopted a constitution. The country was almost immediately plunged into further conspiracy and revolution and the political pendulum swung between conservative Centralists—who favoured a vice-regal style of government—and the nationalist Federalists. But the politics of Mexico turned on the enigmatic personality of Santa Ana, a *caudillo* with a natural bent for nationalist sentiment and a populist interest in military glory. In 1834 he became president of Mexico, with the support of the Federalist Party.

On 6 November 1835, one hundred and thirty men, most of them North Americans, embarked at New Orleans bound for Texas. The border of Texas—one of Mexico's nineteen states under the constitution of 1824—had been closed by the Mexicans who were fearful of the growing number of immigrants moving in from Louisiana, who posed a threat to the security of Mexico's borders. The US doctrine of Manifest Destiny—which held that all the territory of North America should be part of the Union—represented a more ominous threat.

It is not clear why the one hundred and thirty passengers outward from New Orleans changed their course from Texas to Tampico, but they landed at the northern port and seized the fort without much difficulty. When they tried to take the town they were repulsed and twenty-eight men—two of them French—were captured. All were executed one month later.

France entered a claim for compensation, which included a demand for damages to be paid to the relatives of the two dead Frenchmen, one of them a pastry cook. The conflict that followed has become known as the "pastry war". Such a minor incident was overtaken by the declaration of the independence of Texas. This was crushed in March 1836, when General Santa Ana led his army—all dressed in the operatic-looking uniforms left behind by the Spanish—and defeated the North Americans at El Alamo. But he was then defeated in April by Sam Houston, who made Santa Ana prisoner for eight months.

The French minister in Mexico pressed demands for damages for the 1835 incident until, in 1838, the reclamation took the shape of an ultimatum. A correspondent of *The Times* gave the following account:

> The French minister demands by his ultimatum, not only the payment of 600,000 dollars, but also that several Mexican functionaries should be dismissed, and that several additions should be made to the treaty about to be ratified between France and Mexico. Should the answer of the Mexican government be in the negative upon only one point, should it even be doubtful upon one point, or should it be delayed beyond 15 April, he should place the continuation of the affair in the hands of the commander of his [French] majesty's naval forces, to put into execution the orders he had already received... The Baron Deffaudis brings forward what he designates the "butchery at Tampico in 1835", when twenty-eight foreigners (two of them French) were made prisoners by the Mexican troops, in consequence of an attack which they meditated on the territory of the republic in favour of the Texanos, that they were put to death a few days afterwards in a yard, where they were surrounded and shot like wild beasts; and the Mexican government, although solicited by him to do so during a period of two years, has never been able to show by what law they were sentenced and executed. [12]

Baron Deffaudis demanded that "General Gregorio Gómez, who ordered the assassination in Tampico of the two Frenchmen, be dismissed, and that he pay an indemnification to their families of 20,000 dollars (100,000 francs)." As Mexico failed to consider the claim, France declared a blockade of Mexican ports. The Mexican reply was, perhaps naturally, that "the President of the republic can enter into no treaty until the French naval forces shall have retired from the coast."

On 9 June 1838, the *Manchester Guardian* published the announcement by the French government declaring the blockade. Count Molé, the foreign affairs minister, explained to Earl Granville, then ambassador in Paris, that Mexico had "refused to redress the numerous grievances" to France. On 23 June, under the headline "Continued blockade of the Mexican ports" the *Manchester Guardian* reported that:

> The *Delight* packet brings a full confirmation of the active blockade of the Mexican ports by the French squadron, which commenced on 16 April and was maintained vigorously... although not a gun had been fired by either party... The privileges of the packet service were fully recognised and respected by the blockading squadron.

These privileges were admitted under a post office agreement reached in June 1833.

On 22 August the paper reported preparations for an attack on the fort of San Juan de Ulloa, at Vera Cruz.

> The British packet, which sailed from Vera Cruz on 27 May, had been detained a week after the regular day of sailing at the request of the Mexican government, for the purpose of taking out a request to the British government to become mediator between the French and Mexican governments.

Hence, while the British were angered by the French action in the Americas—for this blockade pleased England no more than had the events in Buenos Aires—the French were also to be infuriated by the continued pre-eminence of Britain in the continent. This influence had reached the point where in each event the Foreign Office was summoned to help in arbitration.

On 25 August the *Manchester Guardian* speculated that the blockade was still without hostilities "because their force [the French] was not sufficiently heavy for an attack on the Castle of San Juan de Ulloa till reinforced with a line of battle ships, or that the commanding officer waited the results of the Baron Deffaudis' return to Paris..." Yet, on 15 September the paper reported that:

> the first blood has been drawn between the French and the Mexicans. It appears that on or about 22 July, a Mexican vessel was pursued between Vera Cruz and Tampico by a boat filled with armed men from the French squadron. She could not escape and the crew abandoned her in their boats. The vessel dived into the surf, and the French, in taking possession of her, were fired upon from the shore, and several of them wounded—one or two are not expected to live... this act is likely to lead to retaliation.

The French fleet, commanded by Admiral Baudin, prepared to attack the fort. In London, a group of merchants from the main industrial towns of England and Scotland expressed their indignation. The committee of the South American and Mexican Association established what, in the present circumstances, might be described as a siege of the foreign secretary and at regular intervals subjected him to an epistolary barrage. Eventually, to bring its lobbying into the open, the Association published its correspondence.[13] After providing a summary of the commercial damage suffered by Britain, the committee's chairman, one J. D. Powles, also told Palmerston that Admiral Baudin had met Mexican officials at Jalapa—where Santa Ana had been born and still had his *hacienda*. Admiral Baudin had then presented a list of exaggerated demands, all of which had to be added to the ratification of the treaty of commerce with France. These demands included payments for damages to French nationals, compensation to the French government, an inquiry into the executions of 1835 and "$200,000 towards the expenses of the squadron sent from France to the coast of Mexico".

On 26 November, the Mexican minister advised Admiral Baudin that all the conditions would be met except payment of the expedition expenses. The Mexicans insisted on their recommendation that arbitration be sought in England. Wrote Mr Powles:

> Admiral Baudin received this letter on 27 November and after recommending his countrymen in Vera Cruz to the humanity of the Mexican commandant there, and his countrymen in Mexico to the known humanity of the Mexican people and government, he proceeded, with the aid of his 27 vessels of war and the experienced artillerymen aboard them brought from France, to bombard and take the castle of San Juan d'Ulloa.
>   The history of modern times affords no precedent of actual hostilities being resorted to on such utterly insufficient grounds.

The shelling of the castle by Baudin's three double-banked frigates, four sloops of war, four brigs and bomb vessels began shortly after lunch on 27 November. The bombardment demolished the castle and buried more than one hundred and fifty men in the ruins, but the battle continued until nightfall. On 4 December, Baudin was advised that Mexico rejected the terms of the convention and declared war on France. French nationals were given sixty days in which to leave Mexico.

> On the following morning before daybreak he [Baudin] surprised the town of Vera Cruz and spiked the guns on those batteries which faced the castle. He was, however, attacked by the Mexicans under General Santa Ana, and driven to his boats. The town was then bombarded by the French, and the Mexican general, in order to deprive them of supplies

ordered it to be abandoned; the inhabitants, including of course the British merchants, consequently shut up their houses and retired, leaving their property wholly unprotected.[14]

The British took refuge in the packet which had arrived off Vera Cruz. Baudin resumed the blockade, concentrating on Vera Cruz and removing his boats from Tampico when he learned that a rebellion had broken out there against Santa Ana.

Contemporary writers, and merchants expressing their feelings in their correspondence, had little sympathy for either side in the conflict, but their worst adjectives were directed at the French, who were seen as responsible for disrupting their livelihood.

In the battle of Vera Cruz, Santa Ana's horse, a white charger, was shot from under him and grapeshot wounded the general's leg, which had to be amputated. The event allowed Santa Ana to become a national hero again. A funeral mass was said for his leg, buried in a cemetery in Mexico City. The substitute wooden leg was after that regarded with respect, being the prop of a hero. Fanny Calderón de la Barca, the English wife of Spain's ambassador to Mexico, went to visit the general at his *hacienda* in Jalapa. He was:

a gentlemanly, good-looking, quietly dressed, rather melancholy-looking person, with one leg. He has a sallow complexion, fine dark eyes, soft and penetrating. Knowing nothing of his past history, one would have said a philosopher, living in dignified retirement... It is strange, how frequently this expression of philosophic resignation, of placid sadness, is to be remarked on the countenances of the deepest, most ambitious, and most designing men... It was only now and then that the expression of his eye was startling, especially when he spoke of his leg, which is cut off below the knee. He speaks of it frequently.[15]

A peace treaty was signed on 9 March 1839, with the mediation of Mr Pakenham, the British minister. Mexico paid three million francs to French nationals who had entered claims before the outbreak of war. The damages suffered by Frenchmen expelled from Mexico were to be assessed. But the greatest advantage won by the French was the Mexican consent to place commerce from France on an equal footing with that of the most favoured nations, among which was Britain.

NOTES:

1. See Chapter 2.
2. PRO FO 6/47, p. 134.
3. PRO FO 6/47, p. 144.
4. PRO FO 6/63, p. 194.
5. PRO FO 6/63, p. 198
6. *The Times*, 5 September 1838.
7. *Manchester Guardian*, 12, 16 September and 15 August 1838; *The Times*, 21 October 1838.
8. PRO FO 6/75, p. 256.
9. *Manchester Guardian*, 15 September 1838.
10. From a moral point of view, Rosas' victory came at the wrong time, in 1840. He had beaten France; his army had defeated Lavalle in Corrientes during July (see PRO FO 6/75, p. 73); and he was even further flattered by the publicity he received from the reception of formal notification of the engagement of Queen Victoria to Prince Albert, to whom he sent

his good wishes (See PRO FO 6/75, p.1). But in contrast to this, and which makes his victories unfortunate, was the growth of his despotic power. The number of outrages against his opponents made that year the bloodiest of his long government. Every night many of his enemies, or suspect enemies or just suspected sympathisers of suspected enemies, "disappeared". On this subject Mandeville wrote to London: "The excesses committed in Buenos Ayres for the gratification of public and private vengeance have arisen to a height rarely recorded in the annals of history. During the preceding three months until the last few days not a night passed but from two or three, to twice and three times the number of assassinations took place in the town and suburbs." (See PRO FO 6/75, 14 October 1840). Rosas' bands of law enforcers, the members of the *Mazorca* organisation which was a "society like the secret tribunals in Germany in the Middle Ages, issues its decrees and immolates its victims." All the persecuted were either active in or sympathetic with the Unitario party, Mandeville said, or simply suspected of possible links with the party. Mandeville "called together the British residents in Buenos Ayres and made known to them the personal danger which in my opinion they would risk by remaining in the country."

11. PRO FO 6/75, p. 288.
12. Reproduced in the *Manchester Guardian*, 25 August 1838.
13. *The Times*, 23 February 1839.
14. *The Times*, 23 February 1839.
15. Frances Calderón de la Barca, *Life in Mexico*. (Chapman & Hall, London, 1843), p. 27. Quoted in Pendle, *Latin America*.

Chapter Six

ANGLO-FRENCH BLOCKADE IN THE RIVER PLATE, 1845-1850

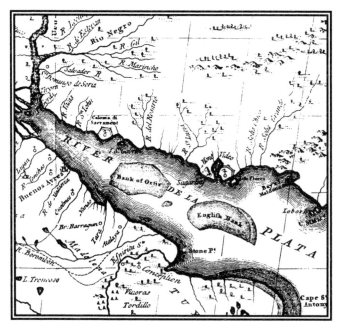

Nineteenth-century map of the River Plate (private collection)

During the French blockade of Buenos Aires, initiated in 1838, Admiral Leblanc sought shelter and provisions for his ships at Montevideo. General Manuel Oribe, who had succeeded General Fructuoso Rivera as the second president of Uruguay since independence, invoked his friendship with the Governor of Buenos Aires, Rosas, in refusing to give the French any more than the assistance that might be considered basic and essential.

Oribe's refusal was used by General Rivera as an opportunity to accuse the president and his *Blanco* (National) Party of consorting with a dangerous tyrant across the River Plate. Rosas was suspected of spending all of his waking hours—and not a few of his sleepless nights—planning the annexation of the Banda Oriental to the Argentine Confederation. Rosas was also accused of planning a similar fate for Corrientes, briefly declared a republic and the stronghold of General Lavalle; and for Paraguay.

Rivera's accusation against Oribe aroused the sympathy of the Unitarian fugitives and other opponents of Rosas living in exile in Montevideo. The Unitarians found an ally in Rivera and his conservatives, who identified with a certain political liberalism inspired by Europe and opposed the Federalists—whom they saw as semi-feudal. *Unitarios* and *Colorados* toppled Oribe. The French, who were blockading Buenos Aires, supported Rivera, seeing it to be to their advantage.

The displaced president, Oribe, was given moral and material support by Rosas and in 1839 organised a campaign to regain his office. That was the beginning of a war which is remembered in both countries for its length and cruelty. It is, in world history, another small war; but in the River Plate it was the *Guerra Grande*—the Big War—which lasted for twelve years.

To terrorise his enemy, Oribe announced that no prisoners would be taken. All prisoners would be "executed by the cutting of the throat" (*pasado a degüello*). Such a policy, which was also the practice of Rosas' troops since the civil war in the 1820s, made the occupation of the *degollador*, with the rank of non-commissioned officer, one that was respected as well as feared. The brutality of such open surgery was obvious; yet the men took pride in the sharpness of their steel and the swiftness of their arms. The prisoners, with their hands tied behind their backs, were ordered to kneel on the ground in a line and the executioner crept up behind them whispering to each, "A mother suffers more in labour," or "Such a beautiful young throat, my blade cannot resist this temptation." It is said in the littoral of Argentina and in western Uruguay that fruit grows well in the soil which was so irrigated by the blood of many unfortunate men.

Lord Palmerston, foreign secretary in the Whig government of Lord Melbourne, looked on Rosas, and later on Oribe, with the horror natural to contemporary Europeans; but he considered that such tyrants were at least in control of their countries and were governments that could be referred to and dealt with. The British disapproved of France because the blockade threatened British trade and because the French were thought to be trying to establish some form of protectorate in Uruguay, to compete from there with English commerce. Britain also feared that French intervention would lead to the collapse of local governments and lead to anarchy. The British minister in Buenos Aires, Mandeville, was in favour of Rosas in the contest with France, because the governor had not hampered British commerce and had even favoured it. With only a few exceptions, resident Britons were generally well treated, though they had not escaped the widespread sense of fear that existed in the city.

But in 1841, the Conservative government of Robert Peel took office and the foreign secretary, Lord Aberdeen, adopted a friendlier attitude towards the French. Rosas and Oribe appeared destined to win the war in Uruguay and hence the French would soon be out of the River Plate. British trade there could be resumed without hindrance. On this issue at least, Britain could afford to appear friendly with France.

The evidence supported this assumption. Initial skirmishes between Oribe and Rivera had led to successive defeats of the latter. On the river, for it was a naval war as well as one on the land, Admiral William Brown, commanding Rosas' fleet, defeated the Uruguayan navy—which in 1841 was commanded by John Halsted Coe, a former United States citizen born in Springfield, Massachusetts. Coe had served with Lord Cochrane in the Pacific, and with Brown in Buenos Aires until a few years before.

While Brown began a partial blockade of Montevideo after his success against Coe, the battered navy of Uruguay was to be reorganised by Coe's successor, Giuseppe Garibaldi. The Italian liberator, who had fled Italy and an execution order, had first gone to Brazil, where he had been fighting for the republicans in Rio Grande against the Imperial authorities in Rio de Janeiro. He had arrived in Montevideo in that year.[1]

Still the war was to go against Rivera. During 1842 he was to lose heavily to Oribe's army—supported by Rosas' army in Entre Ríos, led by General Urquiza — and Garibaldi was defeated on the river by Brown. In February 1843 most of Uruguay was controlled by Oribe. He laid siege to Montevideo, the last stronghold against his return to power. He appeared to be just a few days away from victory; there was no reason to doubt such an expectation. But he delayed the final attack fearing that his *gauchos* would massacre the population. The delay would last nine years.

Montevideo's administration was in the hands of foreigners. The partisans of Oribe had left the town fearing reprisals from the *Riveristas*. The *Riveristas* were squabbling between rival factions. The foreigners in the capital, who numbered over 20,000 out of the total population of 31,000, organised local commerce and a civil service. They also organised an army to defend the city against Oribe. The French formed the largest legion, with 2,900 volunteers out of 5,300 residents. They had their own newspaper, *Le Patriote Français*, and a strong conviction that they were fighting a noble cause and could beat the enemy, and live to collect the rewards of land and cattle promised to all foreign volunteers by the Montevideo parliament. Garibaldi managed to recruit only 215 Italians out of a community of 4,200; their paper, *L'Italiano*, folded just when they needed it most. The British community numbered about 600, so the volunteers joined the Montevideo regulars or entered the French legion—which was seen as the best group for a good fight. But the British had their own paper, *Britannia*, which became a powerful organ of propaganda to counter the pro-Rosas English-language paper, *The British Packet and Argentine News*, which Thomas George Love had started in 1826.

The Uruguayan government split. Some of its generals defected and splinters reunited, while the foreign communities defended the city against Brown's blockade of the port and Oribe's siege to the north. The population and the politicians in Montevideo viewed the foreigners with mixed feelings. They disliked having to rely on them, but had no choice.[2]

Oribe's army and Rivera's propagandists—the able intellectuals who had fled Buenos Aires—appealed for sympathy in Europe. The *Riveristas*, supported by their foreign legions, contacted numerous MPs in England to try to turn Lord Aberdeen around from his policy of waiting for Montevideo to fall. Rosas, with the support of a far more powerful British community in Buenos Aires, sought the sympathy of Europe's governments to discipline the armed foreigners in Montevideo. France opposed Rosas, supported Rivera, but was not totally out of sympathy with Oribe, whose desire to reconquer the government he had been expelled from by a coup was understandable.

The *Riveristas* and the *Unitarios* won an early supporter in Sir John Purvis, commander of the British naval units outside Montevideo. He had been stationed off the coast of Uruguay to watch the French ships there since the blockade of Buenos Aires had been lifted and Oribe had been overthrown. Purvis was attracted to the idea of a liberal cause: the idea of supporting the weak besieged town against the vast armies threatening it, the idea that Montevideo was fighting for enlightenment. Samuel Fisher Lafone, one of the British merchants in Montevideo, who felt a strong dislike for Rosas, helped to convince Purvis of the justice of the Unitarians' cause. Lafone, an Anglican, had been imprisoned by Rosas for marrying a Roman Catholic woman in Buenos Aires without the dispensation of the local Bishop. Lafone was largely responsible for financing the Uruguayan army from his own fortune.[3] He was then in the process of acquiring a large part of the Falkland Islands, to be known as Lafonia.

Purvis ordered Admiral Brown, under the terms of the Foreign Enlistment Act of 1819, to withdraw from the command of Rosas' army. It was obvious that Brown would refuse, because of his sympathies and his duties as an officer; and perhaps too because he had been told that Purvis hated the Irish. Purvis used the refusal to justify assisting a group of Garibaldi's troops under attack by Brown. Purvis' intervention outraged the British in Buenos Aires; but in London it did not elicit any reprimand.[4] Purvis also used his naval strength to order Oribe to rescind a declaration that he would treat foreigners in the legions as if they were native enemies. *The Gaceta Mercantil* of 6 May 1843, published in Buenos Aires, said that:

> Commodore Purvis, in conjunction with the Unitarian savages, has trampled on the natural rights of man, of nations, and of the human race. The war, which was about to end, is renewed and rendered more bloody. Commodore Purvis will be responsible for all its disasters, for all its horrors.

Purvis was quietly recalled to London some time later.

Rosas ordered Brown to intensify the blockade of Montevideo and Oribe tightened his ring around the city by land. There were always cattlemen and fishermen prepared to defy the siege or run the blockade to sell food and wine at good prices to the besieged Montevideans. The escalation of the dispute prompted Britain and France to agree to seek an end to a war which was causing so much damage to trade, and to impose peace terms by force if necessary. John Gore Ouseley was appointed by Britain and Baron Deffaudis—he of the blockade of Vera Cruz and Tampico—by France to deliver a peace plan to Buenos Aires and Montevideo in May 1845. If Buenos Aires did not accept the plan, its port would be blockaded. Under the peace terms, Rosas would recognise Uruguay's independence, which he readily acceded to out of respect for his friend Oribe, and because he had never publicly disputed it. His troops would evacuate Montevideo, Oribe and Rivera would abandon their pretence to the government of the Banda Oriental, and new elections would be held to renew the government. All these sections Rosas rejected. The forces in Montevideo agreed to these terms.[5] Britain and France then declared Buenos Aires under blockade.

Admiral Samuel Hood Inglefield, commander of ten ships in the British fleet, and Admiral Laine, in charge of ten French ships, decided to demonstrate the powers' anger with the seizure of three of Rosas' ships, and forced Brown—and all his British officers—to abandon the blockade of Montevideo. Brown agreed and retired.

Brazil, its politicians and court long split into groups supporting Buenos Aires or Montevideo, finally decided to back the stronger and put its navy under the orders of the French and British admirals to defeat Rosas. The United States was shocked: it saw the European powers' intervention to be in breach of its Monroe Doctrine. The concern was expressed in a report in the *Washington Union*, the official organ of President Polk's administration.

Hostilities have been conducted, so far as we have heard, according to the laws of civilized war. Meantime a large squadron of British and French vessels has been lying in the waters of one of the belligerents; and now it appears that, without notice or explanation, or rendered reason, this neutral squadron, availing itself to the fullest extent of the right of the strongest, has quietly taken possession of the naval force of Buenos Ayres...

It was, the paper said, "a monstrous violation of hospitality" in the harbour of a friendly power.[6]

Henry Mandeville, the minister in Buenos Aires sympathetic to Rosas, was recalled to London. On 24 October 1845, *The Times* explained to its readers what the fuss was all about.

The intervention of France and England in the affairs of the river Plate has been carried on with sufficient energy by Mr Gore Ouseley and Baron Deffaudis to prove that the fears of delay arising from a want of distinct and vigorous instructions and powers were wholly unfounded. The two governments of the mediating powers must have foreseen precisely the events which have occurred—the refusal of Rosas to put an end to the war, and the resolution of Oribe to maintain himself as long as possible in the Banda Oriental; and we must believe that the two greatest states in Europe do not deliberately engage in an affair of this kind without providing the means necessary to accomplish their object...

It must not be lost sight of that the real object of this intervention is to liberate the Banda Oriental from an invading army, and to restore the proper independent government—not to attack Buenos Ayres. In this respect it may be compared to the intervention of the great powers in 1840 in the affairs of Syria... If hostilities occur between England and the Argentine Republic they will probably be occasioned, not so much by the part we have taken in favour of Montevideo, as by the arbitrary acts inflicted by Rosas on British commerce in the course of the war on the river.

The Times complained strongly against a letter written by the British merchants at Buenos Aires in favour of Rosas.

> The absurd exaggerated language of this paper at once denotes its origin. There has long been at Buenos Ayres an English party, with which we fear the late minister, Mr Mandeville, had connected himself, determined to remain blind to all the barbarities and insolence of the government of Rosas... The principal organ of the Argentine dictator is a journal written and printed in English at Buenos Ayres, in which every act of cruelty or oppression he has ever committed is palliated or defended...

The target of such odium was Mr Love's *British Packet*, which could hardly be described as the dictator's principal organ, although it was sympathetic to Rosas, and tried only to be a little more level-headed than the Spanish-language press. The letter which had caused such anger in London had been written by several members of the Buenos Aires Commercial Rooms, where Mr Love was a prominent member, to Lord Aberdeen.

> ... it is utterly impossible for us to leave the country we are in, where many of us are engaged in trade with Great Britain, hold large stocks of British goods consigned to us for sale, have heavy outstandings in a paper currency daily depreciating from the political events around us... Some of us have resided in this country for a great number of years, and to all of us during the period of our residence in this country the most ample, generous, and efficient protection has been afforded, and especially so during the administration of His Excellency Brigadier General Don Juan Manuel de Rosas... against which we have no cause of complaint... The privileges we have in commerce, pastoral, or agricultural pursuits, inland navigation, or any other branch of industry we may please to adopt, place us on a better footing than the natives...[7]

The Times argued that if Rosas "protects these renegades about himself, it is only the more effectually to injure the general interests of their country elsewhere."

On 15 November 1845, one of *The Times*' leaders on events in Buenos Aires filled a column. Every line was one of outrage and indignation as the writer described the character of Rosas.

> A sanguinary monomaniac like Marat might at such a period as the French revolution rouse the passions of a frantic people to a sort of sympathy with his own diabolical projects; but the most violent diatribes of the *Ami du peuple* of 1793 are literally surpassed by the language which the official journal of Buenos Ayres has been holding for years. Our readers will scarcely believe that the war-whoop of death to their political opponents is the common heading of every document which emanates from a public office in Buenos Ayres. The ordinary statements of the current expenses of the Treasury are preceded by the shibboleth of these monsters: "Long live the Argentine Confederation! Death to the Savage Unitarios!"

The occasion for such anger in these moderate columns was the arrival in London of the message, dated 16 August, from Rosas to his legislative assembly, relating to the transactions to date between his government and the British and French envoys.[8]

In the meantime, in the River Plate, the British and French commanders had agreed on a show of force to demonstrate to Buenos Aires that it could not stop the navies of the two powers from sailing up the river when they wished to. On 20 November, French and English forced their way up the River Paraná and attacked the coast batteries placed at the bend of Obligado to prevent any progress north to the province of Corrientes and to Paraguay, which were opposed to Rosas.

Rosas' government evinced great apprehension at the consequences of the expedition of the allied powers to open up the navigation of the Paraguay river... It was generally thought that this measure of opening a free commerce to Paraguay would create so general a feeling of hostility to Rosas, he being the only impediment to an unrestricted intercourse with foreigners...

said *The Times* of the preparations. [9]

The action, which lasted nine hours, ended with the complete destruction of the shore batteries, but the defenders fought bravely: "The allied squadrons, we hear, had destroyed the batteries erected by Rosas at the entrance of the river, and the large fleet of trading vessels assembled at Martín García were expecting immediate orders to proceed to their destinations."

There were one hundred and thirty-three merchantmen in the harbour of Montevideo. "Great anticipations were entertained of extended commercial relations which would flow from the opening up of the rich country of Paraguay to the enterprise of our merchants..."[10] *The Times* used the occasion to praise the use of steam in sea warfare, then a subject of much debate: conversion of the Royal Navy's units to steam was resisted by an older generation of seamen, who thought the new system was ugly, noisy, and no more effective than sail.

This action is another instance (and several similar ones have occurred in the course of the undertakings in which our naval forces have of late years been engaged) of the advantages to be derived from steam power in river operation, and the necessity of obtaining perfect proficiency in that species of operations.

No attack would in all probability have been directed against the forces of the positions of Rosas upon the right bank of the stream, if he had not endeavoured to convert the authority which he undoubtedly exercises in Buenos Ayres into a sovereign right over one of the principal rivers of the world... An internal blockade of independent territories by the stoppage of one of nature's great channels of communication could no more be permitted at the mere caprice of Rosas than the blockade of Montevideo could be allowed to paralyse... trade. This action is one of the most remarkable feats of maritime warfare which has taken place for many years if we consider the length of the engagement, the relative forces of the parties, the strong positions carefully prepared by the Buenos Ayrean government, and the small size of the vessels bearing the English and French flags up the river. [11]

The paper found much to praise in the joint French and British action and commended the unity of the two countries.[12]

This was to be the only significant action of the long Anglo-French blockade. After Obligado, the ships proceeded north to Paraguay. By January the war had lingered sufficiently to deserve a paragraph in Queen Victoria's speech at the opening of Parliament.

For several years a desolating and sanguinary warfare has afflicted the state of the Rio de la Plata. The commerce of all nations has been interrupted, and acts of barbarity have been committed unknown to the practice of civilised people. In conjunction with the King of the French I am endeavouring to effect the pacification of these states.[13]

The British in Montevideo thought Britain's responsibilities should be far greater and suggested that England take charge of the territory.

There is a very generalised impression here, that in order to maintain a settled tranquillity in the country, it will ultimately be necessary that England and France, or better England alone, either take charge of the country or exercise so direct an influence in its government as to afford security for the maintenance of its tranquillity.[14]

By then the president of Paraguay, Carlos Antonio López, had declared war on Rosas with a rousing proclamation. "Paraguayans!—let us march to victory—for victory will gain us days of greatness, prosperity, and joy. Viva the Republic of Paraguay! Independence or Death. Viva Brave Paraguayans."[15] What was more important than the declaration of war in this decision was that Paraguay, its frontiers closed for years by the dictator Francia, had been opened.

In March 1846, as England heard of the defeat of the Sikhs in India, of a *coup d'état* in Spain, and Earl Grey told the House of Lords that "the condition of Ireland was one of lawlessness and wretchedness"—and famine relief committees received new instructions on the assistance to the starving—Lord Palmerston demanded to know of the Prime Minister whether or not England was at war with Buenos Aires. Peel told the Commons that there was a blockade, but that war had not been declared. The Prime Minister came under some criticism about the interpretation of what was war and what not, in view of the fact that there had been considerable loss of life. After some discussion, he took refuge in the argument that confusion about policy should not be made to sound derogatory to the fighting men: "The gallant officers, sailors and marines engaged in the expedition, are entitled to all the credit of their bravery, whatever may be thought of the policy or of the instructions of the Government (Cheers)."[16]

It was perhaps natural that after the action at Obligado there should be concern about the course of the war and also a desire to know what was being fought for. Hopes for a peace treaty were aroused. "Strong hopes are entertained that the government of General Rosas will find itself compelled to give way, before long, to the demands of England and France..."[17] But the battle of Obligado had only increased Rosas' popularity in Buenos Aires and he was not ready to give up. Oribe had again defeated General Rivera, this time at one of the Colorado chieftain's strongholds at Maldonado. British and French forces were garrisoned there, but did not enter action.

Rosas propped up his economy at home by "issuing 2,500,000 paper dollars monthly to meet the demands upon his treasury." A dollar of these was only worth two pennies, down from about three shillings a few years before.

> A law has been passed for the purpose of bleeding all foreigners, in the form of a contribution to support the war effort. The result of such arbitrary measures all must know: the design is, doubtless, to intimidate the governments of France and England.[18]

As the year progressed the war between the United States and Mexico, as well as the news from India, tended to compete for space in the British newspapers. Yet the war in the River Plate was still taking up several columns each week. In August and September, the progress of the returning convoy of merchantmen that had sailed north after Obligado had a successful outcome.

> We learn from Montevideo under date of 13 June that the expedition up the Parana had been highly successful in a mercantile point of view, all the goods taken up having been sold at very satisfactory prices; the province of Corrientes and the Republic of Paraguay were

able to absorb a much larger quantity being both bare of British manufactures.[19]

Rear Admiral Inglefield, commander of the British fleet, notified the Admiralty that one hundred and ten ships had returned to Montevideo, only two being lost as they ran aground near San Lorenzo, not far from Obligado. The progress and return on the River Paraná of so many ships was an impressive sight. Though the craft were subject to the occasional action of snipers from the coast—whose fire was always returned—the local population was reported more in awe than anger at the passage of such a fleet. Lachlan Mackinnon, a lieutenant aboard one of the British ships, was, in turn, overwhelmed by the beauty of the coast; though he did admit that his attention was drawn to large groups of women and children bathing naked in the shallow water at the edge of the river.[20]

Efforts to achieve peace progressed slowly. The contacts of Mr Thomas Hood, the British minister at Montevideo—who replaced Ouseley in the mediation efforts—were reported to be a mystery.[21] Progress was evident to the foreign minister of Buenos Aires, Arana, who, acting on a letter from Aberdeen delivered through Hood, had ordered General Mansilla, commander of the forces at San Lorenzo, not to fire on Anglo-French merchant ships using the river. However, disagreement between the negotiators delayed a settlement. A correspondent from Montevideo wrote:

> Mr Hood had arranged everything satisfactorily both with the Buenos Ayres government and General Oribe, but the late ministers, [who were still in the river Plate and still active] Messrs Ouseley and Deffaudis, appeared to be throwing every obstacle in the way of a final settlement and consequently there were some doubts as to a final peace.

At Buenos Aires, Rosas had given assurance of agreement to Hood, which he modified when consulted by Ouseley. The peace deal offered by Hood was simply that the two legislative chambers in Montevideo would elect a new president after Oribe and his aides had entered Montevideo, but leaving the bulk of his army outside the city. Oribe agreed. Baron Deffaudis objected, asking "whether Mr Hood's instructions were definite as to raising the blockade of Buenos Ayres previous to Rosas' withdrawing the Argentine troops from the Banda Oriental..." or after.[22] But the peace proposals remained inconclusive: no formula could be found for all to agree.

The blockade had entered a tedious stage. There was much smuggling between Montevideo and Buenos Aires. Goods arrived daily in Montevideo from Buenos Aires agents for shipment to Europe, "the result of lenience observed by the blockading squadron before that port, and by the free intercourse which our traders happily enjoy with Entre Rios".[23] The Entre Ríos province, between the Paraná and Uruguay Rivers, was the stronghold of General Urquiza, Rosas' army commander and political ally.

Correspondents in Montevideo kept the British public informed of frequent outrages: cutting the throats of prisoners now seemed quite normal to the prosecution of war. Other horrors were far worse. The atrocities which the Montevideans said were committed by Rosas' and Oribe's *gauchos* were attributed by Buenos Aires to the *Unitarios*. On some occasions the *Unitarios* were accused of mutilating their own dead to blame the Federal army. There was no evidence of this.[24] *The Times* correspondent, writing from Montevideo at the end of 1846, said:

> Those who lent an incredulous ear to the appalling descriptions given by a British officer,

Captain Frankland, late of Her Majesty's Ship *Pearl*, of what he reluctantly witnessed in Buenos Ayres in 1842, will here find the best confirmation [The captain had reported the mass murder of a family.]

The ferocity of the soldiery of Rosas is almost without parallel. I have heard from Captain Reed, of HMS *Racer*, that when his ship was stationed off Maldonado some time ago, a man was beheaded by them on the bare allegation of his having facilitated some supplies of fresh beef to the *Racer*; that the severed head was kicked about in sport through the square by the soldiers, and that the officer who ordered the butchery declared in derision of the humane captain's intervention, that "the orders of Rosas must be executed; and if he were told to cut the throat of his own mother he would not hesitate to do so."

It was not only the troops who were authorised to kill their enemies. By a decree dated 1 May 1846, Rosas had ordered the execution of British and French men from the fleets who might be taken prisoners. One of the victims had been a mate of the *Racer*, one Mr Wardlaw, who had been cruising off the coast of Buenos Aires when his small boat had been driven ashore by a storm. He was murdered "with most refined cruelty, being cut, scored, and mutilated in a most dreadful manner."

The Times correspondent had a catalogue of horror.

A lady of Montevideo, Doña Teresa de T., was assassinated at Oribe's camp on pretence of her attempting to seduce men to abandon his cause. A Brazilian subject, who was forced to serve, was seized in the act of escaping, his throat cut and his body mutilated. An Italian, taken wounded at Tres Cruces (near Montevideo) by Don Jorge Carreras, was trailed at the heels of the latter's horse, his throat cut, his legs and hands severed, castrated and flayed, his heart torn out, roasted and eaten.

In England, some readers of *The Times* became vegetarians and the evangelist missionaries of South London were said to have turned to a life of spiritualism after they had finished reading such reports. Peace prospects remained remote, though the forces in Montevideo were regularly reported to be seeking a settlement that would end the siege and allow life to return to normal. The city's economy and its customs house, which acted as a bank, were managed by foreign merchants. Not a day went by without the death of a civilian, hit by the irregular cannon fire from Oribe's army, posted at the Cerro, the hill on the west of the bay of Montevideo, which commanded a view of the besieged town.[25]

On Monday, 1 February 1847, *The Times* reported that Lord Howden, the new minister to Brazil, had left London for Paris three days before.

The object of his Lordship's visit to the French metropolis is to receive the final assent of the Cabinet of the Tuilleries to the modifications which may be necessary to terminate, satisfactory to all parties, the hostilities on the river Plate.

The growing crisis in Europe made peace an urgent necessity. However, it could not be rushed. Oribe, while expressing to Howden his desire for a speedy settlement, organised the murder of a young Argentine lawyer, Florencio Varela, editor of the Montevideo newspaper *Comercio del Plata*, and a prominent propagandist for the *Unitarios*. The murder, on 30 March 1848, spread fear among the more prominent foreigners in Montevideo. Garibaldi, who lived near Varela, left soon after, fearing an attempt on his own life, but also using the occasion to set a date of departure for Italy, where he longed to return. Rebellions in Europe were gaining force in that year of revolutions. The popular uprisings had an unfortunate effect on the peace talks: "Baron Gros, the French ambassador, had arrived and commenced treating with the belligerent parties, but the news of the French revolution having quickly followed him, he was in a perplexing position", reported *The Times*. King Louis Philippe had been driven from the throne.

On 9 June 1848, *The Times* reported that conditions for reaching an end to the River Plate dispute had been reached. These were:

1. the evacuation by the Argentine troops from the territory of the Oriental republic; 2. the foreigners now in the service of the government of Montevideo to be disarmed; 3. Oribe to enter into the city as president for four months, to complete the four years of his presidency; 4. a general amnesty to all Orientals without reference to political opinions; 5. life and property to be guaranteed to all foreigners; 6. if Rosas and Oribe offered any impediment to the carrying out of the intended pacification, the blockade would continue, and the city of Montevideo defended at least by the French until the arrival of new forces, and hostilities would continue; 7. if Buenos Aires accepted these conditions but not Montevideo, the blockade would be lifted with the consent of the former alone.

Palmerston had returned to the Foreign Office in 1846 and was anxious to see Britain out of the River Plate dispute, which appeared to be politically exhausting with little material gain to be achieved. Britain moved its ships to a place of observation outside Montevideo while the French were urged to keep up the blockade by the lobbying in Paris of Louis Adolphe Thiers, the former foreign minister and president of the council. French marines landed at Montevideo, and others remained garrisoned at Colonia del Sacramento, in front of Buenos Aires. Britain withdrew its troops.

Peace with Rosas was as difficult as victory. Henry Southern, founder of the *Retrospective Review*, proprietor of the *London Magazine* and a writer in the *Spectator*, was appointed minister in Buenos Aires in 1848, to arrange the details of the peace. On 13 December 1849, he wrote to Palmerston describing the trouble in dealing with Rosas: "It is now three weeks since the signature of the convention... I looked upon my reception immediately afterwards as a matter of course..." Southern had signed the letter on 24 November, but:

General Rosas is both original and capricious... his defence consisted chiefly of statements of how his countrymen would view his reception of a British minister while the Argentine squadron was still detained by the English... "Let something come in the shape of detained ships, and I shall not look too closely at them. You say these vessels are in a wretched state, that it requires time and money to put them in repair; it is true that the Treaty stipulated that they are to be put approximately in the state in which they were when detained, but let them come, they shall not be looked at too closely". I was having access to the immutable resolutions and the capricious waywardness which is the fountain of all that is official here.[26]

Southern eventually secured the ratification of the convention. Admiral Reynolds patched up two ships, one of them in deplorable condition, for their symbolic return to Buenos Aires, and the minister was formally received by Rosas, who had refused to meet him twice and caused him much humiliation.

But Rosas refused to agree to sign a statement that he would not interfere in Uruguay's affairs. "General Rosas declares he has never interfered and never will interfere in the internal government of General Oribe", wrote Southern. The next day Rosas wrote to Southern on paper "which bears no address, signature or date. It is in this manner that His Excellency has fallen into the way of corresponding with me—confidentially, without any official compromise beyond that implied in unofficial conversation."

Southern, though furious with Rosas, was to write to Palmerston on 10 January 1851:

> It is not wise to judge lightly the motives of a man who has discovered the means of governing one of the most turbulent and restless people in the world, and with such success that, though there is much cause for complaint, and not a little discontent, still the death of General Rosas would be considered by every man in the country as the direct misfortune. It certainly would be the signal of disorder and of intestine quarrels, which would reduce the country to misery.

By then the British public had read of the settlement of the dispute between England and Buenos Aires, "which puts an end to all old animosities, and re-establishes the former relations of friendship and good understanding."[27] Animosity there had been but, perhaps strangely, a great warmth was felt towards Britain. The British had their own newspapers, their own hospital—which offered charitable assistance to all nationalities—their own schools, their own church (which was suspect but tolerated), their own businesses, which gave employment to many. Animosity did subside.

In Paris, Alexandre Dumas the elder published a book on the history of the siege of the Uruguayan capital, *Montevideo, ou une nouvelle Troie*, which was to win the hearts of many Frenchmen and serve the cause of the *Unitario* propagandists in Europe. The idea of Montevideo as a new Troy had been suggested frequently by the opponents of Rosas, but now it was sanctioned by a respected author.

Rosas' rule teetered. The war with Britain and France had ruined the economy and support for Oribe had sapped the army's strength. General Urquiza, governor of Entre Ríos, rebelled against Rosas and marched against Oribe, forcing an end to the siege after nine years. *The Times*, looking back on events in South America, regretted the failure of the blockade but explained the shortcomings of such an operation as attributable to the peculiarities of the region. Now it was delighted that Urquiza had turned on Rosas.

> At length the day of deliverance has arrived. General Urquiza at the head of a considerable force from the province of Entre Rios, and with the support of a Brazilian detachment, marched upon Montevideo, and Oribe was compelled to raise the siege without battle.[28]

By the time of this report Urquiza, who had amassed an immense fortune in the service of Rosas—and boasted that he had sired 102 bastards—had gone from Montevideo back to Buenos Aires and there had defeated Rosas' army at the battle of Caseros, on 2 February 1852.

On 9 February, Robert Gore, appointed minister to Buenos Aires after the promotion of Southern to the Court of Brazil, wrote to Palmerston:

> The morning of the 3rd February was ushered in, in this city, by beating of drums and every possible military preparation to defend the city from an attack of fugitives from the army from pillaging and robbing the city. At nine a report was circulated that Rosas had broken the left wing of the army of Urquiza and that the battle was going well for him, but it was

soon known that his army instead of fighting, with the exception of the Division of Palermo and the artillery, dispersed and fled to the country. The city was in the greatest state of agitation when General Mansilla [brother-in-law of Rosas], commanding the troops and armed forces in the city, requested the foreign agents to proceed to the camp of General Urquiza and offer their good offices to procure some arrangement between the city and the conqueror, by which the useless effusion of blood would be avoided. This took place at noon, and having been much occupied during the afternoon I did not return before half past four to my house, where, to my astonishment, I found in my bed General Rosas who had entered there half an hour previously disguised as a common soldier. He talked to me with as much calmness as if he had been quietly at Palermo, and told me that he was secure under the Protection of the British flag; that he had written a note to the President of the Sala resigning into the hands of the Sala of Representatives the power that they had done him the honour to invest him with, and that he was about to leave the country. I made no remark; in fact I had very little time, as I was obliged to accompany the rest of the foreign agents to the camp at 6 p.m. I gave orders that no person was to be admitted into my house, and then informed his daughter of her father's safety. I then accompanied the foreign agents to Palermo where we found the Advance Guard of the army of Urquiza had just arrived and had taken up their quarters under the command of Colonel Galán, minister of Government of General Urquiza, who received us very civilly, when we informed him of our mission. He sent an aide-de-camp to the field of battle, where General Urquiza was to inform him of it. No answer having arrived at half past ten, I deemed it advisable to return to the city and arrange and execute a plan to embark General Rosas and his daughter before daylight. Rear Admiral Henderson, with whom I at once communicated, immediately saw the necessity of General Rosas leaving my house as the consequence of his remaining there might prove most injurious to British interests. I then proposed to embark him on board the *Locust*, steam vessel (which we had agreed to send to Montevideo with a dispatch to catch the *Packet*), and transfer him and family to the *Centaur*, until the *Conflict*, steam vessel, might arrive here from Montevideo to carry him to some place of safety. I returned to my house with General Rosas' daughter, at midnight, and, after some conversation, convinced General Rosas of the absolute necessity of embarking that night, which I effected at 3 a.m. with his son-in-law and daughter. This plan was all done without the knowledge of any person but those absolutely necessary for its conduct. On my return at 4 a.m. General Mansilla requested me to accompany a commission consisting of the Bishop, and the President of the Bank... to wait on General Urquiza, which I accordingly did, and arrived at Palermo at 6 a.m., where we found the foreign agents waiting for the arrival of that General, which event took place at 10 a.m. By this time the town had given in its adhesion to General Urquiza, who received the commission and appointed Don Vicente Lopez the provisional governor. We were all presented to General Urquiza, who said a few civil words to each and returned to the city, which we found in the hands of the rabble who were pillaging and sacking the shops, chiefly those of the jewellers, General Mansilla having taken refuge on board the French steamer of war *Flambert* and the garrison retired to their houses. The Marines from the various foreign vessels of war having been previously landed, the Custom House and bank [were] put under the protection of the British and French, and guards stationed at each of the foreign agents' houses where the national flags were hoisted. The provisional governor appointed General Guido military commander, and immediate steps were taken to restore order, which was not accomplished before some two hundred persons were shot by virtue of a decree which was issued.[29]

Poor Mr Gore. While he wrote this long explanatory letter, he sat fearing for his life. After he had tried to sleep he wrote again to Palmerston asking if he could be transferred away from Buenos Aires, given a holiday or six months leave. In the last week, since the fall of Rosas, he had been threatened often by people passing his house. The town had learned almost immediately that Rosas, who had antagonised the governments of the world's great powers for nearly ten years and caused England no end of bother, to say nothing of the damage he had caused to British and French trade, had then sought refuge in the bed of the English minister...

On 26 April 1852, *The Times* began over a column of editorial comment with the remarks:

> The tolerant hospitality of England has seldom been put to stronger proof than it is at this moment by the arrival in an Irish port, and probably ere long in the metropolis, of the late Dictator of Buenos Ayres. If further demonstration were needed that the soil of Britain is alike open to refugees of every clime, and is not even shut against the representatives of the most atrocious forms of despotism... a land that consents to receive General Rosas...

Henry Southern died in Rio de Janeiro in 1852, General Oribe died in Montevideo in 1857, but the civil war continued, and the Colorado Party won control of Uruguay in 1865, with Brazilian support. General Urquiza became the founding father of the new Argentine Confederation, but within ten years his rule was challenged and he was defeated. He was murdered at his palace, San José, in Entre Ríos, in 1870. General Rosas died at Burgess Farm, near Southampton, in March 1877—his name and actions a matter of controversy in Argentina to this day. Woodbine Parish, the first British minister to Buenos Aires, died at St Leonards on Sea in August 1882.

NOTES:

1. Jasper Ridley, *Garibaldi*. (Constable, London, 1974), p. 94.
2. Ridley, *Garibaldi*.
3. Andrew Graham-Yooll, *The Forgotten Colony*. (Hutchinson, 1981), p. 131.
4. Ridley, *Garibaldi*.
5. Ridley, *Garibaldi*.
6. *The Times*, 17 October 1845.
7. *The Times*, 24 October 1845. As a historical curiosity, it is interesting to read the British Merchants' text in comparison with some of the text written by the British community in Buenos Aires to the British prime minister, Margaret Thatcher, in 1982, a propos of the Falkland Islands dispute: Telegram to Thatcher from the British Community Council in the Argentine Republic "...Argentina has always shown every consideration towards the British community allowing it to run its own schools, churches, hospitals, old people's homes, etc. In addition, members of the British community have integrated themselves into all aspects of Argentine life, playing prominent roles especially in business and agricultural circles. In spite of the difficult moments we are living through, the President of the Republic has continued to emphasize that the community and its institutions will be safeguarded, and no animosity has been shown towards the community by the population as a whole. We therefore strongly urge you to seek a peaceful solution to this situation and give due consideration to the strong British presence in Argentina..." (17 April 1982).

    The Association of British and British-descended Farmers in Argentina also sent a telegram to Mrs Thatcher: "...we have lived and worked happily under Argentine governments of differing political persuasions. We have led our traditional, British way of life without any hindrance and our experience has led us to believe that the inhabitants of the Falkland islands have nothing to lose and much to gain by coming under Argentine sovereignty..." (13 April 1982).

8.   See also the "Manifesto of the ministers of England and France", *Liverpool Times*, 16 December 1845; *The Times*, 17 December.

9.   *The Times*, 15 January 1846.

10.   *The Times*, 21 January 1846.

11.   *The Times*, 29 January 1846.

12.   *The Times*, 29 January 1846. Policy of France in the Plate.

13.   *The Times*, 23 January 1846.

14.   *The Times*, 23 January 1846.

15.   *The Times*, 4 December 1845, 1 March 1846, 8 April 1846.

16.   *The Times*, 24 March 1846.

17.   *The Times*, 26 March 1846.

18.   *The Times*, 6 April 1846.

19.   *The Times*, 13, 17, 24 and 26 August 1846.

20.   Lachlan B. Mackinnon, *Steam Warfare in the Parana*. (Charles Ollier, London, 1848).

21.   *The Times*, 22, 24 September, 1, 5, 22 October 1846.

22.   *The Times*, 3, 14 November 1846.

23.   *The Times*, 15 January 1847.

24.   *The Times*, 24 December 1846.

25.   *The Times*, 8 January 1847.

26.   PRO FO 6/145.

27.   *The Times*, 9 February 1850.

28.   *The Times*, 20 February 1852.

29.   PRO FO 6/167. See also Andrew Graham-Yooll, *Así vieron a Rosas los ingleses*, ed. Rodolfo Alonso (Buenos Aires, 1980), reprinted as *Rosas Visto por los ingleses*, published by Universidad de Belgrano, Buenos Aires, 1997.

Chapter Seven

GUNBOAT DIPLOMACY (PART ONE), 1853-1867

'Zouave of Bahia', 1865-70 (Museu Histórico Nacional)

The second half of the nineteenth century was marked by the growth and economic expansion of the British Empire. In many places, direct intervention was abandoned as impractical because of its cost. The mere threat of use of naval might and commercial pressure all over the world was a preferred and cheaper weapon. The hint of displeasure in one of the great centres of power and finance in Europe became as worrying as the presence of an invading army to the vanities of the ruling classes of Central and South America. These were the conservative landowners who thought of themselves as liberal and progressive because of their acquaintance with the history and cultures of the Old Continent. When a sign of irritation was insufficient, the presence of a gunboat was enough to make the wayward repent for the annoyance caused.

This sedate extra-colonial progress, which Britain applied in Latin America, was at times in conflict with the southbound encroachment of the United States in the implementation of its concept of Manifest Destiny.[1] In pursuit of this doctrine the United States' eastern provinces had annexed Texas in 1845. In the war of 1846 Mexico had been reduced to about half of its size by the loss of California, New Mexico, Arizona, Nevada, Utah and part of Colorado. Oregon joined the Union in 1859.

But the United States and Britain avoided direct conflict. Britain maintained its commercial interests in South America and tried to preserve them in Central America too. It had long found, however, that British ethics and policies could not come to terms with the Roman Catholic ethics of Spanish America.

Bolivian Stand-off

After the war against the Peruvian-Bolivian Confederation (1836-9), Chile withdrew its army to behind its borders; but did not remove political pressure for eventual concessions from its northern neighbours. Bolivia, in turn, lived in fear of Chile. It was perhaps this fear that caused Bolivia to produce eccentric *caudillos* who gained domestic sympathy by, among other things, thunderous promises to defend the country from foreign intervention. Inevitably, there were many European merchants in the area who regarded with some contempt the mismanagement of Bolivia by the successors of General Santa Cruz. It may have been the eccentric behaviour of one such *caudillo* that caused Queen Victoria to remark that Bolivia "must be erased from the map," or that "we must rub out Bolivia from among the civilised nations."[2] The incident in question occurred while Colonel John Augustus Lloyd was British chargé d'affaires at the port of Tacna, Peru.

In a letter written by Lloyd to Lord Clarendon in April 1853–it is for us to wonder, without hope of clarification, whether such correspondence was ever read by their lordships, or by anybody except historical researchers–the diplomat described Bolivia in flattering terms.

> The valleys [approaching Cochabamba from Tacna] are intersected by veins of silver, copper, lead and tin... The city of Cochabamba is one of the most favoured of Bolivia, enjoying a delightful climate quite peculiar to itself, and different from the frigid, rarefied atmosphere of the other cities. In Potosí, La Paz, Oruro, there is a silence, a savage stillness and a cold listlessness in the people which is most remarkable. On entering the city [Cochabamba] which is built in perfect Spanish symmetry, the hum of busy voices and the joyful laugh of the contented and thriving artisan is for the first time heard in Bolivia. Every

trade known in these countries is in comparative perfection here. The consequence is that everything is extraordinarily cheap... All is joy, goodwill, and industry... It is the only province where glass blowing is known. The young men generally are well versed in history, most of them speak and write English and French, and are particularly attached to English... 3

Even as he wrote such kind words, however, Colonel Lloyd had no sympathy for the government of President Manuel Isidoro Belzú.

Belzú had seized government in 1848, and was to become one of the great South American *caudillos* of the mid-century. He strengthened his peasant power base with the support of the urban working class. He disliked the local aristocracy and the foreign merchants whom he thought had impoverished the country. His statements and speeches on these, his chosen subjects of hatred were, by any standards, inflammatory.

> Comrades, an insensitive throng of aristocrats has become arbiter of your wealth and your destiny; they exploit you ceaselessly and you do not observe it; they cheat you constantly and you don't sense it; they accumulate huge fortunes with your labour and blood and you are unaware of it. They divide the land, honours, jobs and privileges among themselves, leaving you only misery, disgrace, and work, and you keep quiet. How long will you sleep? Wake once and for all! 4

The rousing manner of Belzú's talk prompted some peasants to overpower their landlords and seize land. Belzú took the side of the indians against the landowners, who tried to put down the revolt. This put Belzú out of favour with the local upper class and with the foreign entrepreneurs they dealt with.

One of the victims of this dislike between Belzú and the foreigners was an American, a Mr Cuningham, who was an agent for several British houses. When he asked the president to expedite the payment of Bolivia's debts to the English business houses, Cuningham was beaten up and forced to leave La Paz.

Belzú's attitude prompted Lloyd to write to Admiral Moresby, commander of the British station on the Chilean coast, to explain that the "conduct of the Bolivian government has been a continuous series of oppressive and dishonest acts."5 But the "immediate cause of disagreement was the act of oppression to Mr Cuningham, an American, but agent of the English house of Hogan Ltd." Hogan and Company were claiming compensation of 15,000 pesos for losses caused by a Bolivian ban on the export of tin. There were Bolivian debts to Hogan for another 30,000 pesos. Debts were also claimed by two other companies, Myers, Bland and Co, for a return of a loan of 110,000 pesos, and Bolton and Co, which had lost 30,000 pesos as a result of the forcible closure of its warehouses.

The chargé d'affaires approached the government after Mr Cuningham had failed to collect his money, only to be threatened, too, with expulsion from Bolivia. Colonel Lloyd then travelled from La Paz to Tacna to seek the intervention of a gunboat of the Royal Navy, as the only way to protect British interests and collect the debts. "Bolivia has been running an unchecked career in villainy... I left after being affectionately embraced by this despot, the President offering to receive me as a brother on my return." Lloyd said that it was not only the British who suffered: Bolivia had insulted the

Brazilian envoy, "insulted Peru and thrust their minister out at the point of the bayonet...
They are coining base money faster than ever... Chile has been rejected in its claims...";
the United States also expected to be insulted because of a memorial detailing extensive
claims. He continued:

French subjects have been beaten, imprisoned, and banished without any charge or trial...
Lastly they have expelled an innocent British subject without the least form of complaint
against him, injured British interests, treated with contempt their claims, and to wind up
offered a gratuitous insult to the British representative. The country is in a state of anarchy... The Peruvians will close their ports of Arica and Islas against Bolivia. Cobija will be
the only available port for Bolivia; *that* taken or blockaded, with about 12,000 tons of inferior guano... would partly pay English claims... and the whole country would rise against
the insupportable yoke of this ignorant man.[6]

The navy was not convinced, however, that a gunboat would bring the satisfaction desired. Rear Admiral Moresby wrote to the Admiralty:

relative to an insult received by Mr Lloyd, Her Majesty's Chargé d'affaires, from the
Bolivian government.

Any coercive measures taken by HM's naval force at Cobija, an insignificant port, the
only one the Bolivians possess in the Pacific, would be jeopardising the vast capital of our
commercial community now floating in the republic. It is from Arica, in Peru that the mar-
kets of Bolivia are supplied; taking the initiative against their open defiance of all civilised
usages would be a hasty proceeding and probably not to be approved by HM's government.[7]

The Foreign Office decided to consult a former minister in Bolivia, Frederick Bruce,
before taking action. He counselled against a blockade.

The subject is not new to me... I was led to consider seriously whether Bolivia could be
brought to reason by the employment of force... However, after mature reflection I was
unable to suggest any hostile measures which were not open to the objection of being insufficient to obtain their object [and would damage British interests]... The position of Bolivia
is such that her only vulnerable points are the guano deposits, and the port of Cobija...
which is an insignificant village with a small natural harbour formed by a projecting ledge
of rocks, but without quays or any accommodation for shipping... It is surrounded by a
sandy desert, which extends from the seashore to the Cordillera... [8]

There was no vegetation, food came from Chile and Peru; Potosí, the nearest town, was
200 leagues away...

When I left Bolivia some Englishmen held copper mines of considerable value in Corocoro,
and a few others were dispersed in different parts of the country. The fate of these persons,
if exposed to the first outburst of the vengeance and blind fury of such men as Belzú and
his advisers deserves serious consideration...
It is true that in countries such as Peru and Chile it has been found possible to cause
HM's subjects to be respected even in the midst of violence and anarchy, and to create for
them an exceptional position which secures them from the evils incident to an unsettled
political state. But these countries have large and populous sea ports, which afford ready
points of coercion and by this immunities in favour of foreigners have been obtained
although they are looked upon as odious and unjust. In the present state of Bolivia no secu-

rity for person or property is to be looked for.

Colonel Lloyd acquiesced to the recommendation that Britain should not blockade Cobija, confident that Belzú would soon be overthrown. Lloyd was withdrawn, which was tantamount to breaking relations, and the causes of his departure from Bolivia were widely publicised in Peru and Bolivia.[9] Belzú remained in government until 1855, when he stepped down peacefully and handed over to his nominated, though constitutionally ratified, successor.

Britain did not restore diplomatic relations with Bolivia until 1903.

We Are Not Amused

The following anecdote is a digression, but Queen Victoria and the map have also been mentioned in connection with it. The only difficulty is that some Bolivian historians have found no record of the incident.[10] Readers will probably agree that this is to be regretted because, were it to be true, this short history would be far more entertaining.

The Bolivian president, General Mariano Melgarejo, one of the last leaders of Bolivia's *caudillo* era, was known for violent outbursts. In 1869, for instance, when the Haichu indians of Lake Titicaca demanded the return of communal lands, Melgarejo ordered their massacre. Melgarejo is reputed to have held a strong distrust of all foreigners residing in his country and an equally strong feeling that these foreigners flaunted too frequently their self-inspired opinion that they were superior to the native Bolivians.[11]

This feeling of distrust was exacerbated after the general married a native woman, a *chola*, in whom the Europeans saw no beauty and imagined that she wore her bowler hat even in her matrimonial chamber. It was only natural that the titters in the *tertulias* of local society and the salacious and deprecating gossip that circulated in the political clubs and commercial offices should eventually reach the ears of General Melgarejo. He was naturally quite angry.

Melgarejo ordered his aides to organise a party, a grand occasion, at which the president's wife would be introduced in society. It was announced as a formal affair. The generals dressed in their best uniforms, and the ladies in the finery brought from Europe or held from their grandmothers' youth. All went to the presidential palace, their mockery muted by respect and fear.

The British minister arrived in full regalia and in the legation's best coach, and on entry to the palace was informed that the greeting to the president's wife would have to be addressed to the lady's bare posterior. The minister's mutterings at the thought of bowing to a pair of buttocks were not recorded by any contemporary scribe, but the minister refused to take part in such a ceremony. The president was outraged, and would not accept the minister's apologies; the refusal was an offence to the president, to Bolivia, and to the lady—in that order. Without further debate, the minister was stripped of his regalia, flogged before the rest of the gatherings, and expelled from the palace, sitting naked and facing backwards on a mule, which delivered him to the legation.

It is said, and this is the part of the story that is not documented, that when the news of this ill-treatment of a British minister reached Queen Victoria, she first had to be shown a map of South America and be told where Bolivia was. Without hesitation, she picked up a quill from her writing table, dipped the point in a pot of ink and ran a thick stroke through the map of Bolivia. She said that a country which acted in such a manner deserved to be struck off the map.

William Walker

On 2 February 1848 Mexico signed a treaty with the United States by which it formally surrendered 51 per cent of its territory to its expanding northern neighbour. Some time before, towards the end of a two-year war, two North American generals, one advancing from north to south, a second invading Vera Cruz, and supported by a smaller force which seized New Mexico, had won a thorough and humiliating victory over Mexico.

The American advance in pursuit of its Manifest Destiny had alarmed Britain, which wanted to contain such southbound progress. In 1849, Britain posted Sir Henry Lytton Dalling and Bulwer, an experienced diplomat, brother of the novelist Lord Lytton and biographer of Palmerston, as ambassador to Washington. He was ordered to find a way to prevent the United States expansion from extending in Central America. The diplomat was not without a record of success. He had secured significant trade advantages from the Ottoman Empire by a treaty with Turkey in 1838. This personal victory, and his expulsion from Spain by the dictator Ramón Narvaez for making public his sympathy with the constitutionalists, made Bulwer a popular figure in Washington.

On 19 April 1850, Bulwer signed an agreement with the US secretary of state, John Middleton Clayton, to be known as the Clayton-Bulwer Treaty, which aimed to harmonise US-British interests in Central America. By that treaty the US renounced the right to build a canal across the Isthmus of Panama, leaving such a task and the ensuing control of shipping and trade to Britain. In return, Britain was to renounce the occupation of British Honduras (Belize) and the Bay Islands. But Britain, determined to protect its trade and not allow US shipping to move freely between the Pacific and the Caribbean, did not construct the canal. Neither did it move out of the territory east of Guatemala. Lytton Bulwer's popularity waned as the relations between the US and Britain became strained and their traders more aggressively competitive in the Americas. The ambassador returned to England in 1852 and was later to be instrumental in drawing up peace terms at the end of the Crimean War in 1856.[12]

In the meantime, the United States had moved south of Mexico to Nicaragua. In October 1853, William Walker, aged 29, an American adventurer and member of an upper-class family, invaded western Mexico, declaring Baja California and Sonora an independent republic. After an unsteady five-month presidency, he was forced by the Mexican army to return to California. On 24 April 1855, the *San Francisco Placer Times* reported that Walker, formerly editor of the *Democratic State Journal* of Sacramento, California, had sailed for Nicaragua with between fifty and one hundred mercenaries whom he named the "American Phalanx of Immortals". On arrival at Realejo port, in Nicaragua, Walker seized the assets of the Accessory Transit Company, a subsidiary of Cornelius Vanderbilt's American Pacific and Atlantic Ship Canal Company. With that financial support he took over the country and appointed himself commander-in-chief of the Nicaraguan army. He defeated the conservatives who held government and installed a member of the Liberal Party, Patricio Aivas, replacing him the following year. On 29 June 1856, Walker proclaimed himself and on 2 July was inaugurated as president of

Nicaragua. He did not stop there. He aimed to take over all five of the small Central American republics. Costa Rica, however, had become alarmed by the United States' designs on the continent and was convinced that Walker was acting with official backing. This suspicion was not unreasonable: the new president of Nicaragua was also a source of worry to Britain.

Britain armed the Costa Rican forces to defend the country against Walker and also won the support of Vanderbilt–disgusted by Walker's filibustering–in drafting the Dallas-Clarendon pact, which exempted British Honduras from the terms of the Clayton-Bulwer agreement.[13]

On 24 September 1856, armies of Costa Rica and Honduras attacked Walker's forces. It took them seven months to defeat him. When he saw that he was beaten, Walker submitted to a US naval force at San Juan del Sur, in April 1857, to avoid surrendering to Costa Rica. Walker organised a second attempt to take Nicaragua that same year; but he was arrested in the US. On his third expedition he planned to invade Honduras; on this occasion he was captured by HMS *Icarus*, off the coast of Honduras, before he could make a landing. The British handed him over to the Hondurans, who executed him at Trujillo on 12 September 1860.

Mexico's Emperor

While Walker was still holding out in Nicaragua, Benito Juárez, a young lawyer of indian extraction, was revolutionising Mexico. As Minister of Justice of Mexico, Juárez won the promulgation of a new constitution in February 1857. Juárez's aim was to make a modern country out of one ravaged by war and by a despotic class system. He brought in sweeping reforms: he abolished slavery, dissolved monopolies and expropriated ecclesiastical property. These and other changes reduced the power of the landowners and of the Church, which had always had a predominant position in Mexican society.

Juárez went further. In 1861 he suspended payment of the Mexican foreign debt of eight million dollars, as well as that of the usurious dividends of a fifteen million dollar French bond issue. France's ruler, Napoleon III, encouraged by the enemies of Juárez, conservative Mexican exiles in Paris, proposed to Britain and Spain that they jointly invade Mexico to secure payment of the debt. France considered that the time was appropriate because the United States was involved in a crippling civil war (1861-5), and a European garrison in Mexico would check US advances into the southern areas of America. France presented its move against Mexico as a crusade, a search for a "Latin link"–which led to the use of the phrase "Latin America". The French plan for intervention appealed to Britain and to Spain because of the possibility of preventing the spread of US influence. Britain trusted her own experience in the Americas to prevent France from gaining any further advantages. When France introduced its bond issue into the debate about the intervention, however, Spain and Britain abandoned the Mexican adventure. They nevertheless assured France that they would support the operation with financial assistance.

Napoleon III shipped over thirty thousand troops to Mexico in 1862 and 1863. In the meantime he sought throughout Europe for a member of a royal family who might successfully represent the crowned heads of Europe—the French in particular—as monarch of Mexico. He was not to be called viceroy, but Emperor. Napoleon III settled on a relative, the Archduke Maximilian, a member of the Habsburgs, and younger brother of Franz Josef I of Austria.

While this selection process was underway, the commander of the French army in Mexico, General Élie-Frédéric Forey, rode victorious into Mexico City in June 1863. Juárez fled to organise a movable Republican government which went where his army did. The following year, Maximilian arrived at Vera Cruz with his wife Charlotte and, on 12 June 1864, was proclaimed Emperor of the second Mexican Empire.

He ruled through three years of turmoil until, in 1866, the US recovered in part from its civil war, and pressed France to withdraw from Mexico. Napoleon III embarked his army for the return to France and abandoned the Archduke Maximilian—who refused to leave—to defend his throne with a small force of Austrian volunteers and Mexican conscripts. The emperor hoped to defend himself for a time and then negotiate an honourable exile. But Benito Juárez rejected pleas for talks or for clemency and after besieging the imperial army to the point of near starvation, he ordered the execution of Maximilian in June 1867.[14]

However, such events of European concern overshadowed incidents of local relevance. It is time to return to these.

Trouble in Brazil

The Brazilian empire was by far the most friendly link Britain had in South America. But such good relations did not prevent the use of gunboat diplomacy against Rio de Janeiro. Britain had got accustomed to the practice and to getting its way in the world.

Next to the frequent and lengthy accounts of the French army's exploits in Mexico, and even lengthier reports of the civil war in the United States, *The Times*, on Tuesday, 3 February 1863, carried a notice out of Lisbon reporting "further details of the late disagreement between the English minister and the Brazilian government".

The report of events was rather late. The shipwreck of the merchantman *Prince of Wales*, near Rio Grande do Sul, had taken place in April 1862. The "late disagreement" to which the paper referred was the demand for indemnity by the British minister, William Dougal Christie. However, the paper assured, rather prematurely, that the Brazilian government would pay indemnity, "the amount of which is to be fixed in London... Much excitement had been produced at Rio by these proceedings, but the agitation had partly subsided at the departure of the mail."

Two incidents were involved; the disputes they had given rise to were running concurrently. The first had been the shipwreck. The British owners of the *Prince of Wales* argued that after the ship had gone against the shore, the surviving crew and passengers had been killed and the property stolen. Three months after that incident, the second had taken place, in which three officers of the HMS *Forte* were beaten up while on shore leave in June 1862. The protest over this incident had been referred for arbitration to the King of the Belgians.

A few days after publication of the first report in *The Times*, the paper supplied ample details of both incidents in its edition of 6 February. It referred to "the 'difficulty' in Brazil". The correspondent was obviously delighted by the events which had made for some change in a humdrum life.

We have had a little excitement here during the last few days... Some time ago an English ship called the *Prince of Wales* was wrecked on the coast of Brazil, near Rio Grande do Sul; three of the crew were murdered, and the ship plundered by the natives. A British man-of-war was sent to the spot in April last to inquire into the circumstances and report upon them; and the result has been a demand upon the Brazilian government for £10,000, as some compensation to the murdered men's families, and for the loss sustained by the plunder of the wreck. Another cause of the excitement is that in June last, three naval officers belonging to HBM's ship *Forte* left Rio early one morning on a walking excursion through the beautiful mountain pass of Tijuca, intending to walk up one side of the mountain and half way down the other, and return the rest of the distance to Rio in the *Marcham Bomba*, a sort of tramway. They reached the pass after a walk of 18 miles and stopped at Bennett's Hotel for rest and refreshment during the heat of the day. The last omnibus of the *Marcham Bomba* started at 8 p.m. They remained at the hotel until a quarter to seven; they had several miles to go, and, fearful of being too late, ran. About half way down to the omnibus they had to pass a guard-house; one of the officers was ahead of the other, and, as he was passing the guard-house, a sentry stepped out in front of him with the evident intention of stopping him. The sentry was asked what he wanted, when he struck the officer with the butt of his musket and called out the guard; the other two officers came up and were also assaulted; they had nothing to defend themselves with but two light sticks and an umbrella, so were made prisoners and lodged in the guard-house. About ten minutes afterwards the officer of the guard made his appearance, to whom they gave their names and ranks in writing, but they were shut up for the night, and next morning, at 9 o'clock were marched under escort of seven soldiers into Rio (a distance of seven miles) and through the streets to the police-office. They asked permission to hire a conveyance, but were refused. At the police-office they again made known their ranks and names, but in spite of this, they were locked up in the common prison with about 70 of the lowest class of the people, slaves & c. As they were being locked up, the turnkey in attendance was asked "if he was aware of their rank and position" when he answered "Yes". They remained there four hours, while the British consul was being communicated with, when they were removed to a cleaner part of the prison, in another part of the city, where political offenders are confined, but they received good treatment. They were kept prisoners from Tuesday night until the following Thursday, at 11 a.m. when they were released without any trial or inquiry. Three weeks afterwards a charge of drunkenness was preferred against them, but was not substantiated; and then the British minister, Mr Christie, demanded an ample apology for the indignities shown them. These two demands have now been pressed home, but were refused, and Mr Christie, in an ultimatum insisting on their being complied with, gave the Brazilians until the evening of 29 December to consider the matter when both demands were again rejected. Next day two British men-of-war, the *Curlew* and the *Stromboli*, steamed from the harbour, and their mission was soon made known by a signal from the telegraph hill saying "A Brazilian ship captured and in tow of British man-of-war". This created an immense sensation in the town; many would not believe it and ran to satisfy their own eyes, but all doubts were put an end to on the 4th of January by the arrival of the *Stromboli*, and it soon became known that she had detained five sailing vessels and a steamer, the *Parahyba*, all Brazilian and of more value than the sum demanded. She left them at a place called Palmas Bay, in charge of the *Curlew*, but brought on the passengers she found in them, who speak in the highest terms of the kindness and hospitality shown towards them. In the meantime the excitement became intense, the public squares were filled with angry people, and some

Dutch officers, being mistaken for British through the similarity of their uniforms, were very severely handled, before the mistake was found out. In the evening a council was held, presided over by the Emperor in person, and, after sitting many hours, the demand for the money for compensation was agreed to and the case of the officers is to be submitted to the arbitration of the several foreign ministers in Rio, their decision to be subject to the approval of the English government. The detained ships were immediately released. The mail packet has been detained 36 hours, but the decision of the arbitration is not known yet. The excitement among the people still continues.

The British minister involved, Christie, inclined towards the use of force. He had previously served in Buenos Aires, where, in October 1856, he had strongly recommended that the Foreign Office use gunboats to enforce demands for payment of the still unpaid 1826 Barings bond issue.

While Brazil said that it would pay compensation, it also said that it would do so under protest, which the British government rejected. The owner of the *Prince of Wales*, the Newry, Dundalk, Drogheda, and Dumfries Screw Steampacket Company, increased the claim for compensation. The Brazilian government rejected the higher demand on the grounds that it could not be held responsible for every act of plunder. The British minister demanded the investigation and trial of the culprits of the plunder but these could not be found and the local justice of the peace could not be charged with negligence.

On 6 February 1863 *The Times* also carried a statement of the alarm caused to the merchants in Liverpool trading with Brazil, for they feared severe damages to their livelihood. At a meeting, they moved a motion to advise Earl Russell, the Foreign Secretary:

> that this meeting has learnt with alarm and regret the unfortunate disagreements between the Brazilian government and the British minister at Rio de Janeiro, and is astounded at the summary and extreme measures taken by the British admiral against a friendly power.

The matter did not stop there. Admiral John Pascoe Grenfell, of the Brazilian navy, wrote to *The Times* on 17 February to question whether the shipwreck had really been followed by murder.

> Evidence was found of the total wreck of a vessel, the debris of which and some corpses were scattered along the coasts; of plunder little evidence was found, and none whatever of murder... the coast is a very dangerous one; hard sand, deepening very slowly out to sea at the estimated rate of a fathom a mile, upon which there is little rise or fall... but upon which the whole swell of the Southern Ocean breaks with irresistible fury... Woe betide the ship caught inshore there... Hopeless is the prospect of the crew of the vessel that once touches the sand reaching the shore alive.

However reasonable the explanations, the diplomatic battle had begun. Neither side could emerge without some damage to their honour. By 25 February *The Times* expected to see a solution arrived at soon. The paper was being lobbied by the Brazilians and the British, both expressing concern for the good relations between the two countries. "We have reason to believe that a satisfactory settlement of the dispute with Brazil is likely to be promptly effected..." It reminded readers of the two incidents involved in the dispute and for the first time introduced an element of doubt into the British stories. One of the incidents, it said, "involved the destruction of British property, if not the murder of those of the crew who survived the shipwreck." The paper frequently carried letters from people with knowledge of the area of the wreck–all of them describing it as a desolate area where the rule of law was not known and not expected.

On 28 May 1863, Earl Russell, the Foreign Secretary, expressed to Parliament his "regret at this needless interruption of diplomatic relations" and complied with a request from the Brazilian minister in London, Commander Moreira, to be given his passport to leave the country. Moreira had, on 5 May, proposed that Britain apologise to Brazil for the offence caused by the seizure of the merchant ships and offer compensation to the injured proprietors "by means of an arbitral liquidation".[15]

On 30 June, under the heading "The Brazilian Difficulty", *The Times* published the decision of Leopold I of Belgium "in the case of the officers of the *Forte*": "We are of the opinion that in the mode in which the laws of Brazil have been applied towards the English officers, there was neither premeditation of offence nor offence of the British navy."

In less formal language it was explained in Rio de Janeiro that the sentry who had battered the English officers had been asleep and, on hearing the voice of the running man, had awoken with a start, reacting with violence. He had afterwards had to make his story stick with his superiors. As English sailors were expected to be drunk and as there was the smell of beer on their breath from the stop at Bennett's Hotel, the Brazilian authorities had made the best of a bad job. The sentry received his own punishment, for he was arrested. However, he was told that he could rest in the security of fame: it was not often that a *siesta* caused an international incident between two friendly countries. The Belgian king's decision saved honour. The claim on the shipwreck was not as simple to solve as the patching up of honour. The proprietors wanted their money, and the widows needed it.

The following year, relations were on the way back to normal. Commerce was already normal–in fact, it never had been affected. The trouble with the incident was that it had led to a scrutiny of Brazilian relations, and there it was discovered that Brazil still had a slave trade. Britain had tried to bring the slave trade to a stop by official pressure, and naval interference with shipments. But meddling could not be too forceful. Nobody could afford to get too cross. The volume of trade between Brazil and Britain was £12 million a year. Brazil's debt to Britain amounted to £9 million; and three English companies were operating on a £5 million guarantee in the construction of Brazil's railways.[16]

Contacts reached a happy arrangement when both Britain and Brazil apologised. The formality was kept as quiet as possible.

NOTES:

1. John O'Sullivan, *United States Magazine and Democratic Review*, July-August 1845. Manifest Destiny was a phrase that embodied the idea that North America was, by right, designed to spread its influence along the length and breadth of the New World.

2. Roberto Querejaza Calvo, *Bolivia y los ingleses*. (La Paz, 1973).

3. PRO FO 11/15, Lloyd to Clarendon, 15 April 1853.

4. Bradford Burns, *Latin America*, pp. 116-17.

5.   PRO FO 11/15, 6 April 1853.

6.   The demand for compensation was in fashion. At that time, 1853, HM Consul at Guayaquil, Ecuador's principal port and industrial centre, reported that the admiral of the French station had exacted 7,000 dollars, with an apology, as satisfaction for injuries to local French merchants (PRO FO 11/15).

7.   PRO FO 11/15, Admiralty, 31 May 1853.

8.   PRO FO 11/15, 30 July 1853.

9.   PRO FO 11/15, 12 July 1853.

10.   Querejaza Calvo, *Bolivia y los ingleses*. The author contends that a thorough search of the Foreign Office files has not revealed such an incident. However, it has been recorded by several other authors.

11.   Angela Caccia, *Beyond Lake Titicaca*. (London, 1969).

12.   In 1901 the Hay-Pauncefote Treaty superseded the 1850 agreement; and Britain ceded to the United States the right to build, and control, the Panama Canal. On 3 November 1903, Panama seceded from Colombia—which was just recovering from the tragedy of civil war, the War of the Thousand Days, 1899-1903. Though the US denied involvement it later paid Colombia 25 million dollars in compensation. The US gained the Canal Zone from Panama in perpetuity by a treaty signed on 18 November 1903, which was enshrined in a constitution adopted in February 1904. The Panama Canal Zone was formally returned to the Republic of Panama in 1999.

13.   Eduardo Crawley, *Dictators Never Die. A Portrait of Nicaragua*. (Hurst, London, 1979).

14.   Jasper Ridley. *Maximilian and Juárez*. (Constable, London, 1993).

15.   *The Times*, 3 June, 18 June 1838.

16.   *The Times*, 19 July 1864. Parliament, Osborne. See also: *A presença britanica no Brasil (1808-1914)*. A bilingual history of Brazil. *The British Presence in Brazil*. (Panbrasil, Sao Paulo, 1987).

Chapter Eight

TRAGEDY IN ARCADIA: THE PARAGUAYAN WAR, 1865-1870

Detail from 'La Paraguaya', J.M.Blanes,
Museo de Bellas Artes, Montevideo

On 18 July 1838, *The Manchester Guardian*, quoting from a Dutch newspaper out of Paraguay, announced that:

Dr Francia is dead, and with his death ends the most singular government that ever existed. His slavish adherents, dreading the vengeance of the inhabitants of Ascunción have left the country and fled to Monte Video. This singular man retained his character to the day of his death. It is said that he has left several unpublished manuscripts, one of which is "Proof of the character and the simplicity of the Spanish Americans, and the means which a governor must employ to make himself necessary to them". The inscription which he affixed to his portrait is very original; it is as follows: "Despotism is increased either by having in a country very numerous laws at variance with each other, or no laws at all. I have chosen the latter course, because it is more adapted to the frankness of my character, and to the bad memory of the people of Paraguay."

Dr José Gaspar Rodríguez de Francia, *El Supremo*, was not dead; but that is irrelevant to this tale. Dr Francia lived for two more years after that premature obituary, to die in Asunción, aged 76, on 20 September 1840.

In the same year as the *Manchester Guardian* report, John Parish Robertson's *Letters on Paraguay* were published in London, and in the first volume he recalled meeting Francia some years before.

I turned round, and beheld a gentleman of about fifty years of age, dressed in a suit of black, with a large scarlet capote, or cloak, thrown over his shoulders... I was invited to sit down under the corridor, and to take a cigar and *maté*. A celestial globe, a large telescope, and a theodolite were under the little portico... He made some display of his acquaintance with Voltaire, Rousseau, and Volney, and he concurred entirely in the theory of the latter. But he was most of all proud to be known as an algebraist and astronomer... In Paraguay, an acquaintance with French, Euclid's Elements, equations, the mode of handling a theodolite, or with books prohibited by the Vatican, was, in point of knowledge, so much the exception to the general rule that the man who had it... was deemed something of a magician and a demigod.[1]

Francia had inherited a mysterious country. The history of the native Guaraní indians was lost in pre-Columbian mists; the Spanish founder of Asunción, Domingo Martínez de Yrala (1510-56), had encouraged—by his own example—miscegenation to a degree that a society of mixed blood was established like no other in the Americas; the Jesuits, perhaps inspired by the Utopia of Thomas More, established six cities, or Reductions, with indians working in peace and remarkable social advancement which has sometimes been called an example of Christian Communism in practice. This socialist experience alarmed Spain, leading Charles III to believe that the Jesuits were creating, in Paraguay and elsewhere, their own states within the empire. The followers of St Ignatius were then expelled from Spain and from all Spanish possessions in 1767.[2]

Francia was an honest ruler, frugal, and horribly cruel. He entered government in 1811, after independence from Spain, and was elected dictator for life in 1814. He modernised the country's industries, agriculture and social structure. He then closed it completely to outside influence, which helped its culture and his control; he conserved Paraguay as a South American Arcadia and prison camp. After his death, his rehabilitation began in England, when Thomas Carlyle published an essay, *Dr Francia*, in 1843, which questioned whether the late dictator was a fiend.[3]

He was succeeded by a man of mixed blood, Carlos Antonio López, who became Paraguay's first president and promised to rule by a newly-drafted constitution. He brought to Paraguay under contract a large number of British artisans, physicians, and engineers, who built the country's arsenal, shipyard, hospital service and railways.[4] But, though he strove to open up Paraguay to world trade, after three decades of isolation imposed by El Supremo, López was unable to establish good relations with his neighbours. To the east he suspected Brazilian expansionism. To the south there was Rosas, who was also suspected of planning the annexation of part or all of Paraguay and, when rejected, closed river communications on the Paraná River, once more isolating Paraguay.[5]

Although López tried to liberalise Paraguayan society, improve education—young men were sent to Europe to study—and modernise industry, the president remained attached to many of the absolutist forms of Francia. An English scientist, C. B. Mansfield, who visited Asunción in 1852, said of López:

> Everybody is obliged to stop and take off their hats when he passes; so of course I did so and received a most gracious bow in return. In Francia's time everybody was forced to take off their hats to every soldier, and the country boys, who wear no clothes at all, were obliged to wear hats for the purpose of saluting them... The President himself rarely sees or receives any society: he is, I suppose, more utterly alone than any man in the world, for, unlike other kings, he has neither ministers nor advisers of any kind; everything is arranged by his own head, every officer of the executive appointed by him. The President is immensely fat; as he sat to receive me with his hat on, cocked a little to one side, he looked like George the Fourth.[6]

His eldest son, Francisco Solano López, was thirty-six when he succeeded his father to the presidency in 1862. One biographer described him as a little sultan in his home. His father, who pandered to him, had made him a brigadier-general in the army at eighteen.[7] At twenty-seven he had been sent to Paris to buy armaments for Paraguay and to receive the education which contact with European society was supposed to give. In Paris, in 1851, he had met a young Irish girl from Cork, aged sixteen, Eliza Alicia Lynch, recently divorced from a Frenchman. Eliza became López's mistress and returned to Asunción with him.

There are no impartial opinions of either López or Eliza, who entered history as "Madame Lynch". When he became marshal-president, as he had himself named, he inspired strong loyalties and fear; she the hatred of local society. His biographers have described him as physically repulsive, a megalomaniac who dreamed of being a South American Napoleon; she as his Josephine, a greedy tart, too attractive and too ambitious for Asunción, a woman who used her experience as a successful courtesan of the Deuxième Empire in alien surroundings. She bore him four sons.

> Francisco Solano López is a very stout man... He is short, but has a commanding presence... He is careful of his appearance, fond of military finery, especially in his staff, and has a somewhat peculiar strut when walking. His legs are short, with a decided bend backwards. He has a good seat on horseback, and when young used to be a hard rider. Now, however, it is a labour for him to get on and off his horse. He is of very indolent habits; will sit down for many hours, talking, or stand an equally long time, his walks limiting themselves to one

or two hundred yards. He is extremely fond of Mrs Lynch's children, but not of his other ones, of whom he has a number by different women. He entertains friendly feelings for no one, as he has shot almost all those who have been most favoured by himself, and who have been for years his only companions. He is a great smoker, and lover of the table; he eats enormously; after dinner, when in a good humour, he occasionally sings a short song. López speaks French fluently, always conversing in that language with Mrs Lynch, who was educated in France. He knows a very little English, and of course Spanish well, that being the official language of the country; however, he never spoke anything but Guaraní to the men and officers, including myself... López is a good speaker, especially in the kind of oratory likely to inspire his troops with confidence in himself and themselves, and with contempt for the enemy... He has an iron will, and an intense pride... He is, when he likes, very smooth and gentlemanly, and capable of imposing, even on diplomats, and making them believe anything he wishes.[8]

The preceding paragraph reflects the mixed feelings of an English engineer who remained loyal to López in the most difficult circumstances. Another of the marshal's officials was rough and uncharitable in his description of López and Lynch.

Madame Lynch gradually and insiduously imbued López with the idea that he was the greatest soldier of the age, and flattered the vain, credulous and greedy savage into the belief that he was destined to raise Paraguay from obscurity, and make it the dominant power of South America... The influence she exercised over a man so imperious, yet so weak, so vain, and sensual as López, was immense. With admirable tact, she treated him apparently with the utmost deference and respect whilst she could really do with him as she pleased, and virtually was the ruler of Paraguay... That lady occupied a very prominent place eventually in Paraguayan affairs and, I believe, by her evil counsels and boundless ambitions was the remote cause of the terrible war which... utterly depopulated the country.[9]

Sir Richard Burton, the Victorian traveller and writer, was less certain: "Those who write have in almost all instances allowed their imaginations and their prejudices to guide their judgment and mostly they have frankly thrown overboard all impartiality."[10]

President López had to his advantage that he led a united people, who were to become known for tremendous courage and determination and who were undivided by party political rivalries. Such divisions were all too evident in Buenos Aires and were growing in Rio de Janeiro as the imperial rule of Dom Pedro II adjusted to some reforms and resisted others.

López became concerned at Brazil's assistance to the Uruguayan general, Venancio Flores, the leader of the Colorado Party, in taking over the government in Montevideo and thereby ending the Civil War—which had started in 1839. Paraguay feared that this involvement would be followed by annexation. López, in turn, wanted to expand Paraguay by regaining some of the Brazilian territory of Matto Grosso, which had formed part of a *Paraguay gigante* during the Spanish Empire. Brazilian landowners had taken that land from the Jesuits.

On 30 August 1864, Paraguay lodged a protest with Brazil for occupying Uruguayan territory in support of General Flores. Brazil replied by invading northern Uruguay and blockading Montevideo until Flores' enemies were defeated. Paraguay persisted in its protest by capturing a Brazilian ship, the *Marques de Olinda*, on 12 November. That incident led to speculation about the imminence of war between Brazil and

Paraguay. It also attracted the attention of the Buenos Aires papers, whose reports were lifted and reproduced in London.

The British press had not previously given much attention to Paraguay. An incident in 1859, when a British naval vessel attacked the Paraguayan gunboat *Tacuarí*, in the River Plate, in reprisal for the arrest in Asunción of a British subject, James Canstatt—who was charged with taking part in a conspiracy—had gone unnoticed by the press. The Foreign Office had later authorised the consul in Asunción to apologise to the government, but the apology had been kept secret.[11]

On Thursday, 15 June 1865, *The Times* published its first account of the "war in South America". A correspondent, dating his copy "Parana river, 26 April" wrote:

> Passing events in this part of the world are of such a nature as to make one believe that the Virgilian atave *Arma virumque cano* might be chanted here in perpetuity, for no sooner has the civil war in the Uruguayan republic been put a stop to by the success of Flores, aided by the Brazilians, than the battle trumpet is sounded in the upper part of our river.
>
> General López, President in name but in reality the Emperor and Dictator of Paraguay, has invaded the Brazilian territory in his neighbourhood, taken possession of Coimbra, Albuquerque, Curamba, San Lorenzo, Dorados, Miranda and Nivao, and finished these achievements by laying hold of the diamond mine territory of Matto Grosso.
>
> On the 13th of last month an extraordinary session of Senators and Deputies was summoned at Asunción, the capital of Paraguay, to hear the President's address. This message, which is a composition of chaste and dignified style, although regarded, by many persons as somewhat fractured with special pleading, sets forth the recent sanguinary events in the Uruguay and violation of equilibrium in the River Plate as the causes of rupture with Brazil and coolness with the Argentine republic. It charges Brazil with having violated the Treaty of 1850, for the maintenance of nationalities in this part of South America, by allying itself with the rebel band of Flores. It alludes to the Paraguayan government having offered to join with the Argentine in mediating between Brazil and Uruguay, at the same time complaining that the Brazilians still carried on the war without condescending to take notice of the offer made by President López. This, of course, as the message says, outraged the national honour and dignity as well as compromised the security and integrity of the Paraguayan republic. It further states that the territory of Matto Grosso, of which López has now taken possession, had been usurped by Brazil, although belonging to Paraguay by virtue of discovery, possession, and treaties; and that an additional justification for taking it—if such were needed—existed in the fact of Brazil having collected these great military resources to prepare new inroads to Paraguay. [12]

Paraguay asked Argentina for permission to cross Corrientes province to reach southern Brazil and Uruguay and was refused; instead, Argentina granted Brazil the use of the inland rivers to reach Paraguay. López ignored the Argentine refusal and Argentina protested that Paraguayan troops had crossed its northern province of Misiones. That was the formal start of the Paraguayan war against three countries, Brazil, Uruguay—Brazil's ally—and Argentina. It became known as the War of the Triple Alliance.

> The Paraguayan Senate conferred on President López the dignity of a Field Marshal. The salary proposed to be attached to the post—namely, 60,000 silver dollars per annum—he peremptorily refused, but accepted a sword of honour, and agreed to the proposal... that he should lead the army in person.
>
> Exactly one month had passed away after the reading of the message when a fleet of

five Paraguayan war steamers came down from Asuncion, and captured the Argentine war steamer *25 de Mayo*, as well as the government hulk *Gualeguay*... at anchor in the harbour of Corrientes... Coincident with the arrival of the war steamers, the city [Corrientes], being perfectly unprepared for such an invasion, was occupied by five thousand Paraguayan infantry and a like number of cavalry.

President Mitre of Argentina declared war on Paraguay: "Argentines! The moment has arrived. In the name of the country and by the authority of the law I call upon you to take your places as citizens and soldiers of a free state whose banner has been always accompanied by justice and victory." General Urquiza, the *caudillo* of Entre Ríos, who had turned against, and defeated, Rosas in 1852, and in turn had been defeated by Mitre at Pavón in September 1861, was now called out of retirement by his former victor and put in command of the army of the Argentine Confederation. Urquiza's rallying cry was "in the barracks in 24 hours, we march in 15 days; within the walls of Asunción in three months." It took somewhat longer than that.

Urquiza was initially given 5,000 men and ordered to march on Corrientes. López was estimated to be able to raise an army of 60,000 men—45,000 infantry, 10,000 cavalry, 5,000 artillery. *The Standard* in Buenos Aires said that Paraguay's artillery commander was a European veteran "who served under general [Richard Debaufre] Guyon [1803-56] in the Hungarian campaign." Paraguay had no British officers, with the exception of the surgeon-general, Dr William Stewart of Edinburgh, and "his corps of army doctors. There are about thirty Englishmen employed in the arsenal at Asunción," *The Standard* said.

On Tuesday, 1 August 1865, *The Times* commented editorially on the first big action of the war, a river battle which ended with a Brazilian victory, on 11 June. This prompted the leader writer to forecast an early end to the war, although the Paraguayan army had crossed the River Uruguay and invaded the Brazilian territory of Rio Grande do Sul and had also defeated an Argentine advance against the city of Corrientes. *The Standard* and the *Anglo-Brazilian Times* had estimated that there were approximately 25,000 Paraguayans at Corrientes. *The Times* said:

> The Brazilian squadron in the river Paraná has nearly destroyed the Paraguayan squadron, after an engagement of nine hours, and with a loss of from 1,700 to 2,000 men; while on the other hand the Paraguayans have invaded Brazilian territory and captured the city of Borja, on the eastern bank of the Uruguay, after five days' fighting... The Paraguayans fought, no doubt, with South American fierceness and cruelty at Borja, and the event is judged of sufficient importance to induce the Emperor of Brazil to join the army.[13]

For the benefit of its readers, the paper supplied a short history of Paraguay which began with the statement: "Most educated people have at some time felt a curiosity as to the mysterious Paraguay", which sounded as if the writer was also informing his readers that he had at last found something on the funny little place in his Handbook.

> This Christian Japan, which, first under the Jesuits, and again under their high-handed successor, Dr Francia, for so long kept itself apart from the world, has always been one of the wonders and puzzles of modern civilisation. A country into which, even when it was under Spanish dominion, Spaniards were forbidden to enter, a people secluded from mankind, and yet possessed of luxury and art, well-built towns, splendid churches, wealthy convents,

and pursuing industry sufficient for all their wants, with hardly even a mercantile connexion with the outer world!

Paraguay was no match for Brazil:

> López and his people must eventually be beaten, and there will be every reason to rejoice at the event, for the opening of the Paraná and Paraguay to free navigation and the establishment of a more hospitable system will be the probable result. Such a policy as that pursued by the rulers of the country for so many years cannot but be broken down by the advance of civilisation, and if this war does its part in the work so much the better.

In the opinion of *The Times*:

> The Argentine Confederation, after being torn by political passions for so many years, appears now to be in a fair way of prosperity under the presidency of General Mitre, a man more respectable than the generality of South American politicians, and endowed with considerable talents.

López's slogan in the war was "Victory or Death". He did not accept surrender by any of his officers. As a result of this order, it was the men in the ranks who demonstrated their loyalty to López and in combat preferred to fight until they were killed rather than ask for clemency. The death toll in combat was always high.

On 2 July 1866, *The Times* published the first hint of the existence of a secret treaty between Brazil, Argentina and Uruguay, which had not been reported before[14]:

> From Montevideo we learn that an unpleasant feeling has arisen, affecting the honour of British diplomacy, owing to the publication, among the documents furnished to the British Parliament by Earl Russell's government, of the text of the secret treaty of alliance against Paraguay, of Brazil, the Argentine Confederation, and the Banda Oriental. This Treaty, it seems, was furnished to Mr Lettsom [the British minister] upon his urgent demand for information as to the purpose of the allies with regard to the independence of Paraguay, by Señor Carlos Castro, the Oriental Minister for Foreign Affairs, who, seeking to dispel any suspicions of the ulterior intentions of the allies on the part of the British government, handed him a textual copy upon a pledge of strict secrecy, which Mr Lettsom states he gave and also mentioned in the letter enclosing the copy to Earl Russell. As, notwithstanding this pledge, the treaty was made public by the British government, Señor Castro considered his honour aggrieved and had resigned his post, addressing besides a letter of a very warm [angry] nature to Earl Russell.

It is safe to assume that the British politicians held South America in such contempt that they considered it unnecessary to honour a commitment made to them.

For the next few months reports on the war in Paraguay were drawn mainly from those published by *The Standard* in Buenos Aires, and the *Anglo-Brazilian Times*, of Rio de Janeiro. Few of the London papers' reports were from their own correspondents. It became obvious that while *The Times* gave the war its concerned attention, it was not clear to the British public why a country like Paraguay could not be defeated by the combined armies of the allies.

In the middle of May 1867, however, there was a new cause for British interest in the war in Paraguay. A letter from a reader, dwarfed by two and a half columns of description of the Great French Exhibition, stated that "a considerable number of

Englishmen employed in Paraguay were forced by President López... into the military service at the commencement of the war," including, the correspondent said, his own brother.[15] Such an allegation, which might have brought pressure from a Britain already hostile to Paraguay, was refuted by the Paraguayan envoy in Paris: "The statement is calculated to throw unlimited alarm among the families and relatives of the Englishmen who are in Paraguay, employed for the most part in the government arsenal... his letter is completely devoid of foundation."[16] The letter-writer was not satisfied, however. On 20 May, he suggested that:

> Paraguay is not Abyssinia, inaccessible to our forces. A threat could easily be executed there by England. With the help of the Americans, who now appear on the scene as opponents of the war, and with that of the allies, it is reasonable to suppose that our countrymen could be rescued...

Events in Europe had almost completely overtaken the peculiar conflict near the centre of South America, when reports of a plot against López were published, which alarmed the British public, concerned for the safety of subjects residing in Paraguay. In a deposition later given by one of the suspects, the apothecary George Frederick Masterman, it was stated:

> He was arrested a second time in October 1868, because he was thought to be one of the pretended conspirators against López. There was not the slightest truth in that charge, or in the alleged conspiracy itself. He was sure no one believed in it, but about 800 people were arrested on account of it, and all, except six or seven, perished. He was taken from the American Legation, of which he was then an attaché, to the police office, where irons were brought up and riveted by a bar, with rings round it, upon his ankles. They would weigh at least twenty-five pounds, probably thirty pounds. He was put sideways on a horse, and sent a distance during the night of about twenty-three miles, enduring intense pain. As the bar rubbed backwards, and forwards, on his ankles, it tore through his boots and socks and ground on the bare flesh. His captors refused to give him food, and left him lying exposed to the burning sun until about four o'clock in the afternoon, when he was sent for by one of the judges appointed by López. He walked with great difficulty, and after he had gone some little distance he was severely flogged by a corporal to make him go faster. The judge told him he had been apprehended as a prisoner, and that Mr Washburn, the American minister, and others were traitors and ordered him to confess. He replied that he was perfectly innocent. "Oh," he said. "we will see if we cannot make you confess." He called some soldiers, who came and bound him and tortured him by binding him with his head on his knees. His mouth was cut and he fainted. When he came to himself he was lying on the ground quite exhausted. He was asked once more to confess. Feeling that he could only die, and that death was preferable to such torture, he made false confession, and said he was a traitor.[17]

In Argentina, President Mitre handed over to his elected successor, President Domingo Faustino Sarmiento, in 1868. The new head of state made it his policy to withdraw Argentina from what he considered an unfair war. Urquiza was relieved of his command of the army. In Montevideo, General Flores, who had fought for so long to gain control of Uruguay, was murdered in a street in the capital.

At length the war ended, but only when López himself, at the head of his Third Army Corps, was run through by a Brazilian's lance at Cerro Corá. López had been re-invading Matto Grosso, on his way to Concepción. What had seemed an impossible war had lasted just under five years.

The Times, Wednesday, 13 April 1870:

Termination of the war in Paraguay—Death of López. The Liverpool, Brazil, and River Plate mail steamer *Tycho Brahe*, from Brazil arrived here this evening. The intelligence of López's death [1 March] as signalled to Holyhead this morning, is fully confirmed. General Camara marched from Concepción and defeated López at Aquibana. López refused to surrender and fell fighting. The remnant of his army were made prisoners. There was a great storm at Buenos Ayres on 9 March, doing damage to the amount of half a million dollars. The *Tycho Brahe* took Count d'Eu's aide-de-camp to Rio de Janeiro with official dispatches. Business in Brazil was nearly suspended owing to rejoicings.

Three days later the paper reported that López's eldest son by Eliza Lynch had been killed with his father. On 11 April, in Entre Ríos, Argentina, General Urquiza was murdered by his political enemies. Two mighty and opposing *caudillos*, both despots, both heroes in their countries, had ended their lives violently within a few weeks of each other.

In Richard Burton's view of the war, "seldom has aught been more impressive to the gaze of the world than this tragedy; this unflinching struggle maintained for so long a period against overwhelming odds."[18] On 14 April 1870, the *Manchester Guardian* assessed the war as making "a profounder impression on the minds of competent observers" than anything else taking place at that time:

It has destroyed a remarkable system of government. It has overturned the only South American state wherein the native indian race showed any present likelihood of attaining or recovering such strength and organisation as to fit it for the task of government. No other state in South America has been able to boast of so much internal peace.

The article implied that had the Paraguayans been more numerous they might have won. There was a sense of romance in the idea of the resurgence of the Guaraní nation.

Paraguay was devastated. Its male population had been reduced to almost one tenth of the pre-war numbers. Paraguay's casualties from war, disease and hunger were estimated at 220,000. An exact figure could never be expected from the country which had lost almost everything, even a large part of its records. The male population was reduced to 28,000—even lower figures were sometimes given—and outnumbered by fourteen to one by the 221,000 surviving women and children. Among its enemies' casualties, estimated at 190,000, Brazil had lost one hundred thousand. Argentina and Uruguay shared the rest. Argentina had withdrawn from the war before the final encounter at which López had died and while it sought large land gains—which it did not get—in the final arbitration, Buenos Aires also tried to show charity and co-operation towards Paraguay.[19]

Brazilian troops marched into Asunción, looting all that had not been taken by López in the cause of war and defence. Churches were stripped bare, houses cleaned out. A shortage of paper for lighting fires and wrapping food was made good by sacking the national archive. Historical documents were sold by the sackful to wrap bread, meat and soldiers' rations. It was to the credit of a few people, among them the officers on the staff of Luis Felipe Maria Fernando Gastao d'Orleans, Count d'Eu—son-in-law of Pedro II and commander-in-chief of the allied forces—who, to stop the loss of the documents, bought as many sacks full of paper as possible for their preservation.

Britain had taken a position in favour of Brazil early in the conflict, because of its trade and acquaintance with the Brazilians. And because in the end there could be no other victor. But a natural admiration for courage moderated the criticism of López towards the end of the war. It was not easy for Europe to understand what had happened. Other conflicts had made too many demands on the European public's attention. In the United States the civil war was just ending as the war of the Triple Alliance began; the fate of Maximilian of Mexico in 1867 was of far more importance to the crowned heads of the Old World because he was a Habsburg and because he had 30,000 French troops with him. In Japan, which was considered as remote as Paraguay, but had more wealth, a combined British, French and Danish fleet had been posted off the Japanese coast to protect their respective commercial interests there. Britain had sent an expedition to Ethiopia to liberate British prisoners held there in 1868. And, perhaps more notable, there was Otto von Bismarck's political and military sweep through Europe to secure regions in dispute. That policy would lead Napoleon III of France into war and then to humiliation and defeat by Prussia.

But of all these wars and local conflicts, the Paraguayan war had been the most savage and its results the most horrifying. The military ingenuity and cunning of López had ensured that, as well as the destruction. Eliza Lynch was placed under arrest by the Brazilians. Late in 1870 she returned to England with her three surviving sons. What money she had left she spent in lawsuits fighting libel actions and trying to recover López's property. A sum of £4,000 which López was said to have given his surgeon-general, Dr Stewart, of Edinburgh, for safe keeping for the education of López's sons and the well-being of his mistress was never handed over to her. In court in Edinburgh, Stewart denied he had ever been given the money and when presented with receipts signed by him he alleged that they had been acknowledged under duress. When, finally, he was pressed to agree that the money might have been given to him, he declared himself insolvent. Eliza Lynch got nothing.[20] She returned to Buenos Aires to try to recover some of her property. She received only a fraction. Her youngest son died and the two remaining stayed to live in Argentina.

Robert Cunninghame Graham, who had taken a strong dislike to López, recalled meeting Eliza in London "several times in 1873 and 1874" near her house in Thurlow Square or Hyde Park Gate. He described her as still attractive, though putting on weight and with a few wisps of grey in her still blonde hair. She went back to Buenos Aires once more, to press claims for what had been her rightfully gained property, but again won little. From there she returned to Europe, travelled to Constantinople, then to Palestine, and died in poverty in a Paris lodging house in 1886, aged 51.[21]

Sarmiento, who had pulled Argentina out of the war, died in Asunción, in 1888. Mitre, who had taken Argentina into the conflict, died at the grand old age of 85 in Buenos Aires, in 1906.

The war of the Triple Alliance forced changes on all the participants. For Argentina it was the first time that the country had entered united into a conflict—even if some provinces were far from sympathetic to a war declared by Buenos Aires against a country which had the friendship of several Argentine provincial chieftains. Though political continuity of sorts had been achieved, the conflict had also caused a severe economic crisis.

Brazil, which after Paraguay was the country with most casualties in the war, suffered the beginnings of social transformation. The war had brought men from isolated farming communities into contact with people from the cities, and with army bureaucracy. The death, mutilation or retirement from battle of professional officers, whose lives and customs had been ruled by a class system within the empire, permitted the promotion of raw recruits and non-commissioned officers. Some of them made a career of the army. The social structure of the force was changed. Victory gave the army a new confidence and its senior officers, who had been responsible for preserving the empire, demanded a say in politics.

The farming men who returned to civilian life received small plots of land, creating a new class of smallholder. There was also a new attitude towards the black man—who had fought alongside the white man for five years. The war strengthened the advocates of the abolition of slavery, which the old conservative landowners had resisted because it represented cheap labour for them. Liberal European ideas gained ground: some Brazilians began to see slavery, for example, as an anachronism. The Emperor, Dom Pedro II, was caught in the middle of opposing groups of conservatives and liberals. Himself a liberal, he abolished slavery and abdicated in 1889.

The arbitration of the post-war land settlement by President Rutherford Hayes of the United States, in November 1878, gave Brazil the border territory it claimed, but Argentina's desire for a large piece of the Chaco territory, which would have given Buenos Aires the land of the Jesuit missions in Eastern Paraguay, and a common frontier with Brazil, was rejected. The US arbitration granted Paraguay most of its pre-war territory.

Paraguay degenerated into a state of near anarchy. Only the rivalry between Brazil and Argentina ensured an early withdrawal of the occupation forces from Paraguayan territory.[22] In Uruguay, though the civil war was over, the post-war period was one of economic and social disorder. A decade of political instability would follow.

NOTES:

1.   John Parish Robertson, *Letters on Paraguay*, vol I, p. 330.
2.   C. Lugon, *La République Communiste Chrétienne des Guaranís*. (Paris, 1949). Philip Caraman, *The Lost Paradise*. (Sidgwick & Jackson, London, 1975).
3.   Robert Bontine Cunninghame Graham, *A Vanished Arcadia*. (Heinemann, London, 1901).
4.   Josefina Pla, *The British in Paraguay, 1850-1870*. Trans. B. C. MacDermot (Richmond Publishing Company, 1976).
5.   See Chapter 6.
6.   C. B. Mansfield, *Paraguay, Brazil and the Plate*. (Macmillan, London, 1856).
7.   R. B. Cunninghame Graham, *Portrait of a Dictator*. (Heinemann, London).
8.   George Thompson, *The War in Paraguay*. (Longman, London, 1869).
9.   George Frederick Masterman, Apothecary General to the Paraguayan Army, *Seven Eventful Years in Paraguay: A Narrative of Personal Experience amongst the Paraguayans*. (Low, London, 1869).
10.   R. F. Burton, *Letters from the Battlefields of Paraguay*. (London, 1870).

11. *The Times*, 19 July 1864. Parliamentary questions, Osborne.
12. *The Times*, 20 October, 7 November, 3 December, 5 December, 7 December 1865, 21 January 1866. *The Standard*, Buenos Aires, 26 October 1865, reports the existence of a secret treaty between Buenos Aires, Brazil and General Flores for war against Paraguay.
13. *The Times*, 4 August 1865. Gives details at length of the battles of 10 and 11 June.
14. The first full account was only published in *The Times*, 15 June 1870.
15. *The Times*, 13 May 1867.
16. *The Times*, 16 May 1867. The letter appeared beside another from one Roderick Murchison, of Belgrave Square, who said that he was happy to report new evidence that Dr Livingstone was still alive and a boat party would set out on 9 June to ascend the north side of Lake Nyasa.
17. *The Times*, 15 May 1871.
18. Burton, *Letters*.
19. Max von Versen, *Historia da Guerra do Paraguai*, Revista do Instituto Histórico e Geográfico Brasileiro, LXXVI, part II (Rio de Janeiro, 1913).
20. *The Times*, 15 May 1871.
21. In March 1936, a presidential decree published in Asunción fully rehabilitated Francisco Solano López, who was declared a national hero without equal. The remains of Eliza Lynch were shipped to Asunción, from Paris, to rest by those of the marshal in the Pantheon of the Heroes.
22. PRO FO 6/326, 26 June 1875. Sackville-West to Derby. Brazil was angered by the publication in Buenos Aires of the agreement on the troop withdrawal.

Chapter Nine

GUNBOAT DIPLOMACY (PART TWO)
ARGENTINA, 1870-1876

Welsh school in Patagonia, 1911 (private collection)

This chapter is one of speculation.

A massacre of the native indians of Patagonia by the Argentine army took place in the 1870s. The matter for speculation is whether or not the massacre was a direct result of pressure from Europe—especially from Britain, but also from Germany and Italy.

Argentina needed to show Europe that it was putting its Patagonian hinterland in order. Argentina therefore mounted a campaign against the natives, called the Conquest of the Desert, which ended in mass slaughter. This conquest of the wilderness also freed land for further European settlement and agriculture.

In Argentina, political crises had preceded the war with Paraguay, and economic crisis followed it. Especially affected were the provinces, in particular Santa Fe—where the allied headquarters had been installed. Economic breakdown led to civil disorder in the cities and towns. Urban upheaval meant neglect of the countryside. In the south of Buenos Aires province and in the west—where the government had tried to promote European immigration—the indians raided farming colonies frequently, making life and business precarious. In the central and northern provinces, the threat to foreign settlers came less from local indians than from strong anti-foreign feeling which erupted occasionally into violence. Britain, Germany and Italy became worried about their investments and about those of their subjects who were concerned with business in Argentina. Britain's investments, of which railways were the most prominent, were greater than those of Germany and Italy.

Argentina's railway system had been started in 1853 with the help of British money and had been expanded through the following decade by British companies, of which the two larger were the Central Argentine Railway Limited, running across northern and central Argentina from west to east, and the Buenos Aires Great Southern Railway Limited, which ran South from Buenos Aires through the province towards Patagonia. The railways had been built by the combined initiative of British landowners and the Argentine government—which could not convince its own landowning classes to finance such projects and therefore had to seek the assistance of foreign business.

Reliance on foreign enterprise, and later dependence on British administration of those enterprises, as well as the need for foreign immigrants who would inevitably keep their loyalties to their old countries rather than establish new ties, eventually became so substantial that Argentina was to be seen as a form of colony. More particularly, it was to be seen as part of the British Empire. Even Lenin would cite Argentina as an example of "informal empire".[1]

One of the aims of the railways, in addition to the transport of regional produce, was to open up the interior to population. This would, in turn, make the railways more profitable. The personnel "imported" from England and hired in Argentina were offered stable wages, higher than those of farm workers and better than those of commercial workers in the cities. Thus the railways created a new social class in Argentina—a middle class that wanted stability and peace.[2]

In that decade of changes, when the conservative government of Buenos Aires tried to pull Argentina out of years of anarchy, one course for modernisation was to populate the provinces with hard-working north European settlers who would make the country safe and productive. North Europeans were regarded as reliable settlers, likely to remain in their new countries. South Europeans—though forced eventually by economic circumstances to settle and assimilate—arrived in Argentina seeing it as a place of temporary residence and employment where the money made would earn them a long and comfortable retirement in Spain or Italy. Argentina set about attracting North European colonists, who, ironically, though not impatient to leave during their lifetime, often watched their children re-emigrate.

Argentina offered free fares, some accommodation, good wages but no land—which meant that it was unable to compete favourably with Canada and Australia, both of which offered free land to new settlers. The award of land was resisted by Argentine smallholders, and by traditional landowners of patrician origin who had divided up the country centuries earlier. The native indians watched with distrust as restrictions were imposed on the open spaces in which they had roamed. But the natives were primitive and nomadic and not averse to the advantages of trade offered by the presence of settlers.

One small group of Welsh colonists had settled on the coast of Chubut province, in northern Patagonia. They had wanted to create a new autonomous Welsh nation in which to preserve their culture and language. The government in Buenos Aires hoped that they would be the instrument by which Patagonia would be inhabited and safeguarded as a national territory. The Welsh had established fairly good relations with the indians. Antonio, an indian chief, or *cacique*, of one of the Puelche and Tehuelche groups that inhabited the Chubut, or Chupat, Valley, confirmed that an element of trust existed between the natives, the Welsh and the government. In a letter to Lewis Jones, a representative of the Welsh settlers and of the British Emigration Society, Antonio stated:

> I am the *cacique* of a tribe of indians to whom belong the plains of Chupat. We hunt between Patagones and the Chupat near the coast of the sea in winter, and in the summer in the interior, where at that season the sun sets... Now I say that the plains between the Chupat and the Rio Negro are ours, and that we never sold them. Our fathers sold the plains of Bahia Blanca and Patagones, but nothing more... I am told to leave you to increase in numbers and not to do anything to you, and also to speak to the other *caciques* that they should not molest you. I promised to do all in my power for you... Now I say that if we had not been contented to trade with good people like you we should not have sold the land. You ought, for my portion of the land, to negotiate with the government. See you what they can pay me for it...[3]

The Welsh felt unable to negotiate on behalf of the indians, but strove to trade honestly and successfully with them and to deny the hysterical reports in the British press—whenever there was a long period without news from Patagonia—that the settlers had been overrun by indians. But to the north of the Welsh settlement, in Bahía Blanca and Patagones, the story was different. There the indians had sold their lands and had been excluded from their hunting grounds. Unable to produce sufficient food in their settlements and villages, or *tolderías*, they went back to the lands they knew to hunt and rob.

Colonies of British and Europeans were established in Buenos Aires, Sante Fe, Entre Ríos, and other provinces well suited to farming. When the native indians attacked, the government in the city of Buenos Aires tried to suppress publication of the news of the raids. Argentina did not want to show the provinces as being out of control and thereby discourage immigration of farming settlers. The authorities could prevent reports from army officers in command of outposts from reaching the local press, but they could do nothing about the correspondence of colonists writing to their diplomatic agents or to their relatives in Europe.

The news alarmed both the public and the governments. In *The Times* of 22 February 1870, a notice inserted by the Emigration Society warned British emigrants against going to Argentina. It said several Britons, as well as other Europeans, had been murdered in Buenos Aires. The notice prompted a reply by the Argentine minister in Paris who, on 18 March 1870, complained about the damage such notices did to his country. He supplied cuttings from newspapers and other reports as evidence of the prosperity of the new farming colonies. Forty thousand Europeans had emigrated to Argentina in 1869. In Buenos Aires the newspaper *La Tribuna* reproduced the minister's correspondence on 15 April, and added to it words of praise for his intervention. Coincidentally, the newspaper *El Nacional* reproduced the same items but instead of adopting the accommodating manner of its rival, it ran a heading that read "125 murders" and in the article beneath it said that "instead of being offended [Europe] should be grateful" that society had been rid of a large number of drunken sailors, ruffians and vagrants caught in riverside brawls.[4] Some time later *La Tribuna* was able to report that the British government had accepted the minister's explanations and the warning notice had been withdrawn.[5]

Promoters of Argentine immigration moved freely about the working men's clubs of England, were thrown out of those in Germany—which wanted to keep its young men for war—and attracted people in most of Europe's capitals. In general, the colonisation effort prospered.[6]

Not all was well. On 17 January 1873, one Arthur Mildred, resident near Bahía Blanca, at the settlement known as *Colonia Inglesa de Sauce Grande*, wrote to the colony's agent, E. P. Goodhall, British vice-consul and a local merchant:

You will have heard of the Indians down here. I will tell you as well as I can what is really true. There were a gang of fifteen of them in the Sierras robbing. An *alferez* [NCO] came across them and killed some of them, also losing a soldier I believe. They attacked Pavón and lost another [indian]. They came to Edwards' trot horse and Walker shot one in the back and natives finished [the indian]. On their way back Heralde met them on the other side of the Sierra, and killed six, and yesterday I heard that some of them came back with some more [indians] and that they killed four. This I give you for what it is worth. I know it is the truth. We spent a very pleasant Christmas day. The three Cobbolds were here and one or two others and we got up some races. I was very successful. I have lately made 700 pesos in racing... I don't know that there is anything more to say. Potatoes are very good. A happy new year...[7]

The writing was not that of an educated hand; it was that of a tough Englishman who was trying to make a living and build up a property in an alien land and culture. The names mentioned were those of his neighbours and fellow-settlers. Henry Edwards and John Walker were cousins, identified locally as *Facón Grande* (Big Knife) and *Facón Chico* (Little Knife) because of the blades they wore in their belts. Both names were later to be immortalised by R. B. Cunninghame Graham, in *Mirages* (1936).

Letters from the colonists to their agent recorded the occasional skirmish, such as that mentioned by Mildred; but the fear of a large indian invasion was ever present among the tribulations of the farmers. At the end of that year, on 20 December 1873, John Walker wrote to Goodhall, incorporating Spanish words into his English.

We have got a high old *golpe* [coup] this journey from the darkies. On the morning of the 12th I as usual went up onto the hill behind the house to look about me with a field glass and couldn't see anything moving in the *camp*;[8] I came down and about a quarter of an hour afterwards let go the animals, but gave them a turn down by the side of the corral to keep them near the house, because a *chasque* [messenger] passing the night before had told me that the brutes were invading and had taken all the indian horses from the Sauce Corto. Well, the animals had hardly got to the bottom of the corral when there was a high old yell and our friends appeared all over the shop mixed up with the cows and driving them for the hills. I was by the milking *palenque* [post] at the time and cleared into the house to get the Mrs out of bed and tell her to go onto the roof as they were all round the corral... Marcos Holmes in the meanwhile blazed away with rifles. I toddled back and got a steady on one coon and hit him hard, but he got away. The fire was too hot for them and they left a *point* [9] of 250 cows which cleared past the back of the house and for the hills. Holmes and self got on horseback and followed them in, Mac doing the infantry business. They camped in the alfalfa and on the highest point between here and Sinclair's and stopped there about four hours, ate a couple of cows *carne con cuero*.[10] We went out into the hills now and then and got stray pots at them at long distance, but I don't think did any harm except when they tried to take the flock. Then Mac gave one of them a quietener at about a hundred yards. He did not come off then, but Mac and Chevengo found where they had buried him the next day with his horse *parado* [standing] over him with its throat cut right across as their custom is... Holmes went up as *chasque* behind them with a letter to Major Brio from me telling him how many indians there were and what they had done and which way they had gone, but he could not *animar* [dare] himself to do anything saying they were too many—he had a force of over fifty men at his orders... The beggar wouldn't even go to Barber's when they were fighting there. He went as far as the top of that hill that divides the two valleys, remarked that there were too many of them and toddled home again... Barber and his people did for a couple of them but the others took them away and also robbed all San Juan's cattle and Barber's house. I have put in a formal complaint at the Comandancia Bahía Blanca... If the forces do not go out quick and hammer them they will be in again soon...

There were expeditions against the *toldos*—a word taken from the cloth and hide shelters used as homes in the indian villages. None was effective and the native indians were thrown back, but not defeated. A strong hatred grew between the white man and the native. The indian was thought of as vermin, to be eliminated.

It was election year. President Sarmiento's liberal spending on his progressive reforms, education and urban planning diverted attention from the problems of the farmers and the indians. The difficulties in local banking, reflecting a crisis in Europe, focused attention on events in the capital. General Mitre, the former president, attempted a military coup to prevent the presidential elections. In the countryside, the complaints of the settlers continued. A farmer at Sauce Grande, George Catty, wrote to Goodhall on 23 January 1874, again with the matter of the native indian attacks among his problems.

You have heard of the grand expedition to the *toldos* and what came of it. We have been expecting the darkies here every day for the last fortnight but have not seen anything of them yet although they paid several visits this month... We have Major Givaleva with a hundred men encamped on the river just by the Paso Grande so that even if they do come we may be able to show claws a bit. I rather think the darkies already know that our bite is worse than our bark. I dare say that you don't know that Holmes shot an indian at the *toldos*... Lieutenant Brown has been staying here for a few days... He and Walker have been composing a letter to *The Standard* on the subject of the frontier... I suppose Buenos Aires is beginning to be livening up about elections. I hope to goodness they will pass over without a row. If the few soldiers we have here were taken away we should be "treed" as the Yankees say.

A fortnight later, another settler, one H. L. Black, wrote on 8 February that indians had killed six men from Bahía Blanca. Black was doing well.

I am now a *fondero* [innkeeper], having rented the *retratista's* [portraitist's] house, furnished with billiard table and all. I have been open about sixteen days now and am doing very well. If you ever know of passengers for Bahía Blanca mind you send them to me. I will give them good and cheap accommodation: man and beast.

They were there to do well. That was what they had uprooted for—not to suffer harassment from native indians, who were regarded as little better than criminals. In October 1875, Walker reported more raids.

Twenty or thirty indians took about three hundred horses and mares from the Indio Rico a few days ago, leaving Edwards only one horse. One hundred and fifty men out from the Sauce Corto are after them. Let's hope they'll catch them.

Only a month later, on 17 November 1875, Mildred told of new raids, in addition to a shooting between two Englishmen.

Collinson shot Barber... The ball entered underneath the right nipple and, traversing the rib, lodged underneath the shoulder blade where it still remains. It was a row about a dog of Collinson's that Barber wanted to kill because it had bitten him. It seems he began knocking Collinson about and in self-defence he drew his revolver. I am awfully sorry that such a thing should have happened amongst Englishmen... An invasion of indians took place the other day... however, [Comandante] Maldonado met them at *El Paso de los Chilenos*, killed nine, took one prisoner, and took away all the *robo*, including their own horses. They only got away on the horses they were riding.

A summary of these letters describing events in Argentina was sent to the British minister in Buenos Aires, then Mr (later Lord) Lionel Sackville-West. And as the correspondence reached Buenos Aires, the British envoy found that the German and Italian ministers were receiving similar epistles from their countrymen in the provinces. The alarming news continued. Mildred wrote to Goodhall on 19 January 1876.

Of the invasion we can only give you very meagre details, but you may distrust reports that say the troops got any advantages over the indians, as from all we can hear the savages had it all their own way. The *galera* [stage coach] passed yesterday with Camacho as *mayoral* [driver] instead of poor Calderón, who was brutally murdered by the indians, four leagues from Azul. The contents of the *galera* were not touched as it was stopping at a post at the time. The indians were driving away the *galera* horses and Calderón went with his two *peones* to stop them, but the *peones* stayed a respectful distance behind, and Calderón went by himself. There were twelve indians. They lanced him, then tied his hands and feet and cut his throat... Mr Edwards who passed yesterday showed us a letter that he had received.

It had been covered with blood and either torn or cut... Camp in want of water which has not fallen copiously. A very good summer lambing in the flock...

Mildred wrote again on the subject to Goodhall on 27 June 1876.

I now just want to explain to you how we are situated in regard to the indians... This month a body of indians, variously estimated at one to two hundred, passed at Cheek's pass, about a league above Jordan's and after *carneando* [slaughtering] seven cows... passed on. All the horses and mares with very few exceptions were cleared off... and at Indio Rico they took all Faramiñan's cattle (two thousand head) and seven hundred at Edwards. Comandante Cessi came out to Jordan's for a day or two but the indians went out another way. They did not kill anybody and went perfectly at their leisure. We have now received official news both from the Justice of the Peace and the Comandante that they have news of a very large invasion of Bahía Blanca and the Quequén Salado [river] which they think will take place on the 12th or 14th of next month. It is to be under the charge of Namuncurá himself, and they will number from two thousand to three thousand five hundred lances.[11] Please make this known in the papers... The indians go about just as they like. Cessi has from one hundred to one hundred and twenty men under his command to protect a town like Bahía Blanca. It is certain too that amongst the indians are many men armed with Remingtons, probably deserters. This life is a misery here now. You cannot get away ten squares from the house without expecting to meet indians. If this enormous force comes here I am sure I don't know how we shall get on. I trust they will pass for where there is more *robo*... The indians are masters of the country, and it is no use disguising the fact... I have now told you the plain truth about the indians, which is better than all the falsified reports you see in the papers. I hope we may none of us lose more than our animals.

The main attack, the *malón*, did not come; the indians continued their war of nerves with quick raids and robbery. Edwards had more to complain about. He had travelled to Buenos Aires for his wedding, and on his return with his bride found that the indians had burned his house to the ground.

By then the Foreign Office, the recipient of frequent enquiries about settlers in Argentina, was asking its correspondents in the River Plate about safety. Invariably the news was bad. The Foreign Office considered submitting a demand for compensation from the Argentine authorities to be paid to the settlers under attack, but did nothing for the time being.

The British government was under greater pressure from bankers, railway and ship owners to demand safeguards for their property in Argentina. These interests were affected by the policies of government, by civil disorder and by economic crisis. Lord Derby, the foreign secretary, asked his minister in Buenos Aires to make strong representations to President Avellaneda, Sarmiento's former justice minister, for the protection of British subjects and property.

While the native indians threatened the white settlers in the south and west of Buenos Aires, to the north, in Santa Fe province, Europeans thought that their livelihoods and lives, were at risk from a strong antipathy for foreigners. Santa Fe had stumbled out of anarchy in the years immediately after Rosas' downfall and into economic distress as colonisation and farming ventures failed. The Paraguayan war had brought a large army headquarters to the province, mainly at the safe river port of Rosario, and this had produced a short-lived, extraordinary, commercial success. Fortunes were made in a week.

Some were lost, but many more were made. After the war the provincial financial system, without the large turnovers which war supplies had brought, experienced difficulties, even though the external evidence of wealth remained. Colonisation had expanded, farming had thrived, and the Central Argentine Railway had been built and extended, to carry the local produce to the recently enlarged port, Rosario, for export to the world.

But the economic crisis in Europe caused a slump in farming prices in South America. Money was scarce. In Santa Fe debtors defaulted. Law and order disintegrated, as did the economy. The lawlessness was accompanied by demonstrations of dislike for foreigners, who were thought to be responsible for the economic crisis as well as blamed for taking over land that it was thought should have been allocated to native owners. The foreign community was numerous. The province was sparsely populated, so any alien presence was therefore a considerable one. On 22 January 1873, the newspaper *La Nación* said that there were 486 British colonists in the farming settlements of Santa Fe—though the figure also took in smaller colonies in Entre Ríos and Córdoba. There were several thousand Italian and Swiss, eighty-two North Americans, two dozen Germans and smaller numbers of Belgians, Danes, Swedes, Poles and other nationalities.

Europeans controlled the local courts, bank branches, and most of the commercial houses. The presence of so many foreigners caused resentment in all classes in provincial society. In some towns the local justice of the peace was a foreigner, with a priority to defend his own countrymen's interests against the local inhabitants, even the police. One case cited as an example of police reaction to the foreign presence was reported to the Foreign Office by the British vice-consul at Rosario, in February 1874. The consular official claimed that he had been threatened by a policeman with a pistol; when the incident was reported to the senior officer the latter merely turned to the policeman and remarked, 'Well done!'[12]

While the Italian government advised its emigrants not to go to Argentina, and especially not to Santa Fe province, in Argentina it was argued that the European settlers were in great measure responsible for the crime rate in Rosario and the larger towns of Sante Fe.[13] The Italians were accused of being the worst offenders. It was not uncommon for European colonists to take up arms against the police when one of their own was arrested; or even to lynch suspected criminals when caught by gangs of settlers.[14]

The gun ruled, and eventually the stricter rule by gunboat was used too. The Italian consul in Buenos Aires ordered a gunboat up the River Paraná after his vice-consul at Rosario was arrested. To free him, the Italian community mobbed the police station on which he was held.[15] A British gunboat sailed up the river Paraná to threaten the port of Rosario after a banking incident in 1875, which finally convinced Britain that the Argentine interior was ungovernable.

A dispute arose between the Santa Fe province bank, formed in 1874, and the Rosario Branch of the Bank of London and the River Plate.[16] The provincial bank, faced with the long-established competition of the British bank's branch, decreed restrictions on the operations of the London and River Plate bank in the province of Santa Fe. The London bank went to court to get the restrictions on its services overruled, but lost.[17] The Santa Fe province bank took advantage of this victory and ordered the liquidation of the London bank and sequestration of its assets, amounting to £18,000.[18]

The provincial bank also secured a warrant for the arrest of the manager of the Rosario branch of the London bank, a German national, Herr Behn, on charges of trying to remove currency from the bank for transfer to Buenos Aires and London. This determined the intervention of the German consul in Buenos Aires, who described to his government the total insecurity of life and property in the Argentine republic. A German protest was lodged at the foreign ministry in Buenos Aires. *The Standard* published a special supplement on the row.[19] On 25 May 1876 the Buenos Aires branch manager wrote to London.

> I asked the British minister to send a gunboat to Rosario... He complied immediately, but Dr Irigoyen, the minister of foreign affairs, having hinted that it would be better not to send her, as it might create ill-feeling on account of its looking like a threat, and his having told [the British minister] that the national government guaranteed the property of the London and River Plate Bank, the British minister consented to let the gunboat remain at San Nicolás, about five hours further down [the river].

The national government demanded moderation from the provincial administration, but was ignored.

The manager of the London bank's Buenos Aires office then asked the British minister to send a man-of-war, or two gunboats which were then in the Buenos Aires harbour, to Rosario. The diplomat ordered the gunboat at San Nicolás to proceed to Rosario. By then Herr Behn had been released. The gunboat remained at Rosario for a few days, but took no action. The minister had been warned that the bank was not a popular outfit in Santa Fe and he was anxious to keep the British government out of the incident.

Herr Behn returned to work after a few days. It was time for a low profile. The bank's lack of generosity in its credits, and its policy of quick seizure of properties mortgaged, had at times made the banking dispute a motive for personal attacks against the London bank's managers. From London, the management wrote on 3 July to regret that the gunboats had not been used to greater effect: "We feel very keenly the shortcomings of our own representative of the British Government, and are endeavouring to stir up the Foreign Office, and a case is under preparation for presentation..."

The Times, on 30 June, had commented that the events at Rosario were the best example of the lack of respect for the law and for society's institutions and private property. This was now a characteristic of the republic, the paper said. *The Times'* anger represented another turn of the screw. Europe was watching Argentina's internal turmoil and institutional breakdown.

The Santa Fe government was forced by the central government to reverse its liquidation order against the British bank. The London bank won only the consent that no other private bank opening in the province would be granted privileges beyond those held by their own branch. In contrast to this moral and financial defeat, the London bank came out of the crisis with large extensions of land in Santa Fe—all repossessed from debtors who had defaulted. It was a tie, in a way, except that in the eyes of the public it confirmed the bank's notoriety as a terror with debtors.[20]

Meanwhile, the British minister in Buenos Aires, Lionel Sackville-West, informed his superiors in London that Argentina was in a shambles. He shared his time between Buenos Aires, where he had been posted, and Montevideo, from where the

British government had removed its representative because there appeared to be no authority with which an accredited diplomat might talk.

In Buenos Aires, according to Sackville-West, the roads were unsafe and the justices of the peace were not paid—hence the administration of justice was lax, and police outside the city hardly bothered to enforce the law. The British diplomat was in fact extracting his information from *The Standard*, which in February 1875 had offered its readers a series of terrifying accounts of acts of violence and public incompetence in the countryside. In addition, Sackville-West wrote on 15 February that there was "a serious monetary crisis", and the country was making "recourse to a dangerous system of paper trading."[21] He had also to report his frequent intervention on behalf of British subjects in difficulties. On 25 February it was the "case of ill-treatment of a British subject at the hands of the government during the last revolution". The Briton in question, a Mr Anan, an Irishman, "was suddenly arrested and subjected to the punishment of the stocks." Sackville-West had secured his release, an apology and compensation of one thousand pesos—the equivalent of £20 16s 8d.

The worst incident at that time was the sacking of the archbishop's palace and a fire caused by arsonists at the Jesuit College. Anti-religious outbursts were frequent, not helped by the untimely proposal by the Archbishop of Buenos Aires that the government should consider returning property seized a century before from the Jesuits. "There was the usual amount of throat-cutting and fire added to the atrocities committed... Eight or ten, priests and others, were assassinated," the British minister reported. The subjects of his concern in the matter were the Irish Order of the Sisters of Mercy who were thought to be in danger. The situation was aggravated by the discovery by Sackville-West that the guards posted outside the Irish order were drunk.[22]

The government blamed the outrages on "foreigners belonging to the international and other secret societies". Mr Stevens, a resident Briton, was accused of taking part in the burning of the college. He was held for "thirty six hours confined in a criminal prison without bed or decent accommodation", because he had refused to sign a confession. British subjects were murdered; the widow of one who was killed by a group of soldiers was raped. The British minister estimated, by progression, that there were "the astounding number of 756 murder cases pending before the courts". "It cannot therefore be a matter of surprise that large numbers of immigrants are leaving," Sackville-West informed both the Argentine foreign ministry, on one of his frequent visits there demanding protection for somebody, and his own Foreign Office.

For Argentina the biggest blow to its prestige came in the middle of the year, when the German and Italian governments threatened to ban emigration to Argentina— rather than have to continue protecting their nationals in the country—if Argentina did not do something to control criminals in the cities and the indians in the country. "The measures reported to have been taken by the German and Italian governments to check immigration have produced a great impression here. There has been of late a gradual falling off in the number of immigrants arriving," reported Sackville-West. Italians were not coming any more, largely because there were few prospects of making any money in Argentina during the crisis. The British minister was of the opinion that Italians were of little use anyway, as they took too much money out of the country for their families in

Italy, and produced very little. Germans, on the other hand, were not as numerous.

> but of more real value to the country. It is useless to conceal that there are elements in this country opposed to the development of good immigration. Chief among these are the insecurity of life and property, and the defective administration of justice...

Argentines, he concluded, "ignore the fact that the laws virtually afford no protection to the immigrant for his property."[23]

Sackville-West recorded all his meetings at the foreign ministry, which were numerous. He had once found great pleasure in Buenos Aires. He had enjoyed rowing in the River Luján, where he had helped to organise the English-membership Buenos Aires Boat Club, two years before.[24] That time seemed very long ago.

Uruguay was marginal to events in Argentina, but the correspondence of Lionel Sackville-West, and of his assistant, Mr St John, also described violent incidents and frequent threats to British property in Montevideo. The Foreign Office received news from the River Plate as a whole, without making much of a distinction between which capital the disturbances were reported from. Both were in crisis. In 1875, events in Uruguay seemed at their worst for years.

Sackville-West was under considerable pressure from the British community in Montevideo—as well as from those Britons in Buenos Aires who owned property in Uruguay—to move a British gunboat into the port to take action. The trouble was, what would the Royal Marines do once disembarked? They could take control of the Customs House and government stores, but it was not certain how long they would have to remain there. The chaos was too great and too widespread for even a British gunboat to overcome.[25]

On 10 January the most conservative wing of the Colorado party overthrew the government in Montevideo, on the eve of municipal elections. Ten or twelve people were killed.

> The government may now be said to be in the hands of bandits and cut throats... I have stated, as I have stated under similar circumstances at Buenos Aires, that the lives and property of British subjects will be protected by Her Majesty's naval forces should any danger to them arise...

These events were, however, a common occurrence in the South American republics, the minister said. So the gunboat departed from Montevideo, leaving behind a terrified British community, which was also extremely angry with Sackville-West. The minister wrote to Lord Derby, the Foreign Secretary, from Buenos Aires.

> The principal bankers [of Montevideo] waited upon me and requested armed protection. I replied that as far as I was aware there was no necessity for landing an armed force, but I was prepared for all imminencies... I was anxious to avoid intervention, although the ex-president, Señor Alaun, had asked for it. I was told by the English residing in the country that if a foreign force landed in the city, they would all be murdered on their estates.

The farmers felt safer organising their own defence: they had guns and their labourers made small private armies. Not so the Britons in the city. Commander Chatfield of the HMS *Amethyst* offered to land thirty marines to "protect the consulate or to take possession of the customs house." But still the minister refused.

He soon came under pressure from Brazilian businessmen in Uruguay, who also wanted the British to intervene. As he refused, Brazil sent a squadron. On 25 March Sackville-West advised London that this has "given rise to the suspicion that the establishment of a protectorate is aimed at and perhaps ultimate annexation contemplated," which could lead to war between Argentina and Brazil.

The new president of Uruguay, Pedro Varela, serving in an interim capacity, decided to restore order in the economy first. He sanctioned a law, passed by the legislative assembly, to suspend payment of the foreign debt and banned payment of interest for the duration of the suspension. Thirty-six British merchants at Montevideo now begged for a gunboat on the grounds that there had been "injustice inflicted on the British community... by the principle of repudiation" of the foreign debt. "The bonds that represented the public debt of this state have always been considered as a means of investment." The Brazilians drew up a plan to force the Uruguayan government to pay, but could not win the support of all the other foreign agents in Montevideo. In his failure, the Brazilian envoy warned Sackville-West that if gunboats would not protect the British, "God help her subjects in a country like Uruguay, where justice is unknown in a court of law." The gunboats were kept away all that year, even though a resident of Montevideo warned that there "is a smouldering excitement and desire for revolution that when it breaks out may induce a lawless and reckless populace to commit, under the cry of communism, any amount of crime..."

President Varela was removed in a military coup in 1876. His year in government was to be remembered as the "terrible year". He was followed by the kind of stability the British and Brazilian merchants wanted. They had military rule during the next fourteen years before civilian succession was introduced.

Throughout the River Plate countries there was disorder. Europe had not intervened directly to protect its interests, but it never failed to remind Argentina—and also Uruguay, which cast a shadow of its own on the Plate—that Europe had considerable interests at stake. And those interests were threatened by disorder. There is no indication that Argentina was pressed directly to restore order within its borders.

Each incident brought a succession of complaints, a stream of warnings that the badly needed immigrants would be prevented from travelling to the River Plate—for they were causing their governments more trouble abroad than they had at home. Every protest produced what seemed like irreparable damage to Argentina's image. The government chose to make a dramatic gesture where it would be most conspicuous: not in the cities where law and order were difficult to impose, but in the country where the corpses of cattle-rustling indians could be shown.

In 1879, General Julio Argentino Roca, a man with good political contacts in the Argentine conservative establishment and a much respected military career behind him, declared war on the native indians of Argentina and on all those who fought on their side: the gun traders, liquor merchants, army deserters and cattle thieves. He set out on the *Conquista del Desierto*, a vernacular winning of the wild west, or rather the wild south, a conquest of Patagonia. The indians did not stand a chance. They were persecuted, captured and killed.

Roca was welcomed back to Buenos Aires as a national hero—just as Rosas had been five decades before. He had made the provinces safe for cultivation and progress. In 1880 he was elected president. He would control Argentine politics for the next thirty years, in and out of office. He would be re-elected for a second presidential term of six years at the turn of the century, and preside over the country's *belle époque*, which saw Argentina's upper class acquire immense wealth. The fortunes were made largely thanks to Britain. "The Englishman has made many native Argentinos wealthy beyond the dreams of avarice," one traveller wrote at the beginning of the century.[26]

The following is a footnote to the war against the native indian. It appeared in a volume published in 1911 in London and entitled *Twentieth Century Impressions of Argentina* to mark Argentina's centenary as a nation. In it an anonymous writer makes a contribution from which the following lines are extracted.[27]

> In the earlier days of white settlement in Tierra del Fuego, the indians gave trouble by killing the settlers' livestock — probably impelled by hunger resulting from the growing scarcity of the *guanaco* and other indigenous fauna on which the aboriginal was want to feed. These depredations naturally gave rise to the organisation of punitive expeditions, in which as short shrift was granted the marauders as is given to the blacks in the remote parts of North Queensland who indulge in similar practices and are promptly hunted down by mounted men with magazine rifles and shot wherever found... No more humane way of effectively impressing the aboriginals of a primitive region with the determination of civilised man to prevail and punish depredation has yet been suggested... A recent issue of the London *Field* on the subject of the indians of Tierra del Fuego speaks of "the dark tales of brutality and rapine told of the early days of settlement in Tierra del Fuego" as being "almost without parallel in modern times". And with shame it must be confessed that these outrages were committed not by the Latin races—for it is only in recent years that the Chilean and Argentine have come into the country—but by men of British birth and extraction... After a while the havoc among stock wrought by the indians grew so great that the *estancieros* paid £1 a head for every *macho*, or indian male, killed. At first the bow had to be brought in before the money was paid; but later on an ear had to be cut off and shown...[28]

NOTES:

1. V. I. Lenin. *Collected Works*, Imperialism the Highest Stage of Capitalism, vol. 22, p. 263 (Moscow, 1963). See also H. S. Ferns, *Britain and Argentina in the Nineteenth Century*, and D. C. M. Platt, "The Imperialism of Free Trade. Some Reservations", *Economic History Review*, vol. 31, 1968. *La Nación*, 11 February 1933, reported the speech of Julio A. Roca, vice-president of Argentina, at a banquet in his honour at the Dorchester Hotel, London, in which he said that economically, Argentina felt it was part of the British Empire.
2. Andrew Graham-Yooll, *The Forgotten Colony*. (Hutchinson, 1981), p.220.
3. Glyn Williams, "Welsh Settlers and Native Americans in Patagonia", *Journal of Latin American Studies* (London, 1979). The Welsh arrived in Chubut in July 1865. The letter is dated December 1865.
4. *El Nacional*, 12 April 1870.
5. *La Tribuna*, 24 May, 28 June 1870.
6. *La Tribuna*, 18, 24 May, 3 June 1870, 4 February 1871. *La Nación*, 22 January 1873.
7. Copies of these letters were given to Andrew Graham-Yooll and other researchers by Miss

E. M. Brackenbury of San Isidro, Buenos Aires, a descendant of one of the Sauce Grande settlers.

8.   From the word *campo*; meaning country, or farm.

9.   Point, from the word *punta*, "a number of...".

10.   Form of roasting meat on an open fire.

11.   [Ceferino] Namuncurá, the last and the most powerful of the indian *caciques*.

12.   Ezequiel Gallo, *El gobierno de Santa Fe vs. el Banco de Londres y Río de la Plata (1876)*. (Instituto Torcuato Di Tella, Buenos Aires 1972), p.9. This text has proved essential in the compilation of this section.

13.   A vernacular Mafia established its headquarters in Rosario towards the end of the century, controlling the drug trade and prostitution. See Albert Londres, *The Road to Buenos Ayres*. (Constable, London, 1930).

14.   *The Standard*, 12 September 1876.

15.   *The Standard*, 17 January 1877.

16.   Later absorbed by the Bank of London and South America; now part of Lloyds Bank International.

17.   Gallo, *El Gobierno de Santa Fe*, p. 11. See also, David Joslin, *A Century of Banking in Latin America*. (Oxford University Press, 1963).

18.   University College London, Library. Bolsa 01/10, 035/6, D1/10.

19.   *The Standard*, 31 May 1876.

20.   *The Standard*, 22 September 1891. During the banking crisis that followed the Baring Brothers collapse in 1890, British flags on British-owned offices were torn down "by men and women in elegant suits", and there was a run on deposits at the Bank of London and South America. (See also *Buenos Aires Herald*, April-June 1982.)

21.   PRO FO 6/326.

22.   PRO FO 6/326, 2 March, 4, 6 March 1875.

23.   PRO FO 6/326, 6 and 17 March 8, 9 and 28 Arpil, 8 May, 1 June 1875.

24.   *The Standard*, 10 December 1873.

25.   PRO FO 6/326.

26.   Hiram Bingham, *Across South America*. (Houghton Mifflin, Boston, 1911).

27.   Reginald Lloyd and others, *Twentieth Century Impressions of Argentina*. (London, 1911), p.827.

28.   In contrast, see the understanding and sympathetic text of Lucas Bridges, *Uttermost Part of the Earth*. (Hodder & Stoughton, London, 1948). Thomas Bridges, a missionary, and father of Lucas compiled the only existing dictionary of the language of the now extinct Yagan indians of Tierra del Fuego.

Chapter Ten
The Manure War.
Chile-Bolivia-Peru,
1879-1883

John Thomas North (private collection)

The nitrate deposits in the Atacama desert were a matter of dispute between Chile, Peru and Bolivia throughout the last quarter of the nineteenth century. The dispute led to the War of the Pacific—a contradiction in terms, for a pacific war it was not.

Since the discovery of the nitrate (saltpetre) deposits in the 1860s, Bolivia had felt threatened by Chilean expansionism. The result of this fear of Chile had been a defence agreement between Peru and Bolivia in 1873. In December 1875, Peru expropriated the private mines within its territory in the hope of raising enough money to pay its own vast public debt with income from the saltpetre deposits. The enterprises affected were mainly Anglo-Chilean mining interests in southern Peru.

Bolivia was encouraged to follow Peru's example; but, fearing hostility from Chile in the area, limited its action to an increase of the existing duties on the product of foreign and private companies. Those most affected were the Chilean mining companies in the Atacama desert. The Chilean companies were funded by English business, in the forefront of which were two groups: Antony and Herbert Gibbs, and Edwards and Company. British capital invested in the Chilean mining companies was close to one million pounds.

The increase in duties on extracted nitrate escalated the conflict from commercial dispute to war. A Chilean fleet blockaded the southern Bolivian port of Antofagasta, which was populated largely by Chilean nationals who controlled much of the local commerce and were most numerous in the city's middle and upper classes. Initially, Peru managed to avoid involvement.

The Times, Saturday, 22 March 1879:

Chile and Bolivia. Santiago, 19 February, via Lisbon. The Chilean troops, acting in cooperation with the fleet, occupied Antofagasta on the 14th inst and afterwards took possession of Caracoles and Mexillones without meeting with any resistance. The Bolivian authorities at those places have been superseded. A Chilean war vessel has been sent to Cobija to protect the Chilean subjects residing there. The Chilean government has declared that in consequence of the Bolivian government cancelling concessions made to Chilean subjects, seizing the nitre mines, and refusing to give any explanations in regard to these measures, it [the Chilean government] has decided to resume the territorial rights it possessed previous to the treaty of 1866 [when a border was drawn and mining rights agreed]. The Peruvian government has refused to mediate between Chile and Bolivia.

On 27 March, *The Times* published a short news item which was the Lloyd's agent's confirmation of the conflict. Queen Victoria was visiting Italy at the time, the British were fighting the last skirmishes of their second war in Afghanistan, the Zulu war was continuing in Africa. Not much space could be given to another minor clash in South America. On 29 March the paper published a lengthier report on preparations for war. It was extracted (a common custom when no correspondent was on station) from the *Panama Star and Herald*, whose reporter wrote from Lima, Peru.

The topic of interest with us is the impending outbreak of hostilities between Chile and Bolivia, and the attitude to be assumed by Peru in the event of such an occurrence. Chilean war vessels are anchored in the harbour of Antofagasta and Chilean soldiers occupy the town. The Bolivian forces are rapidly approaching the coast. The Chilean squadron disembarked a sufficient quantity of rifles to arm the Chilean residents of Antofagasta and the adjacent mining districts, so that at least 2,500 armed Chileans occupy Bolivian territory.

The minister of Foreign Affairs of Bolivia, Señor Reyes Ortiz, has arrived at Lima with the ostensible object of soliciting from this government permission for the transportation of one thousand Bolivian infantry over the Puna and Arequipa Railway to Moliendo, thence to be carried down to the scene of the action. He is in daily consultation with President Prado and the Cabinet, but as yet it seems his request has not been acceded to... The interest of Peru in the affair is apparent. The great salpetre deposits of Antofagasta, once in possession of Chile, would be pushed to an enormous producing power, and prove to be more than a dangerous rival to the Peruvian article now the property of the State... Should Peru take part in the struggle, her powerful ironclad fleet might give a different aspect to the question. As a preparatory measure the ram *Huascar*, and the two monitors, *Atahualpa* and *Manco Capac*, are being docked and made ready for sea in Callao. The ironclad frigate *Independencia*, having just concluded her extensive repairs, is in readiness for action.

The Times also extracted a short report from the *Heraldo de Cochabamba*, which described the pitiful state of the region. Bolivia did not have much with which to resist invasion by Chile.

Cochabamba, the granary of Bolivia and the most productive section of the country, where hands for the purposes of agriculture are scarce, beholds the sad spectacle of numbers of its sons succumbing to the fatal scourge of hunger... the San Juan de Dios Hospital has furnished us with the following data, the truth of which we cannot doubt: from the 1st to the 20th of January last the dead bodies of 81 persons who had succumbed to hunger were found in the streets and conveyed to hospital. During the same period 125 persons died in the hospital of hunger... in twenty days, ten per day...

and it gave details of more deaths from starvation in neighbouring areas.[1]

The Atacama desert—the subject of the dispute—had been the source of conflict between Chile, Bolivia and Peru ever since the three countries existed as independent states. The desert itself was—and still is, for the wars have not moved other than political borders—a plateau about 13,000 feet high on the dry and arid Pacific coastline of central South America. The Andes chain blocks moist air from the Amazon river and jungle from reaching the western coast, which has made the Atacama one of the driest places in the world. Here and there in Atacama there were some artesian wells, but their boron content, though useful for medicinal purposes, made the water extracted from subterranean beds—which were too salty—useless for agriculture. The shoreline of the desert is without rain because of the Humboldt current, which brings water from the Antarctic and causes a thermal inversion (cold air forms at the surface of the water and is blanketed by warm air above). This position of cool and warm airs produces fog, but seldom does it produce rain. Heavy rainfall has only been recorded two or three times in a century. The annual average temperature is 66°F.

During the Spanish Empire, the saltpetre extracted from Atacama was used in the production of gunpowder, and also of fireworks. A few years into the second half of the nineteenth century, it was discovered that nitrate made a good fertiliser. From extracting guano, Chile moved to mining nitrates. The deposits at Atacama were the largest in the world and the mineral fetched good prices everywhere.

The Times, Tuesday, 15 April 1879: "The war in South America. Valparaiso, 6 April (by telegraph from Rio de Janeiro). The Chilean government have formally declared war against Peru." *The Times*, Wednesday, 23 April 1879:

Chile and Peru. Lloyds telegram from Lima, 14 April. The coast is entirely blockaded by the Chilean squadron, and our [Peru's] fleet up to the present time has been of no use. Peru is disposed to accept favourable conditions which, it may be hoped, will soon lead to the conclusion of peace. The duties on nitrate of soda will be lowered or equalised. Negotiations continue. [President Nicolás de] Pierola [of Peru] urges peace. The issue depends upon the reply to his propositions expected to be sent today.

But the correspondent was too optimistic. Chile never for a moment appeared to settle for any kind of peace that did not admit her absolute victory. Chilean troops took the town of Calama with the loss of fourteen killed and wounded, but captured a Bolivian general, ten officers and twenty-six soldiers. The defeated Bolivian army fled. Chile gained territory and soon had the use of the lines of the National Nitrate Railways Company to transport troops and supplies. The line had been completed in 1875 for Peru on a £1.5m British mortgage loan. The Chilean fleet, meanwhile, took up a position outside the port of Iquique—the terminus of the Peruvian nitrate railway—to start a blockade. Chilean naval units shelled the guano loading platforms up and down the coast of Peru.

At length, *The Times* felt it had to explain what was going on. On 10 May 1879 its leader reminded readers that "the war that broke out some weeks ago" had caused concern in England, and then told readers why this should be so.

Chile and Peru and Bolivia are known to the world as petty communities which have hindered their own progress, and inflicted much purposeless injury on people that hardly know of their existence, by aping the political ambitions of powerful states. They boast of an immense extent of territory, stretching along the Pacific coast of South America from the dreary wastes of Patagonia almost to the Equator. They have, it is reckoned, a population of some seven millions, of whom probably half are barbarous or semicivilised indians, while of the rest only a minority are of pure white blood. But their spendings and borrowings have been on a scale proportionate rather to their areas than to their population. The name of Peru, with its national debt of more than fifty millions sterling, is painfully familiar to English investors. Chile has been more modest in her claims and more careful in her outlay. She has borrowed not quite thirteen millions. Even Bolivia, the poorest and least promising of the three republics, has saddled herself with obligations amounting to three millions and a half. We do not mean to assert that there is no difference between the three states. Chile has treated her creditors with honesty and good will, and her credit, though lately tried by various reverses, has in consequence been upheld far above the level of the common run of South American republics. Of Peru and Bolivia it is unnecessary to speak.

Unfortunately, whether poor or prosperous, solvent or bankrupt these states think it is necessary for their dignity to keep up the show of military and naval power. Both Peru and Chile have spent a vast amount of money on their fleets, and each power possesses a couple of very powerful ironclads, concerning the respective merits of which there is a controversy. Bolivia can hardly be said to have a seaboard, and she has yet no navy; she disposes, however, of an army of 2,000 men, commanded by eight generals and 1,013 inferior officers, and this remarkable instrument of war is said to cost her two thirds of her annual revenue. The possession of weapons is a public danger among excitable people, and the South American republics, like the reckless fellows who swagger with revolvers and bowie-knives about their towns, are too prompt in appealing to arms on the slightest provocation.

The paper went on to say what the war was being fought over and to define the quite considerable economic interest Britain had in it. On nitrate it said: "The value of this mineral as an agricultural manure is now universally recognised..." Peru "was jealous of the menaced competition of the Chilean companies" and therefore made a state monopoly of its resources and allegedly persuaded Bolivia to do the same. "A crushing export duty was imposed" on the Chilean companies owning the deposits and therefore Chile

> took the law into her own hands... [and] had a legitimate *casus belli* against Bolivia, if not directly against Peru.
>
> The British farmer was threatened with a further rise of prices, brought about, if the Chilean contention be admitted, by gross injustice and scandalous contempt for treaties... [meaning that of 1866, which set the boundaries between the two countries].
>
> English interests were, therefore, directly involved in the prolonged negotiations between Chile and Bolivia.

It was still too early for *The Times* to know of the other British interests: the volume of investment in nitrates, which would only become evident later.

By 30 April *The Times* reported that "intelligence received at Lloyds from Iquique, dated 23 April, states that all vessels that were in this port and in the neighbourhood have left. Since the departure of the Chilean workmen nothing has been done in the Interior". Ecuador made an attempt to mediate and sent an agent to Valparaíso early in May, but the effort was rejected by Chile.

It became a long war, with a few major battles and many skirmishes. It would be fought with modern weapons and equipment, evolved out of the experience of the Paraguayan war, and more importantly, the technical developments resulting from the Franco-Prussian war. Many families, on both sides, lost all their men. In Chile, a sense of national pride took thousands to their deaths at the front. The army, trained in the tough traditions of San Martín and O'Higgins, fought fiercely. The navy, Chile's strongest force, demonstrated the discipline and courage inherited from the years when Lord Cochrane had led the service.

One of the biggest battles of the war—and certainly the only considerable naval contest—took place at Iquique. Chilean troops and naval units encountered a combined force of Peru and Bolivia over a stretch of coastline between Iquique and Tacna, both in Peru. For Peru it was a difficult contest. Its army, which it thought better, and certainly was bigger, than that of Chile, faced a well organised force from Chile. In the navy matters were similar, though luck played an important part. On 17 June *The Times* published news of the battle of Iquique, which had taken place on 21 and 23 May. Peru had lost the ironclad *Independencia* which had run aground in shallow water while trying to capture a fleeing Chilean ship: "After the crew and part of her armament had been removed, the vessel was burnt to prevent her falling into the hands of the Chileans." Peru's other ironclad, the *Huascar*, had rammed the Chilean wooden ship *Esmeralda*, commanded by one Captain Thomas, with 150 men aboard. Thomas had tried to take the *Huascar* with a group of men from the *Esmeralda*. They had been overpowered and only forty Chileans had survived. Chile, however, won the battle.

The Peruvian action in the battle was heroic and deserving of praise, but the loss of one of their two ironclads was a severe blow to the morale of the navy and to Lima. As if to counter this reverse, Peru learnt that Bolivia had raised an army of 8,000 men; Peru had 9,000 near Iquique and had left another 6,000 at Lima.

But by then whatever Bolivia did was unimportant to Chile. The command at Santiago rejected the possibility of invading the eastern highlands of Bolivia and virtually ignored that rival for the next four years. Chile intensified the blockade of the northern Peruvian coast up to Callao, and its army progressed slowly up the coast towards the Peruvian capital. Once again Chile was accused of putting ashore, among its troops, its most distasteful social elements: criminals freed to fight in Peru, cut-throats who were offered pardon if they survived combat and an assortment of convicted stranglers and thieves.

Twenty months after the battle of Iquique, with the control of the sea long secured and the mining operations under Chilean management, the Chilean army captured Lima on 17 January 1881. The troops entered the old capital; the *Limeños* resisted as far as they could, but they were unaccustomed to fighting and were unaware that their army could be beaten. The occupation of Lima was seen as the end of the war in Britain, even though a peace settlement was a long way off.

On Saturday, 22 January 1881, *The Times* was beside itself with admiration—which is why some figures may seem exaggerated—for Chile.

> The war between Chile and Peru has culminated in the complete defeat of the forces of the latter, and the Peruvian capital is now in the hands of the Chileans... Blow after blow, in quick succession and with decisive effect, has been struck by the Chileans. They have followed up each advantage and pressed their adversaries hard, and now they are masters of Lima. To the number of twelve thousand the Chilean troops landed at Corayaco, and subsequently drove out of Lurin the Peruvian garrison of nine thousand men. The next fight took place at Chorrillos, towards which after attacking Callao, the Chileans directed their operations, and near it... a great battle was fought. It resulted in the overthrow of the Peruvian troops, who were driven from their positions with heavy loss, 7,000 of them being killed and 2,000 being taken prisoners. A third battle was fought with the same result. The Chilean army attacked and routed its opponents at Miraflores. Their overthrow seems to have been complete. The brother of the dictator Pierola and the Peruvian war minister were made prisoners, and the Dictator himself fled. This decided the fate of the Peruvian capital, which was occupied by the Chileans on the 17th... Callao also was captured, a result only to be expected considering the proximity to the fallen capital... [Nicolás de] Pierola is credited with a design to protract the struggle still further and to carry on hostilities in the mountain regions far away from the sea... Guerrilla warfare might be prosecuted there indefinitely...
>
> The Chileans have no doubt accomplished a surprising feat of arms. They have been brave, even to the verge of audacity, and almost uniformly successful; they have triumphed over grave difficulties and a multitude of surprises, in the rapid development of events, in the overthrow of preconceived ideas of superiority, the campaign which has resulted in the capture of Lima is, in South American warfare, the parallel of that which ended in the capture of Paris... The People of Lima and Callao have often talked about spending their last dollar and shedding their last drop of blood in the struggle and they will be reluctant to recognise that they are vanquished in a contest with a state supposed to be inferior in

resources. It will be bitter to own that they who have been somewhat boastful as to their prowess are at the mercy of their foe...

The war had been waged with so much fierceness and obstinacy that many new passions have been enlisted... It is no longer a question of guano and nitrate of soda...

Chilean politicians had "begun to discuss the propriety of obtaining territorial compensations..."

The Chileans looted and pillaged the city which had once been the stronghold of the Spanish Empire. Not since the liberator, General Bolívar, and his southern supporter, General Sucre, had entered the city had the *Limeños* seen such fighting, and never so much robbery. During those warm summer days of January the Chileans, tired by the austerity of a slow progress from southern Peru to the capital, were let loose by their officers. The library of Lima, which contained 58,000 volumes, was set ablaze. Although Lima was no longer a seat of learning as were other cities of the old empire, and although the library was by no means a large one, it was inevitable that comparisons should have been made with the burning of the library of Alexandria. Here was a useful recourse to propaganda which was expected to go some way towards repairing the humiliation of the invasion of the capital. The press of the European capitals regretted the fire and the pillaging, and took their cue from Chile's critics who said that the Chileans had been driven by greed and desire for territorial gain without concern for culture. But then the subject was dropped. It had been a small library.

British sympathy was firmly with Chile, although *The Times* on 1 May 1883 accused the Chileans of delaying a peace treaty and of keeping troops in Lima to exact from Peru all the terms desired. Even this mild remonstration prompted a rejoinder by correspondents, who argued that Britain fully supported Chile.[2] A contemporary account of the dispute, *The War between Peru and Chili*, by the writer Sir Clements Robert Markham—adventurer, former secretary of the Royal Geographical Society, geographer to the expedition to Ethiopia (Abyssinia) in 1867-8, traveller, and explorer of Peru between 1852 and 1854—depicted governments in Lima as responsible for the origins of the conflict, but was nevertheless sympathetic with Peru. Lima had "established a nitrate monopoly in her own dominions which would injure the prospects of Chilean capitalists and labourers."

In general, however, the British heard of this war only by way of occasional and telegraphic reports on the foreign news pages. For the British the real issue would come later, and would concern the competition for nitrate-rich property.

Chilean troops remained in Lima for two and a half years, and for nearly three years on Peruvian territory. When they left, they took with them not only a large piece of Peruvian pride, but also kept several Peruvian coastal towns and all of Bolivia's access to the Pacific Ocean. On 17 May 1883, *The Times* reproduced a telegram dated in New York the day before which said:

> Intelligence received here from Valparaiso states that a treaty of peace between Chile and Peru has been signed by Señor Novoa, representing the Chilean government, and General Iglesias, president of the north of Peru. According to the terms of the agreement Peru cedes Tacna and Arica to Chile for a period of ten years at the expiration of which a plebiscite will be held, in order to determine to which country these provinces shall belong, the state

acquiring them to pay an indemnity to the other.

Thus the treaty of peace was signed at Ancón, the archaeological centre north of Lima.

Once the peace terms were known, the City of London wanted to know what was to happen with the British bonds in Peru. In the "Money and City Intelligence" section of *The Times* on Monday, 4 June 1883, a reader wrote to remind the Foreign Office publicly of the legal implications of the war for Britons: "Since 1870 Peru has contracted in England principally if not exclusively, a foreign debt amounting to about 32 millions nominal capital..." and he wanted to know which government was going to pay the debt on investments in the land now ceded to Chile. He was sure that bond holders should have the first claim on payments as soon as the question was answered.[3]

The British were to be confirmed in the rightness of their sympathy for Chile when some time later, the government in Santiago signed a convention with that in London to satisfy the claims of British investors. Chile had agreed to such an arrangement in order to be able to seek more capital in London for the exploitation of the newly-acquired territory.

> Convention with Chile. The *London Gazette...* contains the convention which was concluded between Her Majesty and the President of the Chilean Republic, on 4 January 1883, for the settlement, by means of a Mixed International Commission, of the claims of British subjects arising out of the acts and operations effected by the forces of the Chilean Republic in the territories and coast of Peru and Bolivia during the then existing war.[4]

Although peace had been signed, evacuation took a little longer still. It was only on Thursday, 25 October 1883 that *The Times'* readers were told the withdrawal had begun three days before.

> The Peruvians are now in possession of the capital. The Chileans have left for Chorrillos. The custom house at Callao was handed over to the Peruvian authorities yesterday afternoon. The population of Lima is quiet. No demonstrations occurred on the departure of the Chileans.

Some weeks later, on 29 November, the paper reported that the Chilean army and navy had completed their removal from Peru. Well, almost; they stayed on a stretch of coastal land which they had not held before. In 1860, Chile's most northern point had been Mejillones, just north of the Tropic of Capricorn. After the war and once the frontier was finally drawn, Chile had extended 330 miles northwards, to a line between Arica, in Chile, and Tacna, in Peru. Bolivia now had no exit to the sea. That too was confirmed by treaty.

The Times, Monday, 7 April 1884: "A truce between Chile and Bolivia for an indefinite period was agreed yesterday [4 April]..." They had hardly exchanged a shot in anger for nearly four years. A few days later, on 10 April:

> A despatch received by the Chilean minister to France states that under the terms of the truce concluded... between Chile and Bolivia, the portion of the Bolivian territory occupied by the Chilean forces will remain under Chilean law. Trade will be free between Chile and Bolivia.

In addition to permitting Bolivia to trade on the Pacific coast through Chilean territory,

Chile undertook to construct a railway from the port of Arica to the Bolivian capital, La Paz.

The war was at an end and Chile had come out of it enriched, in spite of the reparations demanded by foreign investors. The "age of manure" had begun—it was "manure more precious than gold or silver".5

Chile moved from war to prosperity and expansion. Its cities grew, its urban population more than doubled in the next twenty years. Visitors were delighted by Chile's main towns. One, Frank Vincent, had nothing but praise for Valparaíso in 1885. It was a city where English language was used as much as Spanish, and the money was all in pounds sterling.

> I was struck by the very civilised look of the famous Chilean seaport... In the dining-room of the hotel the electric light was used, as well as in very many of the stores... The sidewalks are smoothly and neatly flagged. The architecture of some of the buildings is very fine... The principal streets are threaded by tramways. The trams, or cars, are of two stories as in Paris and other European cities. But a Valparaiso conductor is not paralleled in any other city anywhere—for it is a woman.6

The capital, Santiago, was equally the subject of admiration. A visitor named W. D. Boyce found that Santiago had no equal.

> No city in the world has a finer location. There are many beautiful drives... The Alameda Avenida Delicias, the great boulevard of Santiago, is six hundred feet wide and runs the full length of the city. The finest private houses front on the Alameda. The largest of these are of Spanish style, being built around a courtyard, or patio... Sixty-seven miles of electric tramways are operated by a private company, which also supplies electric light...7

Who were the European empire builders who had brought this sophistication about?

George Edwards is reputed to have jumped ship while on a British vessel which called at Valparaíso during the early years of independence. He earned a living selling eggs. He failed to introduce the custom of an English-style breakfast, but still managed to make enough money to buy a small extension of property. He was a supplier of food to workers in the guano mines in northern Chile, and also to the troops during the war of the Confederation. All this enabled him to increase his profits and acquire more land and some mining interests. These he expanded to become, at the end of his life, one of the several British millionaires in South America, well established in banking and mining.

According to some descendants of Edwards, the millionaire's name entered fiction by courtesy of Joseph Conrad. In Conrad's *Nostromo* (1904), the story of the silver mine owner at the fictitious township of Santo Tomé, in an imaginary South American country, is understood by some to have been inspired in part by accounts heard about the Edwards family in Chile. In the novel, the mine owner sees his fortune as a means to political progress and power, though he is also presented as an idealist. When a military coup takes over government, the mine owner decides to hide his fortune, but it is lost at sea while in transfer to a secret island. The man, Nostromo, entrusted to sail the silver to the island, finds that all believe the fortune to have been lost; he is able to recover it from the sea bed in small quantities and become rich himself. Nostromo is accidentally shot, but confesses his plot to the wife of the mine owner. Conrad is thought to have taken

Nostromo from the character of a first mate on a ship in which the writer sailed, off the coast of Venezuela. How much the author took from the Edwards' life and how much from another character of the time, John Thomas North, is not known. Conrad's own life in those years is a mystery.

Another name, which merits monuments in Chile, is that of William Wheelwright. He was born in Newbury Port, Massachusetts, but from the time of his arrival in South America he was closely linked to English commercial interests. He went to sea at the age of twelve and it was as the captain of a merchant ship that he was wrecked off the coast of Buenos Aires in 1822. He sold all the cargo he could salvage, and went to Chile two years later. His fortune, and fame, started with a small coaster which he bought and used to supply goods to the Pacific ports, before the Spaniards had been fully evicted. For a time he was a United States diplomatic agent in Guayaquil, but returned to Chile and the coastal trade in 1829 and after that went to Britain in search of money for investment in the Pacific. In 1840 he won a charter in London to start a shipping service and with two ships he launched the Pacific Steam Navigation Company, which thirty years later operated with fifty ships. From 1849 he was responsible for laying the tracks for several short railway lines servicing the northern mines of Chile. In 1850 he gave Chile its first telegraph wire. In Valparaíso he built a lighthouse, installed a gas supply and laid the waterworks. From Chile he moved to Buenos Aires where, in 1863, with British money, he obtained the concession to build part of the Grand Central Argentine Railway—one of the country's two main lines. He went on to take part in the construction of other railways and was among the initiators of the Transandine railway—though this was not completed until the first decade of the twentieth century. Wheelwright died in London, aged 75, in 1873, leaving a fortune to his widow and only daughter, and large sums to charity. In Quilmes, south of Buenos Aires, a small monument remembers the man.

And there was John Thomas North, who became known as the "Nitrate King". There are no monuments to him in Chile; but there are many volumes—in English and Spanish—on the fortune he built out of the nitrates boom; the investments he encouraged with the support of British business; and on his attempts to manipulate the politics of Chile.

North was born on 30 January 1842, at Holbeck, not far from Leeds, in Yorkshire. He was the son of a well-established coal merchant. At the end of his apprenticeship as a mechanical engineer, at the age of 23, he married the daughter of a local Conservative and member of Leeds Town Council. In spite of this solid middle-class background, North would always claim a humble beginning. He went to Chile in 1867 as a foreman on an engine construction plant at Carrizal but left that job to work in the town of Iquique, where he learned about nitrates and became acquainted with the many Britons who owned and ran the mines.

In 1878 North took a lease on Iquique's water supply service, a vital commodity in the arid desert. The war of the Pacific came soon after and, even though the water plant installations were damaged, North did well out of the war. He was compensated for losses he suffered and for some which he was said not to have suffered but claimed for anyway. But more important than that was that he bought depreciated Peruvian nitrate mine certificates—with credit from Chilean banks—and thus his nitrate fortune began. By 1884 he had reached agreement with other nitrate producers to arrange a "production combination" (a cartel) by which the world's demand was satisfied, but never in quantities sufficient to force the prices down.

The rapid growth of his nitrate empire came under the severe scrutiny of the *Financial News* and the *Economist* in London. The two papers warned the public against buying the nitrate certificates with eyes closed. But North had not only a remarkable capacity for business and money making, he also had great charm and a warm social manner which rapidly won over banks and investors to his side.

The *Financial News*, though threatened with action for libel, became bitingly sarcastic in its comments on North's riches. On 14 June 1888, it wrote:

> The latest good story about our friend colonel North is that he was heard lamenting there were not more elements in nature than air, earth and water, as they were such nice things to finance. In Tarapacá he has made himself master of all the existing elements. With his Nitrate Companies and Nitrate Railways he controls all the saleable earth in the province. With his sea-water condensers, his water barrels and his Pica concession he monopolises the drinking materials. It is generally understood that before the recent break in Nitrate Railways diverted his attention he was elaborating a scheme for placing the atmosphere of Tarapacá under the care of a limited liability company, with an airy capital of several millions sterling...

Just as he made money he enjoyed spending it, and he revelled in the publicity that his wealth brought him. The most spectacular show of North's concern for contacts and publicity was a party held on 4 January 1889 to celebrate the New Year and North's departure to Chile to visit his domains. Eight hundred guests—peers, knights, bankers, government officials, senior officers of all the services, and business associates—were invited to a banquet and ball at the Hotel Metropole, Whitehall Place. It cost North £10,000 and he thought the money well spent.

When he left for Chile in February he took with him a complete fire station as a gift for Iquique, and many other gifts for government officers and institutions. And to make sure that every step he took would receive adequate publicity his retinue included several journalists. Among these, the most prominent was the former correspondent of *The Times*, William Howard Russell, who published a book on the visit, *A Visit to Chile and the Nitrate Fields of Tarapaca*, in London the following year. Two other journalists in the North tour were Melton Pryor, staff artist on the *London Illustrated News*, and Montague Vizetelly, of the *Financial Times*. North said later that it had cost him £20,000 to take his guests, all expenses paid, to Chile. A ship, the *John Thomas North*, named after the millionaire by one of his associates, would be later remembered in a poem by John Masefield—probably as a result of the poet's visit to Iquique, and short residence in Santiago, during 1894.

In Chile North has been accused of supporting the 1891 rebellion against President José Manuel Balmaceda, who sought greater Chilean participation in the nitrates business controlled by foreigners. The civil war that resulted from the rebellion was in stalemate from the beginning. The Chilean navy and other supporters of the foreign nitrate operations occupied the north; Balmaceda and his army were strong in the south. They had a desert between them, and neither had enough strength to defeat the other. Balmaceda, depressed by the deadlock, committed suicide in September 1891.

In the aftermath, much Chilean opinion became strongly opposed to North and the nitrate production operators. However, North remained the "Nitrate King" until his death from a heart attack in May 1896, a few days after he had given a party for four hundred guests. His estate entered for probate was not large: £260,000 in England apart from properties abroad. Evidently his capacity for spending almost matched his undoubted talent for making money.[8]

The nitrate fortunes grew until the First World War. Chile then supported its British friend while Germany, starved of the mineral needed for explosives, developed a synthetic substitute. The mining industry collapsed. Iquique's theatre, where the opera stars of Europe had performed, fell silent. The town, which had been one of the most modern in Chile, lost its bustle and life.

Before the First World War up to three million tons of nitrate were extracted each year. The duties paid for half of Chile's budget. In the middle of the twentieth century, the average extraction rate was in the region of 800,000 tons a year and that was largely kept for use in the district. The mines which had once employed 120,000 men, and had created a new working class in Chile by raising the workers and their families above the subsistence levels of farm labour, were reduced to a work force of 10,000 in 1970.

NOTES:

1. See Chapter 7.
2. Stephen Williamson, MP, *The Times*, 3 May 1883. Williamson was a partner of Balfour, Williamson & Co. Ltd, which had an interest in the nitrates mining and shipping. There are many volumes on the nitrates war and on the nitrates railways. See Blakemore, below.
3. *The Times*, 8 April 1884, letter from the Committee of English Nitrate Certificate Holders.
4. *The Times*, 12 April 1884.
5. F. A. Kirkpatrick, *Latin America*. (Cambridge University Press, 1938), p. 228.
6. Quoted in Bradford Burns, *Latin America*, p.140.
7. Quoted in Bradford Burns, *Latin America*, pp. 140-1.
8. Two interesting books on the nitrates war and the fortunes made in Chile, and which offer diametrically opposite views, are Dr Harold Blakemore's *British Nitrates and Chilean Politics 1886-1896: Balmaceda and North*. (Athlone Press, London, 1974), and Dr Hernán Ramírez Necochea's *Balmaceda y la contrarevolución de 1891*. (Editorial Universitaria, Santiago, 1958). The English press reports on North are quoted from Blakemore's book.

Chapter Eleven

THE BEAGLE CHANNEL,
ARGENTINA-CHILE, 1902

Royal arbitration (cartoon by Mayol in 'Caras y Caretas')

Argentina and Chile have been redrawing their boundaries for two centuries, and had never been friendly about it. In 1873, during the administration of President Sarmiento in Argentina, Chile laid claim to Patagonia, a territory that was marked as uninhabited on most maps. Chile was in the process of expanding its territory to the north and also wanted possession of the southern wasteland which it argued had been allocated to Chile since the time of the Spanish colony. There was a mountain range separating Chile from Argentina and the land claimed by Santiago. Buenos Aires argued that the southern region was an extension of the provinces of the River Plate. Sarmiento was not too concerned at the time with keeping Patagonia, but he rejected Chile's claim.

The nitrate war of the Pacific prompted Argentina to press Chile to sign away the disputed territory. With the intervention of the United States minister in Buenos Aires, General Thomas O. Osborne, a frontier was agreed. In May 1879 Chile formally gave up its claim to Patagonia, "thus settling this long vexed question," according to *The Standard* 1 in Buenos Aires. In 1881 a treaty drafted by the foreign minister of Argentina, Bernardo de Irigoyen, was approved by the two governments. It gave Chile half of the southern island of Tierra del Fuego and the coasts of the Magellan straits, in exchange for abandoning its claim to Patagonia. The accord was completed by the signature of a Protocol Agreement in 1893.

In the sharing of the southern islands, the ownership of three small rock formations, the islands of Nueva, Lennox and Picton, at the eastern end of the Beagle channel—named after the ship of Captain Fitz Roy in 1830—remained unclear, if not entirely unresolved. For a few Britons, members of the missionary societies of South London perhaps, the only association with those islands can be found on Picton, where in October 1851 the English missionary Allen Gardiner and six colleagues were killed trying to establish a settlement at Banner Cove.

The treaty of 1881 contained seven articles which were an attempt to define the boundary between the two countries. A clause in article 111, known as the "islands clause", also aspired to define the area in litigation.

> As for the islands, to the Argentine republic shall belong Staten island, the small islands next to it, and the other islands there may be on the Atlantic to the east of Tierra del Fuego and of the eastern coast of Patagonia; and to Chile shall belong all the islands to the south of Beagle channel up to Cape Horn and those there may be to the west of Tierra del Fuego.2

The way Argentina wished the division to be seen was that everything on the Pacific side of the continuation of the mainland boundary was for Chile; everything on the Atlantic side was for Argentina. Chile, however, saw the matter differently: the three islands at the eastern end of the Beagle were placed south of the flow of the channel and therefore belonged to Santiago. Buenos Aires interpreted the islands to be "next to Staten Island" and hence to belong to Argentina.

Semantic confusion approached conflict proportions at the end of the century. By then Chile was fully recovered from its war with Peru and on its way to becoming immensely rich from the export of nitrate. Argentina had survived the financial crisis of 1890—which had threatened the collapse of the Baring Brothers banking group, the Argentine government's agents in London—and was inordinately rich on the income from its cattle and grain exports. The two countries began to arm for conflict. Both governments ordered ships and artillery in Europe. Britain watched with alarm: the two countries were customers and suppliers of food, raw materials and dividends. War between them might be more damaging to British interests than to their own. As Christmas 1901 approached, Chile and Argentina were on the verge of war. Britain ordered its ministers in Santiago and Buenos Aires to find a way to prevent an armed conflict.

Five months later war had been averted. Argentina and Chile agreed to put to arbitration by the British crown any future disputes. But the South American arms race had to be stopped too.

The Times, 19 May 1902:

> Santiago de Chile: The good offices of Mr Lowther, the British minister to Chile, have been exerted for some time past with the Chilean government with a view to devising an arrangement for the limitation of armaments. The arrival of the new Argentine minister gives encouragement to the hopes of an arrangement. The first important meeting took place this afternoon between the president, the minister for foreign affairs, the Argentine minister, and Mr Lowther. The most prominent difficulty is Argentine distrust of the Chilean negotiations for a settlement with Peru and Bolivia, as it is suspected in Argentina that the Chileans are desirous of further territorial acquisitions, while, on the other hand, Chile is distrustful of Argentine interference in those negotiations, which she would not tolerate. The boundary dispute between Chile and Argentina may be regarded as having been eliminated with the departure of Sir Thomas Holdich's commission and the subsequent decisions.
>
> Buenos Aires: The minister of foreign affairs authorises the statement that, through the friendly mediation and advice of the British representatives, the difficulties in the way of an arrangement for the limitation of armaments by Chile and Argentina will probably be overcome on the basis of a distribution of the warships now building equally between both countries. It is expected confidently that the negotiations will be concluded in the course of the week.

The dispute occupied snippets of space in the European press during the next few days, and as May moved to a close, so did the negotiations to prevent battle for the three tiny insignificant islands. A series of meetings was held in the two South American capitals. *La Tribuna,* a pro-government paper in Buenos Aires, accused Chile of delaying a treaty. Chilean papers said that in Buenos Aires opposition to eventual ratification of a deal was being organised in the national Congress.

On 26 May, *The Times* correspondent in Buenos Aires assured his readers that the deal had been made.

> I am officially informed that an agreement has been finally concluded with Chile for the limitation of armaments, each country retaining its naval equipment now afloat and rescinding the contracts for vessels in course of construction. No period is fixed for the duration of the agreement. An arbitration treaty has not yet been definitely arranged, but is expected to be arranged this week, forming the basis of a general agreement for arbitration on future international difficulties. It is stated... that the preamble of the proposed treaty embodies the principle of a mutual understanding, Argentina observing neutrality in affairs on the Pacific coast, and Chile abstaining from territorial *aggrandisement.*

It was no small achievement by the British ministers. They had brought Argentina and Chile to agree to cancel orders for warships applied for. Finally, on 28 May 1902, the crisis was over.

The protocol with reference to the limitation of naval armaments and the treaty of general arbitration in the case of future difficulties between Argentina and Chile were signed in Santiago... A further protocol was also signed stipulating that the demarcation of the frontier... shall be under the supervision of British officials... It is recognised that the satisfactory outcome is due greatly to the tact shown and the advice given by Sir W. Barrington in Buenos Aires and by Mr Lowther in Santiago...

In a leading article the next day, *The Times* issued congratulations all round.

For a whole generation the danger of a desperate struggle between these States has overshadowed and retarded the development of South America... Only last Christmas there was a moment when that menace suddenly assumed an aspect of gravity... But the signature of the three protocols which have been completed, and of the fourth which is now under consideration, should go far, in the absence of untoward contingencies, to render the danger remote for many years to come. By these documents the governments of President Riesco and President Roca have pledged themselves to a course which should render a pacific settlement of the controversies between them assured... They have appointed His Majesty King Edward general arbitrator in their differences... The implicit confidence reposed, by the governments and the peoples of both nations, in the perfect impartiality and justice of our Sovereign in matters of the deepest concern to them cannot but be grateful both to King Edward himself and to his subjects... It is no small tribute to our character for judicial fairness that, at a time when others seek to brand us as high-handed oppressors who know no law but our will, two leading States of a great continent should voluntarily submit these large and difficult questions to our judgment... Both have pledged themselves again and again to abide by the award of the arbitrators, and there is no reason to question the sincerity of their intentions. The boundary question itself, as we have often remarked, would not at any time have justified a fratricidal war between twin republics of the same blood and religion and with the same history... Chile was determined not to allow Argentina to interfere in the affairs of the Pacific coast. Argentina, on the other hand, was equally determined not to permit Chile to increase her territory at the cost of Peru or Bolivia, or to reduce Bolivia to the condition of a Chilian province in matters of commerce. Chile imputed to Argentina the design of undermining her influence in the Pacific, while Argentina taxed Chile with an ambition to become the dominant state of the continent. Both countries were well armed. The German military advisers of Chile assured her that this was the moment to strike, and that an invasion of the rich plains across the mountains was certain to prove successful. President Roca, on the other hand, did not conceal his resolve to ensure the supremacy of Argentina at sea, and had actually ordered four costly cruisers, of which the last was to be delivered in September 1903...

A decided victory for Chile would have meant the loss of her Patagonian territory by Argentina and the payment of a crushing indemnity. A decided victory for Argentina would have involved the destruction of the Chilian fleet, the restoration to Peru and Bolivia of the territories conquered from them in 1879-1882, and the surrender to Argentina of ports on the Pacific coast of Patagonia...

To their European creditors a contest must have been hardly less calamitous. The total foreign capital already embarked in Argentina exclusive of the public debts is estimated at the enormous sum of nearly £123,000,000. The amount invested in Chile is not nearly so large, but it is still very considerable... All that is needed to develop the republics is foreign capital, and foreign capital is ready to flow abundantly into them provided they continue to enjoy peace... This country has supplied, we believe, something like three-quarters of the capital invested in Argentine enterprises, and a yet larger proportion of that invested in Chilian enterprises in the past, and it is quite ready to engage in fresh undertakings in both states in the future. All it asks is the security which peace alone can bring.

The deal struck by Britain was a good one. It took Argentina and Chile more than sixty years to agree on the procedure of arbitration.

The incident passed quietly as far as Europe was concerned. Attention was drawn to preparations for the coronation of Edward VII in August; Scott's scientific research aboard the *Discovery*—then in Antarctica—and the difficult aftermath of the Boer War. South America was a place where there were railways, and beef, and also people who sometimes squabbled, but were not expected to go to war.[3] However, for the parties directly involved the matter was far from being closed. Seventy-six years later they armed for war again.[4]

NOTES:

1.   *The Times*, 28 June 1879.

2.   Award of HBM's government pursuant to the agreement of arbitration (compromise) of a controversy between the Argentine republic and the republic of Chile concerning the region of the Beagle Channel (HMSO, February 1978).

3.   In the second half of 1978 the Argentine military dictatorship, under General Jorge Rafael Videla, took Argentina to the brink of war, largely on a false triumphalist emotion generated out of the World Cup football victory of that year. Finally, the Vatican was asked to mediate. On Saturday, 3 December 1978, the *Buenos Aires Herald* reported that the Vatican's peace proposal had been accepted. The three islands in dispute went to Chile.

4.   Barros, Carolina; Fraga, Rosendo; Rodríguez Guaracchi, Eduardo: *Argentina-Chile, 100 Años de Encuentros Presidenciales.* (Centro de Estudios Unión para la Nueva Mayoría, Buenos Aires/Santiago, 1999). See also: Passarelli, Bruno: *El Delirio Armado, Argentina-Chile, la guerra que evitó el Papa.* (Sudamericana, Buenos Aires, 1998), and Tapia, Luis Alfonso: *Esta noche la guerra,* (Grijalbo, Santiago, 1998.)

Chapter Twelve
ANGLO-GERMAN BLOCKADE OF VENEZUELA, 1902-1903

Maracaibo, Venezuela, c.1900 (private collection)

B ritain and Germany blockaded Venezuela in 1902. They received the assistance of Italy and some sympathy from France. All four wanted Venezuela to pay its long overdue debts. The incident was the last in nineteenth-century-style gunboat diplomacy by Europe in the Americas. By now, the United States was no longer prepared to accept European influence in the region, as it was planning its own expansion in the area. Internal strife and economic depression had kept Washington out of the contest for ultramarine possessions and unable to compete with European colonialism, but now it was ready to make up for time lost.

José Martí, the Cuban revolutionary and publicist, writing in the newspaper *La Nación* of Buenos Aires on 22 November 1889, had forecast that the US would begin by imposing its rule on the island of Hispaniola. He had thought that Santo Domingo and Haiti would be the first points to be taken by the US intent on seizing the Caribbean.[1] But it was in his own country, Cuba, that Washington would take its initial action.

Cuba rebelled against Spanish rule in February 1895. The United States used the occasion to press Spain to end its rule in the Americas. After an explosion in one of its ships, the *Maine*, in the port of Havana, and pressure from the North American popular press, the US declared war on Spain on 25 April 1898. It was considered "a fine little war". Spain had been in no condition to wage war so far away, even if Cuba had once been its most powerful naval base in the region. By the Treaty of Paris, the Spanish-American war came to an end and a US-occupied Cuba was declared independent of Spain on the first day of 1899. With Cuba, Spain had lost Puerto Rico. The latter had been granted powers of self-government by Spain two years before, and now became a United States protectorate.

As the nineteenth century approached its close, moreover, the US forced Britain to accept arbitration in a disagreement with Venezuela over the drawing of the boundary with British Guiana.

Britain had seized from the Dutch what was to become its only mainland South American colony in the early years of the century. At the settlement of the Napoleonic wars, Britain had retained the colonies of Demerara, Berbice and Essequibo; the Dutch stayed in Suriname, and the French at Cayenne. In 1831 the three new British provinces had been named Guiana. Holland had disputed its colonial limits with Venezuela, and the dispute had been inherited by Britain. A truce had been agreed in 1847, but in 1879 each had accused the other of occupying border land. In 1887, Britain had been angered by Venezuelan objection to an extension of the western border of Guiana. British ships blockaded the mouth of the Orinoco river, and tried to force the Venezuelans to accept a new border. Venezuela applied for arbitration, but Britain refused it. They broke diplomatic relations.[2]

In 1895, President Cleveland of the United States—who, having come through an economic crisis, had given his attention to the annexation of Cuba, Puerto Rico and the Philippines—stated his views on British influence in the area in a special message to Congress: the US had to "resist by every means" the extension of British Guiana's border. Britain was forced to agree to an arbitration commission, which was formed by North America, Russia and England. A border line was agreed in 1899. It moved Venezuela's limits east of the river Orinoco, but still left Caracas unsatisfied in its claim for about 50,000 square miles of land in the former Essequibo province.[3]

In Britain the loss of land to Venezuela was hardly noticed. Few members of the public knew much about British Guiana, and the Boer War was affecting British households far more. But the United States, and President Cleveland especially, had come out of the border incident with prestige enhanced. Britain could be pushed back. The Monroe Doctrine against European intervention in the Americas, which had not been much invoked during its first century of existence, gained new currency. Washington prepared to extend southwards.

Venezuela had been born into debt to Europe. The republic of Colombia had been awarded a loan on a bond issue in England in 1823. When the republic was dissolved and Venezuela and Ecuador became independent states in September 1830, their debt was shared among the three countries. New Granada (Colombia) had accepted 50 per cent of the obligations and the rest had been divided among the two new states. Interest on the debt had been paid sluggishly, but paid it was and in 1862 Venezuela sent an agent to London to apply for a loan of another one million sterling. This was won without too much difficulty and on what had appeared to be reasonable terms. Before long, however, the repayment became a burden and took more than 50 per cent of the customs house revenue. Repayment had slowed down; the British bondholders felt cheated, but were unable to resort to any authority for help.

Germany, in the meantime, had begun to compete with Britain for commerce in the Americas. German traders took the precaution of learning Spanish and Portuguese and translating their advertisements and instruction manuals. This had won interest in the products of Germany—and of the United States, which operated in the same way—against those of Britain, whose merchants often made it a point of pride not to learn Spanish or Portuguese, and who presented their customers with technical literature in English. At the end of the century, a majority of the foreign merchant houses in Caracas were German, a few were North American, none British. But Britain remained the main source of finance.

Many years of civil strife in Venezuela had left the economy in ruins and with no money to pay the debts for manufactured goods to German importers or British banks. At the end of the century British officials added to their causes for disenchantment with Venezuela the loss of border land in Guiana to Caracas.

German merchants and British bondholders in Europe teamed up to put pressure on their respective governments. The Kaiser's administration gave in first. The British government resisted taking part in favour of bondholders. The subscription of bond issues for new republics was considered in London as an aspect of the British passion for gambling. Despite many disasters since the early years of independence, people persisted in putting large parts of their savings into bond issues for new republics. The enthusiasm for such ventures was, perhaps, a result of the affluence of Victorians. But the Foreign Office had studiously avoided taking action on behalf of bondholders. They were considered to be involved in private schemes which they entered with both eyes open. When they were a success, official London was delighted. When they failed, the Foreign Office looked the other way.

In Venezuela, however, as the Germans took the initiative, Britain was forced into action to avoid commercial, and diplomatic, loss. In 1899 the frequent changes of presidents of Venezuela came to an end in the person of Cipriano Castro who, as sometimes occurs with men suffering messianic delusions, was a mediocre politician who had been graced with a thick skin. After many years of civil war he had taken over an administration with an empty treasury and no means of paying Venezuela's creditors. He asked for patience while he looked for support in the United States. When the European powers pressed him harder for their money, Castro told them he could not pay.[4] Britain threatened to collect by force; Venezuela seized British property and harassed British subjects. That added an emotional content to what had been only a banking row.

On 14 August 1902, the British Admiralty prepared for action. A joint venture with Germany was arranged on 22 October by a memorandum from the British government. Six days later the Admiralty drew up plans for the seizure of all of Venezuela's gunboats. This was to precede formal blockade and the declaration of war. The ships were to be held until Caracas agreed to meet its commitments.

On 11 November, Britain advised Venezuela that any suggestion for solving the crisis, even a signal of good intentions, would be sufficient to postpone action and make way for renewed discussion. While that note was being sent to Venezuela, on the same day, the German authorities closed access to a peaceful settlement with the announcement of their support for the British suggestion of enforcing claims against Venezuela by the capture of the gunboats.[5]

What were described as the "first line" claims were, in the case of Germany, the smaller of Venezuela's debts: 1.7 million *bolívars* arising out of damages suffered by Germans up to 1900, mainly due to compulsory contributions to patriotic funds and the like. The British demands were more complex. However, the bulk of Venezuela's debt to British bondholders played a secondary role to more immediate demands.

the principal claims and complaints against Venezuela are based upon the seizure of several British vessels, the seizure of a railway line, and the ill-treatment of British subjects, together with arbitrary proceedings directed against British interests and property during the civil wars.[6]

Britain and Germany agreed that "in the event of the two powers having recourse to coercive measures" they would both make further demands. Germany wanted settlement of her claims arising specifically out of the 1899-1900 civil war, which amounted to three million *bolívars*, and also the formal guarantee of repayment to German creditors, especially those of the Disconto Gesellschaft Bank, of Berlin, granted in 1896. All of these totalled approximately 41 million *bolívars*.

On 17 November, Lord Lansdowne, the Foreign Secretary, notified the Germans of the British intention to "exact immediate payment of the pressing claims in the first category." Venezuela replied that it had domestic issues which demanded prior attention before the foreign obligations could be considered seriously. Germany, acting on the British notification with what some British banks saw as an obscene urgency, gave instructions that it would be taking action against Venezuela within twenty-four hours of an ultimatum. Towards the end of November, Lord Lansdowne warned Germany:

We observed that the German government proposed to claim an immediate payment of

1,700,000 bolivars, equal to £66,275, in satisfaction of their "first rank" claims. Our first rank claims would probably not exceed £10,000, and we thought it only fair that the cash payment to be made to each government by the Venezuelan government should be of the same amount. We should therefore ask for the same sum as that demanded by the German government as a payment on account towards the satisfaction of the total of our claims, which would reach a very large sum.[7]

It was not a very clear paragraph; but it told Germany to accept smaller payments in the beginning and to moderate demands, because Britain wanted parity and both claims would in the end involve considerable sums of money.

When questioned in the Reichstag, Count Bernhard von Bülow, the German Imperial Chancellor and Prime Minister, explained: "it was for us from the outset simply a matter of winding up a business rendered unusually difficult by the untrustworthiness of the debtor..."[8] It was necessary to "proceed with special coolness and circumspection in order that no disturbance of our relations with the other Powers might arise out of our action." Count von Bülow said that the *New York Herald* newspaper had to be singled out for its "perfidy" in trying to refute the justice of the German claims.

In London, some sections of Parliament were less than happy about the new bellicosity and about joint action with the aggressive and expansionist Germans. Keir Hardie, the Labour MP for Merthyr Tydfil, who had been a strong opponent of the Boer War, asked in the House of Commons if it was wise to become involved in yet more hostilities so soon after the war in South Africa. Hardie, and to some extent Charles Dilke, MP for the Forest of Dean, were concerned about the fate of Britons in Venezuela. But they were even more alarmed by the conditions of Britons in Britain.[9] People were out of work; unemployment figures were swollen by the return to civilian life of soldiers back from South Africa; the increase in the number of beggars on the streets was alarming; the papers carried letters from the Reservists' Society appealing to employers to find work for former soldiers; an early cold snap had made the lot of the poor that much worse, and the *Manchester Guardian* reported on courts hearing cases of suicide due to dire circumstances.

The European allies decided that a first step before action was to explore the views of the United States and were pleased to find "an encouraging attitude". The *Manchester Guardian*, on 25 November 1902, said that:

Great Britain and Germany have... sounded the State Department... in order to learn whether there would be any objections to their taking active measures to secure the collection of debts... The Department has been extremely cautious in dealing with these inquiries, but the substance of its replies in all cases has been set forth in the declaration of President Roosevelt that the United States does not construe the Monroe Doctrine to mean that it should shelter any of the American republics against the result of its own misdeeds... The only condition the President made was that the punishment inflicted by any European must not include the seizure of any American soil.

The German Imperial Navy Department confirmed that it had already given orders to three cruisers—*Amazone, Ariadne* and *Niobe*—to sail "with war equipment for service in Venezuela".

The offhand manner of Washington was due to the fact that it was preoccupied with the terms of an agreement with Colombia on a treaty to open a canal across Panama. The isthmus had seceded from Bogotá with the acquiescence, if not the support, of the United States. With US neutrality assured, the English and German press told one another and their readers that President Cipriano Castro would rapidly surrender to the powers. In the meantime, Britain ordered the second-class cruisers *Retribution, Charybdis* and *Tribune*, the sloop *Alert*, the destroyer *Quail* and the first-class cruiser *Ariadne*, the British fleet's flagship, to sail from Bermuda to La Guayra, and the cruiser *Indefatigable* to sail from Port of Spain. They were later joined by the cruiser *Pallas*. To Britain's seven ships, Germany put four into the operation. Venezuela made a last minute offer to make an annual contribution towards a unified loan until the debts were paid, but it was regarded as too late. The powers wanted a settlement.

Apart from the naval units ordered to the coast of Venezuela, Britain then had a small land force scattered in the Caribbean. In Bermuda it had stationed the 3rd Battalion, the Royal Warwickshires, the 4th Battalion, the Worcestershires, and the 1st Battalion, the West India Regiment—apart from a local garrison and militia artillery and two companies of Royal Engineers. In Jamaica and Barbados it had the 1st Battalion, the Lancashire Fusiliers and the 2nd Battalion, the West India Regiment.

A joint ultimatum was delivered in Caracas to President Cipriano Castro during the afternoon of 7 December. He was told to propose concrete forms of payment immediately under threat of the loss of Venezuela's naval units. The president gained a few hours by making himself inaccessible to the German and British ministers in Caracas, informing them that he was in deep consultation.

The press in England was pleased to note that only some "cheaply sensational" papers in the US had called the ultimatum a declaration of war. The news had been "received generally with absolute calm and indifference. There was something artificial about the sudden friendship of this country [US] for Venezuela seven years ago [in the Essequibo dispute], and the whole sentiment appears now to have evaporated..." wrote the *Manchester Guardian's* New York correspondent on 9 December. In Berlin, Chancellor von Bülow informed the Reichstag that:

> Venezuela, by her treatment of German representations, has given the Imperial government cause for serious complaint... The Germans settled in Venezuela up to 1900 suffered through forced loans, the seizure of cattle, and the pillage of their houses and estates a loss of about 1,700,000 bolivars, and during the last civil war that amount has been increased by three million bolivars... Moreover in the last civil war the Germans have been treated by the Venezuelan government troops with special violence, which, if it remains unpunished, might give rise to the impression that the Germans in Venezuela are to be left unprotected and to the mercy of foreign tyranny...

The day after the delivery of the ultimatums, President Cipriano Castro published an open letter. It was an eloquent expression of wounded dignity. He argued that he had been taken by surprise by two friendly nations which had not exhausted the full recourse to the law and to diplomacy. The statement omitted to mention the claims. That afternoon, the British minister in Caracas, Mr Haggard, and the German minister, Herr von Pilgrim-Baltazzi, made a precautionary withdrawal, to the British ship *Retribution* and the German cruiser *Vineta*, respectively, which were both in the port of La Guayra.

By 9 December both sides had taken action. Reuter's agency reported that one of Venezuela's main naval units, the *Bolívar*, had been captured at Port of Spain, Trinidad, where it had been sent in an effort to avoid capture. In the wake of that seizure, reports out of Caracas said that the Venezuelan fleet had been taken and four ships—*General Crespo, Totumo, Assun* and *Margarita*—had been towed out of La Guayra. Three of the ships—*Crespo, Totumo* and *Margarita*—were reported to have been sunk immediately. But the *Assun* had been spared on a plea by the French chargé d'affaires in Caracas because it was the property of a French resident. According to Reuter:

> in the afternoon several boats manned by 240 British and German sailors and towed by two launches entered the harbour... The Germans boarded the *Margarita*... and revolver in hand compelled the crew to abandon her. The Germans then smashed the torpedo tubes, compass and machinery, and left the vessel in the dock disabled... Sailors from the *Retribution* boarded the *General Crespo* and the *Totumo* and compelled those on board to lower the Venezuelan flag and retire, which was effected without resistance. These vessels were then towed to a station outside the Harbour... At two in the morning the *Retribution* towed both the *General Crespo* and the *Totumo* some distance further out. Since then neither vessel has been seen. The government maintains that the soldiers in the fort at La Guayra saw them blown up... and sunk. It is a fact that the *Retribution* returned alone to La Guayra a few hours later.
>
> The government complains that the German sailors ate the food which had been prepared for the Venezuelan crews of the captured ships.[10]

In evidence of this the correspondent quoted from the *New York Commercial Advertiser* which commented that:

> if the English alone had been demonstrating, they would not have thought it worth while to seize the four or five ramshackle tugs and converted ferry boats which constitute the Venezuelan navy. Certainly they would never have dreamed of sinking them.

When, a few days later, Britain made a disclaimer "of any sinking of the Venezuelan war vessels",[11] the *Manchester Guardian*'s New York correspondent wrote that this had caused "a distinctly good impression... In fact, the tension of feeling is noticeably less than yesterday." However, there was much soul-searching about possible attitudes if the blockaders were to turn away a ship from the United States. In the same edition of the Manchester paper a telegram from Berlin claimed that if any Venezuelan ships had been sunk the action would have been a joint operation of British and German ships, and not one of the Germans alone: "According to orders, the ships were to be captured before the blockade was begun. It is surmised that if one ship has been disabled or sunk military reasons necessitated such an action."

While this little difference was played out, the British press seemed pleased to reproduce the opinion held in the United States of President Cipriano Castro, which was not very high. Leader writers described him as incompetent and accused him of embezzling public funds, including what might have been used to pay the foreign creditors. The evidence for such charges was not offered.

After the loss of its fleet, and the close watch on its ports, Venezuela searched for arbitration, a request for which was transmitted to the State Department in Washington. The US was slow to react. It did not want to be seen to be supporting Venezuela against the powers; but neither did it wish to be accused of sympathising with European bullies in America.

In Caracas, on 11 December the government ordered all males between the ages of 18 and 50 to enrol in the militia: "Any refusing to enrol voluntarily, as patriotism demands, will be declared traitors and sent before a tribunal." There was a sense of imminent war in the town and a strong sentiment of dislike for all foreigners. President Cipriano Castro modified his public position to proclaim Venezuela's right to be negotiated with rather than dealt with. In support of this new line, he ordered the restoration of all property, including the railway stock, taken from Britons and Germans.

Even so, as the United States Stars and Stripes went up over the offices of the former British Legation and an American vice-consul took charge, the interim official was overwhelmed by a rush of terrified foreign residents seeking protection. The foreigners were not at that time the most enthusiastic supporters of their imperial rescuers. What helped to increase tension was the capture of three more Venezuelan vessels ("A fourth was rendered unfit for use"), by the *Panther, Vineta* and *Retribution* on 12 December.

In La Guayra, Venezuelan workers and troops were ordered to remove all the coal in the navy yard. The British-owned cars on the La Guayra railway were taken to the capital to prevent the allies from reaching the city by train in the event of a landing. General Ferrer, in command of the port defences, ordered trenches dug on the north side, facing the sea, of Mount Avila—a hill that separates the port and the capital.

On Saturday 13 December, the conflict took another turn for the worse when a British ship bombarded Puerto Cabello, a small settlement west of La Guayra. According to the commander of the British squadron aboard HMS *Charybdis*, Commodore Montgomerie, the shelling had resulted from the fact that the British steamer *Topaze*, registered at Cardiff, "was confiscated and pillaged while discharging coal. The officers and crew were subjected to great indignities." They were detained for a night without food or water, "then liberated and permitted to return to their vessels... the captain was compelled to lower his flag and the American vice-consul had to be informed." The vice-consul, in turn, had advised Montgomerie that the whole outrage had been committed "by the populace without the intervention of the local authorities".

The British commander demanded an apology and failing that

I announced my intention to bombard the fort, a thick-walled structure within easy range of our guns, and another battery mounting a few Krupp guns some distance away. I was informed that the mob was responsible and that the matter would have to be referred to a higher authority. I replied that if a dog I owned bit a man I should certainly be morally obliged to give satisfaction... Through the American consul I arranged to receive a reply to my communication... If he hoisted the American ensign I was to know that my demand had been complied with. When the hour for the expiration of the ultimatum came the ensign was hoisted, but was then hauled down again. I waited seven minutes and then fired on the fort and battery... There was a feeble response to our fire from the battery, but none from the fort, the soldiers in which fled like rats. One general, twelve other officers, twenty soldiers, and a number of criminal prisoners were, however, left behind in the fort... Our occupation was of brief duration. The *Vineta* took part in the bombardment. Instead of several persons being killed, as was reported, only two men were injured and these had their thigh bones broken in attempting to escape the fort.[12]

But the action served to shake the United States out of its indifference and President Roosevelt and the Secretary of State, John Hay, began to look seriously at the question of arbitration.

Italy ordered a cruiser, then in Canadian waters, to sail to a point off the coast of Venezuela. The Germans hoped that Rome would become a partner in the blockading alliance, but Italy delayed an announcement and said only that it was interested in securing payment of debts that it was owed by Venezuela if the other powers obtained payment of theirs. France also showed greater interest in the blockade, but said its concern was that of a creditor and not of a blockader.

At a meeting of the Bristol International Arbitration Association, members unanimously voted the resolution: "This meeting protests against the British fleet being sent to Venezuela without the question in dispute having first been submitted to arbitration."[13] *The Times* admitted that it had telegrams "many in number and varied in their contents, but when all is said and done, they do not very materially diminish our ignorance of the situation." It was obvious that the punishment was reaching a difficult stage. *The Times's* leader remarked that there was some doubt about how many Venezuelan ships had been captured, and how many had been sunk. President Cipriano Castro appeared to be only trying to gain time by speaking of arbitration.

> Perhaps the most remarkable sign of a change of mind on the part of the President, if it were established, would be his reported recognition of the validity of the claims which Italy has just lodged against his government, and which she apparently means to support by the despatch of a couple of ships. Unfortunately, the President in the course of his daily "interview" assumes an attitude which strengthens the doubts that are inevitable in dealing with a man of his character and antecedents as to the entire sincerity of his desire for peace. He says that it is clear Great Britain and Germany do not wish for a peaceful settlement.[14]

Authorities in Caracas ordered the arrest of British and German residents. "It is understood that the news of the arrest of British subjects at Caracas has evoked a certain feeling of satisfaction as it is thought that they are safer in prison than if exposed to the resentment of a street mob," wrote the *Manchester Guardian*.[15] Police in Caracas had taken 205 Britons and Germans, many of them prominent residents, who caused an accommodation problem at the station. The detainees made a comical gathering. The German railway office clerks addressed Herr Blohm, the manager, and Herr Knoop, a director, with more deference than they granted the police chief. One junior clerk tried to fan both men with a small piece of wood to dry the sweat of their brows. The portly owner of an English warehouse came with his Venezuelan houseboy and ordered him to go to the chief's home and ask the man's wife for a brandy and soda.

Outside the station, an angry mob shouted, "Death to Germans. Death to foreigners. English sons of bitches." The warehouse owner, mopping his face with a filthy handkerchief, was reputed to have assured Herr Blohm: "Well, they always shout these things, old boy. It makes them feel better. We're going to give them a hiding, you know," according to the report of one correspondent.

That night President Cipriano Castro addressed a crowd in front of the government palace and announced that British and German railway property in the country would be embargoed to counter the cost of the ships lost. The crowd marched from the square to the German Legation, where the minister's wife, too ill to leave with her husband, lay in terror. An unsuccessful attempt was made to force the doors. Every window in the building was smashed. After the crowd left, the house felt much cooler. The home of the German minister's doctor, the German Club—which acted as the local residents' commercial rooms—and the German-owned Hotel Klindt, favoured by European merchants for its German-style meats, were all stoned by groups of angry people. The police mistakenly arrested the Belgian chargé d'affaires, who was dragged through the streets protesting his neutrality. He was released within minutes and, in damaged clothes, had to make as dignified a return as possible.

Meanwhile, thirty men from HMS *Retribution* went ashore at La Guayra forced their way through a crowd near the port and rescued three Englishmen, directors of the La Guayra Harbour Company, who had spent the last two days barricaded in their offices. The troops later went to the British Legation and there rescued the vice-consul, one Germanically-named Mr Schunck, and his family.

Mr Herbert Bowen, the young US minister who had been 18 months at Caracas, announced his country's neutrality in the conflict. He agreed to represent British and German interests in Caracas. On his request, President Cipriano Castro had immediately released all the detained foreign residents. The German cruiser *Vineta* remained at La Guayra while the cruiser *Falke* and the gunboat *Panther* sailed for the nearby port of Carupano. The German cruiser *Gazelle* remained at the Dutch colonial port of Willemstad.

The capture of the Venezuelan ships was acclaimed by the British press with the enthusiasm that prominent headlines and pride of place reflect. The *Manchester Guardian* reported on "The seizure of the Fleet" and *The Times* announced "The Fleet seized", until a reader of *The Times* wrote to clarify a possible misinterpretation:

Venezuela does not possess any warship that deserves to be dignified by the title of cruiser, much less by that of battleship. She had a few gunboats and possibly a tramp steamer or two purchased and armed with a few guns. Her most effective vessel appears to have been the *Bolivar*, a torpedo gunboat of 571 tons, and about 18 knots speed.

Venezuela's navy records showed that it had sixteen ships. Its army had nine thousand men in 1901.[16]

What disturbed Britain and Germany more than the size of the fleet was the US reaction provoked by the seizure. *The Times* correspondent in New York wrote in the 12 December issue, as the British sloop *Alert* captured the Venezuelan troopship *Zamora* and the coastguard *23 de Mayo* in the Gulf of Paria, that:

it would be futile to attempt to deny that a bad impression has been created in this country by the events of the last two days in Venezuela. It is not the presence of British and German warships that is objected to. If a fleet ten times as strong had been despatched to Venezuelan waters the people of the United States would not have criticised the action taken... What is objected to is the sinking of Venezuelan warships, which gives the expedition a punitive character. It is significant that there is a general disposition to regard this action as due to the Germans and not to the British.

Questioned in the House of Lords as to what the state of the dispute was, Lord

Lansdowne could only offer the news that President Cipriano Castro's proposal for arbitration had been forwarded through the United States and was being studied by His Majesty's government. As an interesting aside, *The Times* offered the following:

> Incidentally, it appears that the first suggestion of a joint naval demonstration was made by Count Metternich some months ago, while the proposal that the first step in the operations should be the seizure of the Venezuelan gunboats was made by Lord Lansdowne on the recommendation of Admiral Douglas, who advised it as an alternative to a blockade.[17]

France notified the United States, Great Britain, Germany and Italy:

> that any provision for the settlement of their demands must recognise the pre-eminence of the French claims, and has in reply received the assurance that any arrangements made will provide for the security of French interests in the Venezuelan customs.[18]

Which meant that the French had held back their warships but were making sure they were in the front of the queue for the cash. The French wrote to President Cipriano Castro to remind him that Venezuela had signed a protocol in February 1902 by which French citizens would have all their claims up to 23 May 1899 made good, and those claims filed after that date would be considered under the terms of the Treaty of Friendship of 1885. On 20 December the Foreign Office published the formal note of initiation of a full blockade of the Venezuelan ports—to replace the initial measure of ships' seizure—which was expected to last thirty days.

The arbitration proposals began to gain some strength. Britain and Germany made a direct request for a settlement to the US. On 23 December, the *Manchester Guardian*'s New York correspondent wrote that:

> it is safe to say that if England and Germany continue to press President Roosevelt to act as arbitrator he will acquiesce. He will do so reluctantly... but he will do it if a reference to the Hague Tribunal is found to be impossible.

On the same day as this cheerful news was announced, the paper's readers were also told, just as prominently, that war had been declared on Venezuela. It was, the colonial secretary explained, a "proceeding which is merely a formality, intended to legalise the proclamation of the blockade." Vice-Admiral Douglas, on board the flagship *Ariadne*, had announced initiation of the blockade two days before. Further captures by the allied squadrons were the immediate result of the start of the blockade, but the action was now directed at all shipping. HMS *Tribune* and the Italian cruiser *Giovanni Bausan* accounted for the first catches, taking two schooners and three sloops with general cargoes. The German ship *Panther* signalled its greetings as it proceeded to La Guayra with two prizes captured at Maracaibo. The allies released an American owned ship, the *Caracas*, but it was not allowed to complete unloading at the port and was ordered out to sea. Washington lodged its first protest against the blockade. The allies received another unexpected protest, this time from the German community in the capital who objected to the harassment of the US ship.

On Boxing Day Roosevelt announced that he would not be acting as arbitrator, but referred the dispute to The Hague Tribunal and told the allies to submit their protocols there. Negotiations on the protocols' contents were held in Washington. The French congratulated Roosevelt and reformulated their demands. It was progress, even if the proposal for arbitration had to be moved to The Hague. Germany insisted on a first and immediate payment from Venezuela as a pre-condition to lifting the blockade. Germany, having decided to stage the Venezuelan adventure, made it a matter of prestige to secure the first payment. In the next few days, the allies continued to report the seizure of Venezuelan ships as if there was no limit to the country's merchant navy.

However, arbitration was now under way and a solution, which a few days before had been nowhere in sight, appeared to be possible. Venezuela had survived the humiliation of a blockade by weathering the dispute one day at a time. Life began to return to normal in the country's capital. A run on the national bank, when customers tried to convert their certificates for metal currency, was slowed to a more manageable pace by negotiations with the city's principal merchants to persuade them to continue to accept the certificates for trade. President Cipriano Castro regularly addressed the crowds from his palace and, having defeated a rebellion whose leaders had tried to benefit from the blockade crisis, appeared to be in firm control of Venezuela.

The new year began with an announcement by the allies that they had so far captured forty Venezuelan ships. They would be dealt with by a prize court, whether or not they had to be returned under arbitration later. The Germans landed troops at Puerto Cabello on 3 January, but stopped there only long enough to clear the harbour of fifteen small craft. This was to disable coastal trade and make the blockade more effective. As negotiations made progress in Washington, the Germans sailed to San Carlos, their next target. On 23 January 1903, the *Manchester Guardian* reported that:

> three German warships, the *Gazelle*, *Panther*, and *Vineta*, have been shelling the fortress of San Carlos. The fortress returned the fire. The village of San Carlos was burned by shells. Great excitement prevails among the German residents here. They protest against the action of the warships...

The impression caused in Washington was poor and infuriated the Monroe Doctrine partisans, but in Berlin the government explained that the "bombardment of San Carlos is regarded in official quarters as a simple act of force, consequent upon an effective blockade..."

For the next two days the German ships rained shells on San Carlos, until 23 January when Berlin announced receipt of a message stating that the fort had been set on fire by the *Vineta* and the *Panther*. That same day Washington announced with considerable pleasure that the Panama Canal treaty had been signed with Colombia—Roosevelt was on his way to creating a republic.

The attack on San Carlos was the last major action of the conflict. The German commodore explained, through the German chargé d'affaires in Washington, that the *Panther* had been

> in exercise of her blockading duty, navigating not far from the coast in order to enter the channel leading into lake Maracaibo, when she was suddenly fired upon by the fort. The commander of the *Panther* consequently had no alternative but to return the fire.[19]

France entered the negotiations as they advanced. Britain, Germany and Italy secured assurances that 30 per cent of customs revenue in Venezuela would be allocated to payment of the debt. As a settlement grew closer, anti-German feeling in the United States grew stronger. Washington was now keener than ever to reach an agreement quickly. It was not easy: each creditor wanted assurance of a large payment in fear that there would be no second opportunity. Britain's protocol on the method by which Caracas should make its payments was the first to be accepted. The friendliness in Washington towards Britain and discrimination against Germany and Italy became blatant. Finally, all the protocols were signed and their reference to The Hague Court for judgement was agreed. The blockade was lifted shortly before midnight on Friday, 13 February 1903.

Germany received its first payment of £5,500 on 14 March. Britain awaited the arbitration of the international court, as did Italy and France. The court also drafted the rules by which it ordered that never again would a power exact payment of another by violation of sovereignty. Count von Bülow told the Reichstag on 19 March that:

> we succeeded in attaining what we strove for... the matter was carried through to its end without weakness... The costs of the blockade cannot yet be estimated, but they are small. In view of the rather distressing financial position of Venezuela we refrained from claiming their repayment.[20]

President Cipriano Castro, his resignation rejected by the legislative bodies, his enemies at home defeated, his prestige enhanced, remained in office until 1908.

NOTES:

1.   See also *La Nación*, 20 December 1889.
2.   *South American Journal*, 5 March 1887.
3.   When Guyana became independent in 1966, Venezuela's claim was frozen for twelve years by an agreement in Geneva. In that year, Venezuela occupied all of the previously shared Ankoko island. An extension of the freeze expired in June 1982 and both countries reopened sporadic negotiations on a settlement.
4.   Miriam Hood, *Gunboat Diplomacy, 1895-1905*. (Allen & Unwin, London, 1975).
5.   *Manchester Guardian*, 17 February 1903.
6.   Reuter news agency; *The Times*, Monday, 8 December 1902.
7.   *Manchester Guardian*, 17 February 1903.
8.   Reuter, 19 March 1903; *Manchester Guardian*, 20 March 1903.
9.   *The Times*, 12 December 1902.
10. *The Times*, 15 December 1902.
11. *Manchester Guardian*, 11 December 1902.
12. *The Times*, 11 December 1902.
13. *Manchester Guardian*, 13 December 1902.
14. *Manchester Guardian*, 15 December 1902, 7 January 1903.
15. *Manchester Guardian*, 15 December 1902.
16. *The Times*, 15 December 1902.
17. *The Times*, 16 December 1902.
18. *Manchester Guardian*, 19 December 1902.
19. *Manchester Guardian*, 23 January 1903.
20. The reader might like to be reminded of an item of information contemporary with these events: in that year, 1903, the Irish writer Erskine Childers published *Riddle of the Sands*, a popular spy story involving an imaginary German raid on England.

Chapter Thirteen
THE LAST OF THE SMALL WARS

Uncle Sam and the Monroe Doctrine (Minneapolis Journal, 1912)

As the European operations against Venezuela came to an end so did the War of the Thousand Days: three years of strife between the liberal and conservative parties in Colombia.

Other small wars were fought.[1] But as the world advanced into the twentieth century and into wider dispute and greater destruction, the small wars lost their operatic character. Conflicts became less localised and acquired the appearance of appendages to complex international issues. The imposition of ideological hegemony took the place of the real-estate operations which had characterised nineteenth-century colonial expansion. The greed and selfishness that had been the mark of the great power interventions and gunboat diplomacy were still there, but in another guise. In the nineteenth century the powers had invoked more advanced civilisation to impose their colonial rights on wayward outposts. Religious wars had an ideological content, but usually they had a commercial motive equally as strong as the spiritual conflict. The twentieth century brought the argument of a need to defend a way of life, the desire to protect privileges acquired, the need to organise sections of the world within a political system to fight other systems.

President Roosevelt announced that the United States should "speak softly and carry a big stick". By the early years of the twentieth century, the US had wrested control of Panama from Britain and had moved on to strengthen its power in the entire Caribbean. After the Treaty of Panama, the US took into receivership the customs house of Haiti—a country which had been independent for a century but had only been recognised as such by the US in 1862—to demand a number of commercial concessions in compensation for debts. In the same year, 1905, US agents took over the administration of customs revenue of the Dominican Republic, which faced the threat of intervention by European creditors for failure to meet its commitments. The US was then in control of the economy of the island of Hispaniola.

The following year Roosevelt sent a Marine detachment to Havana to replace the tottering conservative government of Tomás Estrada Palma. This was not out of order. Under the Platt Amendment (1901) the US had granted itself the right to oversee Cuba's commitments and administration, and to establish a base there, which was built at Guantánamo. The US Secretary of State, William Taft, was appointed as interim governor of Cuba on 29 September 1906. On the day of Taft's installation, the *Diario de la Marina* praised the US decision and suggested that *de facto* annexation would be the most advisable course of action. Taft's business in the US—among them a campaign for the presidency, which he won in November 1908—then removed him from Cuba. He appointed as governor the man who had been the first US governor of Panama, Charles Magoon, who remained in Havana until January 1909.

The United States made its interventions obvious, almost ostentatious and accepted no criticism of the right to police the Americas. When two US citizens were executed in Managua, Nicaragua, in 1909, accused of aiding a conspiracy to bring down the government, a Marine landing was effected almost immediately. The detachment left soon after, but in October 1912 one hundred Marines were stationed at the US Embassy in Managua as a show of support for a succession of conservative rulers, and as a warning to nationalist rebels. Although the detachment was reduced in 1923, and reinforced again some time later, the Marines remained in Nicaragua until 1933, when their departure became the condition set by Central America's most famous guerrilla leader, César Augusto Sandino, for laying down arms. He was murdered two years later.

Haiti was occupied by the US Marines in 1915, after a wave of civil disturbances which had claimed the lives of two presidents and hundreds of people. Haiti's constitution, which had barred foreigners from owning land in the black republic, was reformed in 1918 to permit foreign ownership in the island. US rule was also imposed in the Dominican Republic (the only Latin American country that had asked—in 1865—for the return of Spanish colonial administration) in 1916, and lasted until 1924. The Marines would return to Santo Domingo forty years later, during the term in office of President Lyndon Johnson.

Cuba saw the Marines return to stay in 1917, and although they withdrew after only a few months, the US watch over the island would be in evidence almost until Fidel Castro's revolutionary victory in 1959.

Under US influence, Central America and the Caribbean became a pit of corruption. The deficiencies of the Prohibition era in the United States helped to make fortunes for smugglers, racketeers and many other undignified elements of a free enterprise gone mad. The landowning classes were happy to let these fortunes be made while they could keep theirs. The dreams of idealistic expansionism, of "manifest destiny", had fallen into a sorry state.

The influence, and the investments, spread down the Pacific. US power in Ecuador, Peru and Chile grew rapidly, while in Brazil and Argentina British interests remained strong. To delegate its policing of the area, the US helped to create the National Guards of several Central American states. They would achieve notoriety as the instruments of repression of the most distasteful dictators. The dictator Rafael Leonidas Trujillo had been a Guard officer in the Dominican Republic. The dictator Anastasio Somoza, in Nicaragua, would use his Guards to attempt to invade Costa Rica in December 1948; and would help the United Fruit Company and the Central Intelligence Agency to overthrow the socialist government of Jacobo Arbenz in Guatemala in June 1954. The ugly war in Central America ran through to the 1990s in Nicaragua, El Salvador and Guatemala.

Yet what might be called the last of the nineteenth-century wars were still taking place. And unlike the ideological conflicts that introduced prolonged warfare, these remained short and sharp.

Bolivia went to war with Paraguay to conquer a stretch of frontier land which was thought to have oil. Bolivia had been cut off from the sea and had been made an inland country by war with Chile. In La Paz, the government thought that a river exit could be obtained towards the Atlantic if territorial gains were made in detriment of Paraguay. Frontier skirmishes began in 1928, without any property changing sides.

A certain number of casualties were reported as a result of the Bolivian attacks against western Paraguayan border posts in the Chaco Boreal. These clashes in the remote region between the Bolivian Altiplano and Paraguayan Chaco forests were soon the subject of the high-sounding statements on the matter of injured honour. Oil, or the suspicion of its existence, made honour even more susceptible to injury. Argentina and Brazil, with the help of the League of Nations, tried to prevent escalation of the dispute, but

Bolivia saw an easy victory and was not to be dissuaded.

Colonel José Félix Estigarribia, later to become marshal-president in the tradition of López, took command of the Paraguayan army and, in July 1932, war began. Bolivia, well-armed with German equipment from the First World War, and its army under the command of a German, General Hans Kundt, advanced quickly. But soon it was found that Bolivia did not have a proper army. Its men were native indians brought from all parts of the High Plain. They were without training for or understanding of the contest.

On the other side were the Paraguayans, united, anxious to overcome the defeat of 1870 which had given them a sense of inferiority, and with a spirit of bravery which only knew of death before defeat. Bolivia sent to war an army of nearly 80,000 men, which was reduced to 7,000 men 18 months after the start of fighting. Paraguay, though it acquired large quantities of equipment taken from the Bolivians, did not have the men for a full-scale invasion of Bolivia. On 12 June 1935, a truce was agreed. Four neighbouring countries joined the United States to arbitrate a solution. In July 1938 Paraguay was awarded the larger part of the disputed Chaco, while Bolivia was granted the right to request transit through Paraguay and Argentina to the River Plate. Argentina's Foreign Minister, Carlos Saavedra Lamas, was awarded the Nobel prize for peace for his part in the negotiations.

Other small wars took place almost simultaneously. In February 1933, Peru and Colombia fought a brief border battle.[2] Ecuador, because of an absence of capital and people, had never settled its Amazonian hinterland and its boundary with Peru was in frequent dispute. The argument grew into conflict, and in July 1941 the Peruvian army invaded the borderland and stayed there. In 1943, with the world involved in another, larger war, Ecuador was forced to sign away much of its Amazon region under the terms of the 'Protocol of Rio de Janeiro'. The lingering disagreement would break out again in an armed clash in 1981, and once more in 1994.

In Central America, resentment between overpopulated El Salvador and more spacious Honduras built up to an outburst of anger at the unfavourable results in three games of soccer. What followed was known as the "football war". Salvadorean planes bombed airfields in Honduras and troops invaded Honduran territory on 14 July 1969. On 29 July, El Salvador withdrew under threat of intervention by the Organisation of American States; but it was not until October 1976 that the two countries accepted the OAS's offer of mediation.

In the southern reaches of the continent anger arose again. On 8 November 1965, in the disputed frontier area of the southern Andes known as Palena-Rio Encuentro, on the border between Argentina and Chile, troops from the two countries exchanged fire. One Chilean officer was killed and an Argentine soldier was wounded. Argentina and Chile agreed to submit their dispute to arbitration by Britain under the 1902 accord. Britain found in favour of Chile.[3]

In March 1972, Argentina advised Chile that it did not wish to extend the arbitration agreement of 1902 after it expired in September of that year. Argentina proposed, instead, that the one outstanding point of disagreement, the delineation concerning three islands in the Beagle Channel, be the last joint submission made under the 1902 pact.

The only trouble was that the Britain they asked to arbitrate was a post-imperial nation with quite a different view of the world to that which it had held at the beginning of the century. Since 1965 Britain had been pressed at the United Nations to negotiate with Argentina to end the British occupation of the Falkland/Malvinas islands. It was politically anomalous that a litigant in one case should have asked its opponent in another case to arbitrate in the first, even if there were protocols which suggested that, diplomatically, this could be done.

The arbitration tribunal appointed by the International Court in The Hague at the request of the British government named five judges: a North American, a Swede, a German, a Briton and a Nigerian. On 2 May 1977 they voted unanimously to award the Picton, Nueva and Lennox islands to Chile.

By then Argentina had a military government, in power since March 1976, which also saw Britain in a post-imperial light.[4] Argentina duly declared the finding "null and void". The fight, as Argentina saw it, was not just over three islands but for a large section of the South Atlantic which Chile could claim by extension of the line of its possessions in the Beagle Channel. Argentina sought direct diplomatic discussions with Chile; reluctantly, Chile agreed to talk. The new negotiations got nowhere. Chile refused to accept reversal of the court's finding, whereas Argentina would not accept the finding. Chile ordered its forces to occupy the three islands. The subject dropped out of the news for a few weeks, as Argentina acted as host to the football World Cup, which its national team won in June 1978.

No sooner had the last whistle blown than the Argentine armed forces set about the serious business of recuperating the islands in the Beagle Channel. The Argentine armed forces acted on the assumption that the defeat of guerrilla uprisings in the 1970s and victory in the World Cup qualified them to defeat Chile in Patagonia. Chile looked on the dispute with alarm. Under General Augusto Pinochet's dictatorship Chile's standing in international forums was not high and it was loath to seek any limelight. The foreign ministers of Chile and Argentina met but failed to move the talks out of deadlock. Senior officers purchased sophisticated armaments in Britain, Germany, France and the United States. Argentina's most belligerent commanders looked forward to "Christmas in Chile". After the Beagle Channel was secured, the British-controlled Falkland Islands would be the next target, they said.

On 12 December 1978, a last attempt at negotiations broke down. The preparations for war were more intense than ever. Chile had resources for a short action, perhaps an invasion that would cut off Patagonia from the rest of the country. The command at Buenos Aires planned a prolonged conflict along the length of the Andes. Argentina warned the United Nations Security Council that tension was reaching a dangerous level. Chile did the same. Both notifications to the UN amounted to appeals for diplomacy to stop two fighters (Chile and Argentina) whose pride prevented them from stopping themselves. It was also an attempt to internationalise the dispute. Each side hoped to gain from the intervention of the UN.

A sense of near hysteria pervaded the two capitals. Peace marchers prayed for a settlement, the respective Roman Catholic hierarchies who had stood aside in caution were called on to avert war and, jointly, they forced their governments to talk. On 22

December 1978 Santiago and Buenos Aires applied to the Vatican for arbitration. Chile gained time; Argentina was left with its frustration.

The next step was, perhaps, obvious. Argentina, having failed to obtain the Beagle Channel, looked to the Falklands. Late in the twentieth century Argentina and Britain went to war in the South Atlantic for possession of the Falkland Islands. It seemed like a small nineteenth-century war.

NOTES:

1. At the end of the nineteenth century a small religious war took place in north-eastern Brazil. A movement of peasants, former slaves, escaped convicts, and a general collection of the poor and the destitute gathered under the leadership of a self-styled preacher, Antonio Conselheiro (1828-97). He promised his followers equality in a socialist society on earth and the Kingdom of Heaven for all. The movement demanded the restoration of the Empire on the grounds that the Republic was godless. The group's growth alarmed the government in Rio de Janeiro, which sent an army to put down the spread of religious rebellion. The battle that ensued was called by Conselheiro "the war of the end of the world". There is an excellent novel on the subject by the Peruvian writer Mario Vargas Llosa, *The War of the End of the World.* (London/New York, Penguin, 1994). See also R. B. Cunninghame Graham, *A Brazilian Mystic: Being the Life and Miracles of Antonio Conselheiro.* (Heinemann, London, 1920). Both authors appear to owe much to the Brazilian writer Euclides da Cunha's, *Os Sertoes* (1902).

2. *Buenos Aires Herald,* 15 February 1933.

3. Valenzuela Lafourcade, Mario: *El enigma de la Laguna del Desierto, una memoria diplomática.* (LOM, Santiago, 1999).

4. See Chapter 11, and Notes.

Chapter Fourteen
THE FALKLANDS/MALVINAS
WAR, 1982

Argentine commandos, April 1982 (Gente magazine)

On Thursday, 1 April 1982, the *Buenos Aires Herald*—Argentina's centenarian English-language daily—reported that a solution to the dispute over the South Georgia Islands, a territory deep in the South Atlantic, was expected to be reached before Saturday: "An array of options drawn up by a four-man foreign ministry team headed by the minister, Nicanor Costa Méndez, has been studied by Argentina's top authorities. Two of the options stand out as the most likely: one is the diplomatic way, the other is not." By then the defence minister, Amadeo Frúgoli, had said after a tour of the Puerto Belgrano Naval Base, Argentina's biggest, 600 kilometres south of Buenos Aires, that "several (Argentine) vessels" were on their way to the South Atlantic. With hindsight, it could have been mistaken for a grim April Fool joke. But unbelievable as it might have sounded to the world beyond Buenos Aires, this was in deadly earnest.

The story went back into the days of Spanish colonial rule and to 1833,[1] when Britain seized the islands from rule by Buenos Aires. But for the more immediate account, this chapter should start on Tuesday, 22 December 1981, when General Leopoldo Fortunato Galtieri grabbed the government of Argentina from his fellow-officer, General Roberto Eduardo Viola. Galtieri was the third general in power since the military coup of 1976, which had ended a weak and corrupt constitutional regime, headed by María Estela Martínez de Perón, widow of General Juan Domingo Perón. Perón had died on 1 July 1974, after only eight months into his third presidency (the previous two were between 1946 and 1955). The first of the three military presidents, General Jorge Rafael Videla, unleashed what has since become known as the "Dirty War" in Argentina.

Three years before Galtieri seized power, in 1978, Argentina under General Jorge Rafael Videla had nearly gone to war with Chile.[2] And two years before, in December 1979, Argentina had been condemned by the Organisation of American States' Human Rights Subcommittee for gross violations of human rights, including the "disappearance" of thousands of people considered opponents of the government.

From January 1982 onwards, the local press was fed a stream of rumours about imminent action, including armed intervention, by the military regime to recover Argentine control of the Falkland/Malvinas Islands. Events saw the following sequence. On Thursday, 18 March, police dispersed over one thousand people who rallied in the Plaza de Mayo, in front of Government House, to demand information on the "disappeared", the opponents and victims of the military dictatorship ruling since March 1976. It is important to note that the rally took place on a Thursday: for more than a quarter of a century, up to the time of this book going to press, the relatives of the "disappeared"— sometimes estimated up to 30,000, but with 10,000 dead or missing clearly identified— have marched in a small circle in the centre of the Plaza de Mayo, every Thursday afternoon at 3 p.m., demanding full information on the whereabouts of the bodies, bones or ashes of their spouses, parents, children or grandchildren—and sometimes all of those from a single family.

The day after police had used tear gas and truncheons on that Thursday rally, an Argentine party landed on the island of South Georgia, a dependency of the British-run Falkland Islands government, ostensibly with a scrap merchant's contract to dismantle the old whaling station. The group of men, whose presence was known to Argentina's foreign ministry and military authorities, raised an Argentine flag on South Georgia and gathered around it to sing the national anthem. The news was first published in London, reflecting British official alarm. It was published in Buenos Aires in the middle of the following week.

At the end of the month, on Tuesday, 30 March, a mass demonstration to protest against economic hardship was crushed by police in the centre of Buenos Aires, close to Government House. There were 1,500 arrests.

On Friday, 2 April 1982, the *Buenos Aires Herald* headlined "Invasion fleet said on its way": "Argentina was reportedly readying last night to invade the Malvinas islands in the South Atlantic at dawn today, after having denounced "the British threat to use force" at the United Nations and the Organization of American States." The leading article commented:

> It is unfortunate that the South Atlantic problem should come to a head just when the country is passing through an exceptionally severe social, political and economic crisis. Even if the islands—and the islanders—are acquired without bloodshed or the loss of valuable ships, the crisis will continue unabated. Indeed, the assertion of sovereignty over the South Atlantic could serve to make it worse. Right now the country does not have much money to spend subsidizing the economy of the islands or to embark on a serious attempt to exploit their resources.

The paper that morning reported three bomb explosions in the city, part of the anti-government campaign, one of them in a ladies' room at the Sheraton Hotel, where the United States Naval Operations chief, Admiral Thomas Hayward, was spending a three-day visit, and where the women in the trio "Los Ángeles de Smith" were performing.

The Guardian in London that same morning announced, with a difference of three or four hours later than Buenos Aires, "Britain fears invasion of Falklands":

> The British ambassador to the United Nations, Sir Anthony Parsons, said in New York last night that an Argentine naval force was steaming toward the Falklands in the South Atlantic and his government feared that an invasion on the disputed islands was imminent. Sir Anthony called for an urgent meeting of the UN Security Council to take preventive action, "before it is too late", and the meeting was agreed.

By then the deed had been done. A communiqué broadcast in Buenos Aires proclaimed that

> The Military Junta, as the supreme organ of state, communicates to the people of the Argentine nation that today, at (blank) hours, the Republic, through the means of its Armed Forces, by means of the successful completion of a combined operation, has recovered the Islas Malvinas, Georgias and Sandwich del Sur for the national patrimony. In this manner, Argentine sovereignty has been assured over all the territory of the said islands and their respective sea and air spaces.
>
> May the entire country understand the profound and unequivocal national significance of this decision, in order that responsibility and collective effort might accompany this enterprise and permit, with God's help, the conversion into reality of a legitimate right of the Argentine people, held back patiently and prudently for almost 150 years.

There were nine other communiqués that day, their contents filled with patriotic self-indulgence.

Communiqué 5 (April 2 - 14.05 hours). The Military Junta communicates that at 10.20 hours today April 2, 1982, the former Radio Port Stanley broadcast as Radio Nacional Malvinas. It began its transmission by playing the Argentine National Anthem.

Communiqué 6 (April 2 - 14.15 hours). The Military Junta communicates that at 11.20 hours on this historic April 2, 1982, the commander of the Malvinas theatre of operations reported that: "the English governor of the Islas Malvinas surrendered unconditionally before the nation's armed forces, the Argentine flag is now flying in the Islas Malvinas. MISSION FULFILLED." [3]

A crowd, estimated at 10,000 people, filled the Plaza de Mayo to celebrate the achievement and hence the military accomplishment. The gathering was addressed by President Galtieri, whose improvised speech was repeatedly interrupted by cheering. In that same square, within the previous fortnight crowds of demonstrators had been battered and arrested by the military government's police.

The British Ambassador in Buenos Aires, Anthony Williams, on leaving the foreign ministry after an early morning meeting when he was briefed on the invasion, told journalists waiting for him, "Leave me alone." Within hours he was packing his bags to return to Britain. He had been in Buenos Aires just two years.

So began two and a half months of conflict and crisis between Argentina and Britain, two traditionally friendly nations.

On 3 April, the *Buenos Aires Herald* headlined its edition "Argentina recovers Malvinas by force".

> Argentina yesterday unilaterally put an end to a century and a half of vain negotiations to establish its right to govern the Malvinas islands by sending in a 4,000-man invasion force to take them over from their British administrators. The pre-dawn landing included members of the three Argentine armed forces who easily overcame the handful of British troops stationed at Port Stanley, the Malvinas capital. The Argentine Navy High Command reported yesterday afternoon that during the landing of the first wave of Argentine Marines, there was a firefight with the British Royal Marines. During the fighting, Captain Pedro Giachino, "who advanced heroically at the head of his men" on the British positions, was shot dead. Wounded were Navy Lieutenant Diego García Quiroga and Petty Officer Ernesto Urbina.

That same Saturday, *The Guardian* ran the headline "Argentine action in Falklands stuns Cabinet". In fact, it was not just the Cabinet that was puzzled. Part of the English popular press and much of its public had to find out where the Falkland Islands were before adequate indignation could be expressed. Britain had been caught unawares. In politics that was one of the severest faults. *The Guardian* continued:

> The Government last night rounded off a day of spectacular military and diplomatic humiliation with the public admission by the Foreign Secretary, Lord Carrington, and the Defence Secretary, Mr John Nott, that Argentina had indeed captured Port Stanley while the British Navy lay too far away to prevent it... The belated confirmation of the invasion which had apparently eluded ministers—though not the world's media, American intelligence, or radio hams—came shortly after it had been agreed that the Prime Minister (Mrs Margaret Thatcher) would open a three-hour debate on the Falkands crisis in the first Saturday sitting since the abortive Suez invasion of 1956.

Challenged by the leader of the Labour Party, Michael Foot, the Tory Prime

Minister, Mrs Thatcher, announced that afternoon that Britain would send a Task Force to recover the Falklands. This dramatic decision overcame the early delay caused at the United Nations, where Britain had failed to get a swift response because the Non-Aligned nations (theoretically not allied to either the United States or the Soviet Union super-powers) and the Soviet delegates said that they would have to receive instructions from their governments before voting.

In Buenos Aires, public joy at the invasion was only comparable to the World Cup victory in 1978. Journalists from all over the world started to arrive in the city. The Sheraton Hotel, one of the few modern facilities in town, became the press headquarters for the international correspondents. The Joint Chiefs of Staff opened an office at the hotel, there to offer information on Argentina to the press, all local news services, maps of the South Atlantic, photocopying machines, free coffee and tea. The foreign ministry offered similar catering to reporters and television camera crews who waited in hope that something might happen to justify their long empty hours.

There was no comfort in the official communiqués, which the military regime produced in abundance:

> Communiqué 12 (April 3, 1982 - 15.40 hours). The Military Junta communicates to the nation that the capture of the Islas Georgias del Sur has been completed with our own forces taking possession of the English settlement in Grytviken. With this event, the entire archipelago composed of the Malvinas, Georgias and Sandwich del Sur, are under Argentine sovereignty.

Earlier, Communiqué 11 had announced that an Argentine plane had delivered the Falklands governor, Rex Hunt, his wife and staff to the British Embassy in Montevideo, Uruguay.

With the benefit of hindsight it was later found that the only truthful information to come out of Buenos Aires during those three months were the official communiqués. These usually brief statements did refer specifically to events.

But no sooner was the invasion made public than every member of the armed forces wanted to be part of the historic event. Hence a wave of rumours about the strength of the landing force, the reinforcements to follow, the political decisions and, later, the military achievements; all were exaggerated out of all proportion or were straight fabrications.

The first casualty of the conflict, apart from diplomatic relations, was suffered by Mrs Thatcher, when Lord Carrington resigned. On Tuesday, 6 April, 1982, *The Guardian* reported that:

> The Prime Minister was engaged last night in plugging the leaks in her own increasingly waterlogged Cabinet just as she despatched the most powerful Royal Navy fleet ever to leave the shores of the United Kingdom in peacetime. Mrs Thatcher spent a day which might otherwise have been devoted to messages of encouragement to the fleet which left Portsmouth yesterday morning in accepting the resignations of her Foreign Secretary, Lord Carrington, and of all but one of his ministerial team (Defence Secretary John Nott), at the Foreign Office.
>
> Two grey leviathans sailed out of Portsmouth harbour yesterday, spurred on by cheering thousands, towards an uncertain destiny 8,000 miles away off the Argentine-occupied

Falkland Islands.

Set against an azure seascape the two aircraft carriers, HMS *Invincible* and HMS *Hermes*—the latter carrying Rear Admiral John Forster Woodward, Flag Officer of the First Flotilla—passed solemnly through the port's narrow mouth to ride into Spithead on the morning's high tide.

President Ronald Reagan of the United States, an admirer of Thatcher, was alarmed by the conflict in Washington's backyard. Anxious to assist his North Atlantic ally, he sent General Alexander Haig, a Vietnam war veteran and then secretary of state, to London and Buenos Aires to negotiate a settlement, the essence of which was the immediate withdrawal of Argentina's occupation force. On Saturday, 10 April, the day before Easter Sunday, a crowd filled the Plaza de Mayo, to show General Haig the strength of popular feeling. General Galtieri addressed the crowd, assuring that he wanted peace in the Malvinas, but stressing that Argentina was prepared to go to war. Haig was reputed to have questioned this warning on the grounds of the lack of balance of combat experience. While the Argentine military boasted that it had won the Dirty War against guerrillas, Haig dismissed that conflict as a "turkey shoot". That same day, the ten-nation European Economic Community announced a ban on imports from Argentina and called on other countries to back efforts to support a peaceful withdrawal from the Malvinas.

Everybody in Argentina wanted to show how much they supported the government's patriotic recovery of the islands. Car bumper stickers showed Margaret Thatcher being buggered by General Galtieri; shops that had English names removed their signs or changed names; newspaper distributors announced a boycott of the sale of the *Buenos Aires Herald*, which throughout most of its 106 years had been owned by an Anglo-Argentine family (since 1968 sixty per cent of its shares had, in fact, been held by a Charleston, South Carolina, newspaper family). But some senior naval officers had decided that it was a British intelligence centre and suggested blowing up the offices and printery; bomb planting had been one of the military's favoured methods for solving domestic issues for nearly ten years. Fortunately, the newspaper distributors suggested that a boycott would be good enough. The paper carried on printing an emergency edition and the most loyal readers travelled to the offices to buy their copies. After ten days the government ordered the boycott to be lifted.

Haig's attempt at "shuttle diplomacy" took him back to London on 12 April, with a demand for British recognition of Argentine sovereignty in the Falkland Islands. The Foreign Secretary, Francis Pym, told the Secretary of State to shuttle off back and demand complete withdrawal for negotiations to begin. Haig returned to Buenos Aires via Washington. On 12 April the first British communiqué announced: "At 04.00 GMT this morning the MEZ (Military Exclusion Zone) was established around the Falkland Islands as announced by the Secretary of State for Defence on the 7th of April. No naval incident has been reported. Nor has there been any report of Argentinian warships or naval auxiliaries within the zone since it was established."

In London, on Friday 16 April, *The Guardian* remarked that "the British Government is bracing itself for a long naval blockade and no longer realistically expects Mr Alexander Haig's mission to Buenos Aires to succeed." A report from Buenos Aires said that the foreign minister, "Dr Nicanor Costa Méndez said that there was no progress in negotiations and regretted Mrs Thatcher's determination to recover the Falkland Islands because 'such words do not help negotiations'."

Countering Argentina's claims of high spirits among the troops on the islands, *The Guardian* reported that "the Falkland islanders are feeding starving Argentinian troops begging for food on their doorsteps, Mr Dick Baker, the expelled deputy governor, said when he arrived back at Gatwick airport." In the early days of the conflict, the news read like propaganda. Eventually it would be found to be true and even fell short of the real deprivation suffered by the Argentine occupation army. Haig left Buenos Aires on 19 April. (He would resign as US Secretary of State on 25 June.)

Argentina called for a meeting of the Organisation of American States (OAS) as a preliminary step to invoking the 1947 Treaty of Rio de Janeiro of mutual defence. Foreign minister Costa Méndez now had a continental stage on which to pursue diplomacy, which perhaps encouraged a sense of his own international greatness. By a vote of 18-0 the OAS agreed to consider measures to be taken against the United Kingdom. Eventually, however, Argentina would get no more than a vote of solidarity from the OAS, and little other defence. In Venezuela's capital, Caracas, a token demonstration of support involved switching off the city's lights for an hour. It was not much to go on.

Communiqué 30, on 20 April, reported the approach of British ships towards the South Georgia islands. In effect, the battle for the islands was shaping up. In London, the official statement of the day said there was nothing new to report. On 30 April, Britain extended the blockade to establish a total air and sea ring around the islands. In Buenos Aires, a decree imposed controls on the press "for reasons of national security". The *Buenos Aires Herald* editorial that morning complained that "what the government is doing is passing the buck on censorship instead of taking proper responsibility for it itself. If there is to be prior censorship during the conflict, then it is essential that it be carried out by specialist personnel, not by those whose job it is to inform the people to the best of their ability." The paper reported that a group of 300 Mothers of the Plaza de Mayo had held their customary Thursday afternoon silent march around the monument to the Republic to demand news of their "disappeared" relatives. Government agents distributed leaflets describing them as "friends of our enemy".

The Battle Begins

On that 30 April the United States formally announced sanctions against Argentina as Alexander Haig prepared to discuss tactical and logistical support for Britain with Foreign Secretary Francis Pym in Washington. And on Saturday, 1 May 1982, British Harriers bombed the airfield at Port Stanley. Argentine anti-aircraft fire brought down two of the jets. It was the first day of fighting.

Communiqué 41 issued in Buenos Aires announced that action had begun; however, "the government of the nation repeats that it guarantees the security of life, property and rights of British citizens and English-speaking Argentines resident in the national territory and the islands of the South Atlantic, and that it will repress with the full weight of the law any action against such rights."[4] That day, the government started a new set of communiqués. Number 1 of the new series announced that "during the attacks on Puerto Argentino (the name given to Stanley) in the Islas Malvinas carried out this morning by English planes, two Harrier aircraft were shot down. Other enemy machines were damaged by their own fire."

The United Nations secretary-general Javier Pérez de Cuéllar offered to mediate, but in truth he was virtually ignored. The President of Peru, Fernando Belaúnde Terry, tried also to find a settlement, but peace never stood a chance.

The looming conflict in the South Atlantic was starting to attract the eyes of the world. For two and a half years, the republic of El Salvador, and before in 1979, Nicaragua, had drawn international attention to the cruelty and vicious nature of their civil wars in Central America. El Salvador had held elections on 28 March, and the new president Álvaro Magana, was offering an amnesty to bring to an end the fighting that had killed more than 30,000 people.

On Monday, 3 May, tragedy struck in earnest in the South Atlantic. Torpedoes from the British submarine HMS *Conqueror* sank an ageing Brooklyn (Second World War) class cruiser ARA (Armada República Argentina) *General Belgrano*. It was to cause the most severe loss of life of the war. Communiqué 15 stated: "the Joint Chiefs of the General Staff communicate that a British submarine attacked the cruiser ARA *General Belgrano* catching it with a torpedo hit that produced damage. It must be emphasised that the attack was carried out to the SE of the Isla de los Estados and outside the designated "exclusion zone". Ships of our own have been detailed to the area to help the cruiser in case it is necessary." By the end of that day 680 crew had been rescued, but another 130 were missing presumed dead. The death toll would grow.

In London, an official Ministry of Defence statement gave its version of events: "At approximately 8 o'clock London time last night, the Argentine cruiser *General Belgrano* was hit by torpedoes from a British submarine. The cruiser is believed to be severely damaged. On Friday, 23 April, HMG warned the Argentine government that any approach on the part of Argentine warships including submarines and naval auxiliaries or military aircraft which could amount to a threat to interfere with the mission of British forces in the South Atlantic would encounter the appropriate response."

The *Buenos Aires Herald* editorial the next day abandoned the paper's disapproving stance and clearly took the Argentine side: "It is time that London stops playing the peace-loving victim in the Malvinas conflict and faces up to the decision it has taken. Peace can only be talked in the context of a cease-fire, not in the midst of full-scale combat. There are no diplomatic victims in this confrontation." Argentina was devastated with concern, fear and sadness. Until the next day.

The turning-point occurred on 5 May, when the British guided-missile carrying Type-42 destroyer HMS *Sheffield* was hit by a French-made Exocet missile from a Super Etendard naval plane and was sunk. No statement was issued in Buenos Aires, where on 4 May, Communiqué 22 had reported an attack by three Sea Harrier planes, adding that "two of the invading machines were shot down by the anti-aircraft gun fire." In London, a ministry statement at 21.15 stated: "In the course of its duties within the Total Exclusion Zone around the Falkland Islands, HMS *Sheffield*, was attacked and hit late this afternoon by an Argentine missile. The ship caught fire, which spread out of control. When there was no longer any hope of saving the ship, the ship's company abandoned ship. All who abandoned her were picked up." The next day, 6 May, the British government defence spokesman, Ian Mcdonald, admitted that "twenty officers and men serving in the ship must now be presumed dead."5

The extent of the tragedy was not really absorbed in Buenos Aires. In Argentina the sinking of the *Sheffield* was rather greeted as a punch in the eye for Britain, celebrated with the senseless enthusiasm of a soccer triumph. The *Buenos Aires Herald*, on 5 May, reported that Prime Minister Margaret Thatcher was "devastated" by the missile attack.

Meanwhile, Britain continued to build up its strength in the South Atlantic. *The Guardian* reported on 13 May that the luxury transatlantic liner *QE2* had sailed from Southampton the day before, to serve as a hospital ship and a base for auxiliary personnel.

After the two sinkings, the world's attention concentrated mainly on the peace proposals at the UN in New York. Argentina said it was prepared to accept them, but Britain insisted on the evacuation of Argentine forces from the islands as a pre-condition for any cease-fire. Argentina, by then, could not withdraw.

Task Force ships shelled Port Stanley, while Sea Harriers strafed Argentine troops and the airport, which continued to be used by Hercules transport planes. On Saturday, 22 May, *The Guardian*'s front page carried the banner headline: "Five warships hit as task force sets up bridgehead. Light tanks go ashore with 1,000 troops":

> British forces have established a firm bridgehead on the Falkland Islands, the Defence Secretary, Mr John Nott announced last night. More than 1,000 Royal Marines and para-troopers were believed to have gone ashore before dawn yesterday in a series of raids and landings. The main landing, believed to be at Port San Carlos at the northern end of the Falkland sound, was unopposed. Mr Nott said there must have been British casualties when Royal Navy warships came under heavy Argentinian air attack. Five ships were damaged, two seriously. The Argentinians claimed that one British vessel was on fire and sinking.

The most famous image of that night was the photograph of HMS *Antelope*, abandoned after being hit, ablaze and lighting up the sky with a dramatic arc of fire.

In Buenos Aires it was Communiqué 86, issued two days later, on 24 May— Empire Day, in the old times, the eve of Argentina's national day—that acknowledged the landing.

> The Joint Chiefs of the General Staff communicated that with regard to the operations being carried out in the Puerto San Carlos area, it can be established with precision that the enemy forces have succeeded in establishing a beach-head, which they are reinforcing by landing material, equipment and personnel, of the order of approximately 2,000 men. The beach-head has a depth of 10 km in an east-west direction and 15 km front in a north-south direction. Our own forces through the movement of army units on the ground, and the support of our air force are engaged in the task of neutralising the advance of the English units.
>
> For the purpose stated and in co-ordination with the forces of our Army, the Argentine Air Force performed attacks whose results were:
> Enemy forces:
> • A troop transport ship severely damaged.
> • A frigate damaged.
> • A Sea Harrier shot down.
> Our own forces:
> • Two planes shot down.

It must be stated that so far there is no knowledge of casualties or prisoners on either side although it is feasible to suppose that there have been some, given the type of operations performed.

In a sea of lies and rumours, the communiqué was surprisingly sincere and clear. Whatever was to follow, it was the indication of the beginning of the end of the war. General Mario Benjamín Menéndez, commander of the Argentine forces and governor of the Malvinas islands, was not at San Carlos. He had expected the British to land at Stanley, and had concentrated his defence there.

On 27 May, the British defence ministry reported that the "Argentine Air Force did not attack any element of the Task Force yesterday." However: "Further reports have now been received about the *Atlantic Conveyor*, the merchant ship which had to be abandoned on Tuesday. She is still afloat, is upright and has normal draught. Although two Exocet missiles were fired only one seems to have hit her. We are looking to see whether we can recover some of the cargo and perhaps salvage the ship." The following day, the ministry spokesman felt moved to issue a clarification:

> I would like to put the record straight on the use of *Uganda*, one of our hospital ships. Argentina has claimed that the *Uganda* was present in the Falkland Sound during operational activity there implying that she took part in that activity. This is a serious charge which if it were true would involve a fundamental breach of the Geneva Convention. She entered Middle Bay of East Falklands for 30 minutes on 27 May to take on board a number of severely wounded casualties.

More significant news followed: "2145. We have just learned the 2nd Battalion of the Parachute Regiment have taken Darwin and Goose Green."

For the British the battle for Goose Green became legendary through the heroic leadership of Colonel Herbert "H" Jones, who died at the head of his regiment on that 28 May. Argentines, for their part, have myriad stories of heroism, displayed by men with inferior weaponry and little training. It was up to the courage of individuals to resist the British advance. But Argentina has not been very good at telling about its war effort, and in defeat and without a history of combat, this is probably understandable. In retrospect, the Argentine war effort was considerable in view of the circumstances, and has to be valued in the determination of individual servicemen, taken separately from the context of their political leadership.

On that day, 28 May, Pope John Paul II met Queen Elizabeth II on his scheduled visit to the United Kingdom. By then the Vatican had decided that an unscheduled visit to Buenos Aires was essential to strike a balance.

Britain suffered another severe setback on 8 June, when Argentine air force planes hit HMS *Plymouth*, and the logistic landing ships *Sir Tristram* and *Sir Galahad*. The newsreel films of helicopters trying to rescue men from the burning ships and of the wounded coming ashore were harrowing and spoke quite simply of the horror of fighting and courage of men in desperate situations. On 9 June, the defence ministry spokesman said: "We know that there were no deaths on HMS *Plymouth* but there were five people injured. They are under treatment and their next-of-kin have been informed. It is, however, feared that casualties from the attacks on *Sir Tristram* and *Sir Galahad* were much heavier; early reports indicate a number of killed and injured." It was an understatement, of course, but in the circumstances it had to be. The horror of the *Sir Galahad* was awesome. The absence of casualty figures caused alarm in London at the possible extent of the deaths and the potential cost of the war.

But by then the Argentine outposts surrounding Stanley had been defeated by the British advance. The Argentine garrison at Stanley surrendered on Monday, 14 June. On that day, Pope John Paul II ended his brief weekend visit to Argentina. On Tuesday, Communiqué 165 did not mention the surrender: "The Joint Chiefs of the General Staff communicate that yesterday, June 14, 1982, the meeting took place of the commander of the English forces General Jeremy Moore and the Commander of the Malvinas military garrison, Brigadier General Mario Benjamín Menéndez. In the aforesaid meeting a document was effected in which the conditions for a cease fire and withdrawal of troops was established. The document referred to will be made known as soon as its text is prepared."

It was the end, but the appropriate words could not be found. The dying euphoria of Argentines who had thought that war was a great idea changed to fury. The country was in economic ruin and the humiliation was unbearable. The idea that the battle for South Georgia had continued until almost the end of the war also had been wiped out days before by news of the ignominious surrender of the commander, Captain Alfredo Astiz, a former torturer and killer during the years of state terror. He had been taken prisoner by the British, who, ignoring French demands for his extradition, delivered him back to Argentina.

A conclave of army chiefs demanded the withdrawal of General Leopoldo Fortunato Galtieri and his replacement by General Cristino Nicolaides, on 17 June. The last communiqué, number 170, on 20 June, sounded like a whimpering attempt to save face: "The Joint Chiefs of the General Staff communicate that today, June 20, 1982, at 09.15 hours, the Corbeta *Uruguay* scientific station, situated on Thule Island, belonging to the Sandwich del Sur group, proceeded to destroy the radio set that they had left, in view of the invasion by British military units that were surrounding them." There was no apology or explanation for the death of nearly seven hundred young men in a ridiculous adventure. By then, in any case, international attention had moved on. The Israeli army had occupied Lebanon, pounding Palestinian positions, following the invasion on 6 June in retaliation for the attempted assassination of Israel's ambassador in London.

Argentina's defeat led to political and economic chaos. The last of the generals, Reynaldo Bignone, installed by Nicolaides as president, called elections in October 1983 and handed over government to the elected president, Raúl Ricardo Alfonsín, in December 1983. The war had helped Argentina return to constitutional rule. But it was not until another change of presidents, following the election of Carlos Saúl Menem, in May 1989, that Britain and Argentina were able to announce negotiations towards full restoration of diplomatic relations, on Friday, 18 August 1989. The official announcement read: "The British Permanent representative to the United Nations, Sir Crispin Tickell, and the Special Representative of the Government of Argentina, Ambassador Lucio García del Solar, met in New York on 16-18 August to discuss the timing, agenda and conditions for a later substantive meeting between representatives of the two countries."

They were on the way to becoming friends again.

NOTES:

1.   See Chapter 3
2.   See Chapter 11.
3.   *The Falklands War: the Official History.* (Latin American Newsletters, London, 1983), p.11. See Bibliography list.
4.   For the reaction of the English-speaking community in Argentina, see the letter quoted in Notes to Chapter 6. For extensive examples of British community appeals to the British Prime Minister, see also Andrew Graham-Yooll, *Committed Observer: Memoirs of a Journalist.* (John Libbey/University of Luton Press, London, 1995) and Andrew Graham-Yooll, *The Forgotten Colony: A History of the English-speaking Communities in Argentina.* (Literature of Latin America, Buenos Aires 1999).
5.   The most important book to come out of that sinking was the posthumously published, *A Message from the Falklands* by David Tinker (Junction Books, London, 1982). The author was an officer killed on the *Sheffield.* The book is a collection of his letters to his father.

BIBLIOGRAPHY

A PERSONAL SELECTION

Latin America—General
Bradford Burns, E., *Latin America. A Concise Interpretive History* (Prentice Hall Inc., New Jersey, 1982).

Calvert, Peter and Susan, *Latin America in the Twentieth Century* (Macmillan, London 1994).

Gott, Richard, *Guerrilla Movements in Latin America* (Doubleday Anchor, New York, 1971).

Humphreys, R. A., *Latin American History: A Guide to the Literature in English* (Oxford University Press, 1958).

Naylor, Bernard, *Accounts of Nineteenth-Century South America.* An Annotated checklist of works by British and United States observers (Athlone Press, London, 1969).

Passarelli, Bruno, *El Delirio Armado, Argentina-Chile, la guerra que evitó el Papa* (Sudamericana, Buenos Aires, 1998)

Pearce, Jenny, *Under the Eagle.* US intervention in Central America and the Caribbean (Latin America Bureau, London, 1981).

Pendle, George, *A History of Latin America* (Penguin, London, 1981).

Romero, José Luis (ed.), *Pensamiento político de la emancipación 1790-1825* (Biblioteca Ayacucho, Caracas, 1977).

Tapia, Luis Alfonso, *Esta noche la guerra* (Grijalbo, Santiago, 1998)

Walne, Peter (ed.), *A Guide to manuscript Sources for the History of Latin America and the Caribbean in the British Isles* (Oxford University Press, 1973).

Journals and Yearbooks
Europe and Latin America (Latin America Bureau, London) annual.

Britain and Latin America (Latin America Bureau, London) annual.

Latin America and the Caribbean (World of Information, Saffron Walden, Essex) annual.

British Bulletin of Publications on Latin America, the West Indies, Portugal and Spain (The Hispanic and Luso-Brazilian Council, Canning House, London).

Hispanic American Historical Review, (Duke University Press, Durham, North Carolina) quarterly.

Individual Countries
Argentina

Ferns, H. S., *Britain and Argentina in the Nineteenth Century* (Oxford University Press, 1960).

Graham-Yooll, Andrew, *The Forgotten Colony: A History of the English-speaking Communities in Argentina* (Hutchinson, London, 1981). Reprinted by Literature of Latin America, Buenos Aaires, 1999.

Scobie, J., *Argentina: A City and a Nation* (New York, 1964).

Bolivia

Fifer, J. Valerie, *Bolivia, Land, Location and Politics since 1825* (Cambridge University Press, 1973).

Querejaza Calvo, Roberto, *Bolivia y los ingleses* (La Paz, 1973).

Brazil

Bethell, Leslie, *The Abolition of the Brazilian Slave Trade: Britain, Brazil and the slave trade question, 1807-1869* (Cambridge University Press, 1972).

Graham, Richard, *Britain and the Onset of Modernization in Brazil, 1850-1914* (Cambridge University Press, 1970).

Chile

Butland, Gilbert J., *Chile* (Royal Institute of International Affairs, London, 1956).

Graham, María, *Diario de mi residencia en Chile en 1822* (Francisco de Aguirre, Santiago, Chile, 1971) (translated from the English).

Colombia

Dix, Robert, *Colombia: Dimensions of Political Change* (Yale University Press, New Haven, Conn., 1968).

García Márquez, Gabriel, *Cien años de soledad* (Sudamericana, Buenos Aires, 1967).

Costa Rica

Torre Rivas, E., and others, *Centroamérica hoy* (Siglo XXI México, 1976).

Cuba

Foner, Philip S., *The Spanish-Cuban-American War, the Birth of American Imperialism* (Monthly Review Press, New York, 1972).

Guevara, Ernesto "Che", *Episodes of the Revolutionary War* (Guairas, Havana, 1967).

Dominican Republic

Bosch, Juan, *Crisis de la democracia de América en la República Dominicana* (México, 1964).

Ecuador

Linke, Lilo, *Ecuador: Country of Contracts* (Chatham House, Oxford University Press, 1960).

El Salvador

Dunkerley, James, *The Long War: Dictatorship and Revolution in El Salvador* (Junction Books, London, 1982).

Guatemala

Plant, Roger, *Unnatural Disaster* (Latin America Bureau, London, 1978).

Haiti

Dash, J. Michael, *Literature and Ideology in Haiti 1915-1961* (Macmillan, London, 1981).

James, C. L. R., *The Black Jacobins. Toussaint L'Ouverture and the San Domingue Revolution* (London, 1963).

Nicholls, D., *From Dessalines to Duvalier* (Cambridge University Press, 1980).

Honduras

Monroe, Dana, *The Five Republics of Central America* (Oxford University Press, 1918).

Mexico

Meyer, Michael C., and William L. Sherman, *The Course of Mexican History* (Oxford University Press, 1978).

Parkes, Henry Bamford, *A History of Mexico* (Eyre & Spottiswoode, London, 1962).

Nicaragua

Crawley, Eduardo, *Dictators Never Die* (Hurst, London, 1979).

Selser, Gregorio, *Sandino, general de hombres libres,* 2 vols. (Triángulo, Buenos Aires, 1978).

Panama

Panama and the Canal Treaty (Latin America Bureau, London, 1977).

Paraguay

Box, Pelham Horton, *The Origins of the Paraguayan War,* 2 vols. University of Illinois, Urbana, 1929).

Machuca Martínez, Marcelino, *Mapas Históricos del Paraguay gigante* (Asunción, 1950).

Pendle, George, *Paraguay, a Riverside Nation* (Royal Institute of International Affairs, London, 1954).

Pla, Josefina, *The British in Paraguay, 1850-1870* (London, 1976).

Peru

Owens, R. J., *Peru* (Oxford University Press, 1963).

Robinson, Arthur R. B., *The Magnificent Field of Enterprise. Britons in Peru 1815-1915.* Lima 1997.

Stepan, Alfred, *The State and Society* (Princeton University Press, New Jersey, 1978).

Uruguay

Pendle, George, *Uruguay* (Oxford University Press, 1963).

Hudson, W. H., *The Purple Land* (Dent, London).

Venezuela

Hood, Miriam, *Gunboat Diplomacy 1895-1905. Great Power Pressure in Venezuela* (Allen & Unwin, London, 1975).

Lieuwen, Edwin, *Venezuela* (Oxford University Press, 1961).

MALVINAS/FALKLANDS: A SELECT BIBLIOGRAPHY

The following list includes mainly the books published since April 1982 in Argentina and Britain on the South Atlantic conflict. This is a personal compilation and by no means can be considered a complete bibliography.

Argentina

Aliverti, Eduardo and Montenegro, Néstor J.: *Los Nombres de la Derrota.* Nemont Ediciones, 1982.

Alonso Piñeyro, A.: *Historia de la Guerra de Malvinas.* Ed. Planeta.

Andrada, B. H.: *Guerra aérea en las Malvinas.* Emecé Editores, 1983.

Arcs, Daniel: *Banderas en los balcones.* Ediciones de la Flor, Buenos Aires, 1994.

Balza, Martín: *Malvinas: Relatos de soldados.* Biblioteca del Suboficial N° 154, Buenos Aires, 1983/1992.

Boletín del Centro Naval - Conflicto del Atlántico Sur. Centro Naval. Abril-Junio 1992, Buenos Aires.

Bramley, V.: *Los dos lados del infierno.* Ed. Planeta, 1992.

Bramley, V.: *Viaje al Infierno.* Ed. Planeta, 1994

Bustos, Dalmiro M.: *El Otro Frente de la Guerra: los Padres de las Malvinas.* Ramos Americana Editora, 1982.

Calvi, Mario Jorge: *Malvinas, el mito destruido.* Ediciones Devoto, 1982.

Carballo, Pablo Marcos: *Dios y los halcones.* Siete Días/Editorial Abril, 1982.

Carballo, P. M.: *Dios y los halcones.* Ed. Abril, Buenos Aires, 1983.

Cardoso, O.; Kirschbaum, R., & Van der Kooy, E.: *Malvinas, la trama secreta.* Ed. Planeta, 1983.

Caron, Carlos María: *Haig y la mediación y otras manías porteñas.* Galerna, 1982.

Cerón, Sergio: *Malvinas: Gesta heroica o derrota vergonzosa?* Sudamericana, 1984.

Costa Méndez, N.: *Malvinas - Esta es la historia.* Ed. Sudamericana, Buenos Aires, 1993.

Crosby, Ronald K.: *El reto de las Malvinas.* Plus Ultra (revised ed.), 1982.

Cuestión Malvinas, un anacronismo colonial. Registro Oficial. 1983.

Cura, María René and Bustinga, Juan Antonio: *Islas Malvinas, Georgias, Sandwich y Antártida Argentina.* A-Z Editora, 1982.

De Estrada, Marcos: *Una verdad sobre las Malvinas.* Ediciones Culturales Argentinas, 1982.

Del Carril, Bonifacio: *El futuro de las Malvinas.* Emecé, 1982.

Desembarco (Infantería de Marina ARA). Magazine.

Destefani, L.: *Malvinas, Georgias y Sandwich del Sur ante el conflicto con Gran Bretaña.* Edipress, 1982.

Destefani, Laurio H.: *The Malvinas, the South Georgias and the South Sandwich Islands, the Conflict with Britain.* Edipress, 1982.

De Vita, A.: *Malvinas '82.* Instituto de Publicaciones Navales, Buenos Aires, 1994.

Esteban, Edgardo (with Romero Borri, Gustavo): *Malvinas diario del regreso.* Sudamericana, Buenos Aires, 1999.

Etchebarne Bullrich, Conrado: *Falklands or Malvinas*. Grupo Editor Latinoamericano, Buenos Aires, 2000.

Ferguson, G. D.: Falklands or Malvinas. British and Argentine documentary evidence. Facts and not hearsay. *Buenos Aires Herald,* June 1937.

Ferguson, G. D.: The Falkland Islands. A historical record. *Buenos Aires Herald,* June 1937.

Ferrer-Vieyra, E.: *List of British Documents related to the Falkland (Malvinas) Islands Controversy.* Cari, Córdoba, 1993.

Gambini, Hugo: *Crónica documental de las Malvinas*. Redacción Sánchez Teruelo, 1982.

García, Prudencio: *El drama de la autonomía militar.* Alianza Editorial, Madrid, 1995.

García Lupo, Rogelio: *Diplomacia secreta y rendición incondicional.* Legasa, 1983.

Gómez R., A. L.: *Prueba - La Búsqueda*. Buenos Aires Edita S.A., Buenos Aires, 1995.

Guardacostas (Prefectura Naval Argentina). PNA, 1993.

Guglialmelli, Gral Juan E.: *La Guerra en el Atlántico Sur; Cronología de la guerra* (2/IV-14/VI) - Documentos *Estrategia 71-72* Instituto de Estudios Estratégicos y de las Relaciones Internacionales. 1982.

Hoffman, F. L. & O. M.: *Las Malvinas/Falklands 1493-1982.* Ed. Inst. de Publicaciones Navales, Buenos Aires, 1992.

Institucional: *El Ejército Argentino.* Ed. IGM, Buenos Aires, 1991.

Kanaf, Leo: *Las batallas de las Malvinas:* Rada, 1982.

Kasanzew, Nicolás: *Malvinas a sangre y fuego.* Ed. Abril, Buenos Aires, 1982.

Kon, Daniel: *Los Chicos de la Guerra.* Galerna, 1982.

Landeiro, José A.: *Malvinas, Cronología de un despojo.* Adrogué Gráfica Editora, 1982.

Lázara, Simón Alberto: *Propuesta socialista frente a la crisis argentina.* Nuevo Siglo, 1982.

Martini, Héctor: *Historia de la Aviación Naval* (Tomo III) Conflicto del Atlántico Sur. Depto Estudios Históricos Navales ARA, Buenos Aires, 1992.

Matassi, Pío: *Malvinas - La Batalla Aérea.* Editorial Halcón Cielo, Buenos Aires, 1992.

Matassi, Pío: *Probado en Combate.* Editorial Halcón Cielo, Buenos Aires, 1995.

Molina, Gilberto: *Reflexiones Sobre la Guerra de las Islas Malvinas.* Ed. Pampa de Olaen, Córdoba, 1995.

Montina, Pía: *Por Londres con traición.* Daipress, 1982 (a novel).

Moreira de Oliva, A. B.; Albornoz, D. S.: *Islas Malvinas. Bibliografía Congreso Nacional.* Buenos Aires, 1984.

Moro, Rubén: *La Guerra Maldita.* Editorial Pleamar, Buenos Aires, 1985.

Piaggi, I.: *El Combate de Goose Green.* Planeta, Buenos Aires, 1994.

Pinedo, Enrique: *Malvinas. Su extraño destino.* Ed. Corregidor, Buenos Aires, 1994.

Randle, P. H.: *La guerra inconclusa por el Atlántico sur.* Oikos, 1982.

Realidad Económica N° 137: *Petróleo en Malvinas: ¿Negociación o rendición?* Buenos Aires, IADE, 1996.

Rodríguez Berrutti, Camilo Hugo: *Malvinas, última frontera del colonialismo.* Eudeba, 1982.

Roth, Roberto: *Después de las Malvina, qué?* La Campana, 1982.

Rotondo, E.: *Alerta Roja.* Baipress, 1982.

Ruiz Moreno, I. J.: *Comandos en Acción - El Ejército en Malvinas.* Emecé, Buenos Aires, 1986.

Schönfeld, Manfred: *La guerra austral.* Desafíos Editores, 1982.
Smiles, J.: *Las Islas, Rotary y Nosotros.* Rotary Club, 1994.
Traba, Juan: *Las Malvinas, pasado, presente y porvenir.* Galerna, 1982.
Trusso, Eduardo Francisco: *Las Malvinas, el fin de la Utopía.* Troquel, 1982.
Turolo, Carlos: *Malvinas, testimonio de su gobernador.* Sudamericana, 1983.
Turolo, Carlos M.: *Así lucharon.* Sudamericana, 1982.
Verbitsky, Horacio: *La última batalla de la tercera guerra mundial.* Legasa, 1985.
Villarino, E.: *Exocet.* Ed. Abril, Buenos Aires, 1983.
Waispek, C. A.: *Balsa 44.* Ed. Vinciguerra, Buenos Aires, 1994.
Zorraquín Becú, Ricardo: *Inglaterra prometió abandonar las Malvinas.* Platero, 1982.

Mexico
Selser, Gregorio: *Reagan, entre El Salvador y las Malvinas.* Mexico: Mex-Sur, 1982.

Britain
Arblaster, Anthony: *The Falklands: Thatcher's War, Labour's Guilt.* Socialist Society, 1982.
Barnett, Anthony: *Iron Britannia: Why Britain Waged its Falklands War.* Allison and Busby, 1982.
Bishop, Patrick and Witherow, John: *The Winter War.* Quartet, 1982.
Braybrook, Roy: *Battle for the Falklands (3) Air Forces.* Osprey, 1982.
British Aerospace PLC: *V/STOL in the Roaring Forties: 75 Days in the South Atlantic.* 1982.
Burden, R.; Draper, M. and others: *Falklands - The Air War.* Arms and Armour Press, Poole, 1986.
Calvert, Peter: *The Falklands Crisis: The Rights and the Wrongs.* Frances Pinter, 1983.
Carr, Roy; Huddart, Arthur and Webb, John R.: *Up the Falklands, Cartoons From the Royal Marines.* Poole: Blandford Press, 1982.
Clarke, Shana: *Soldier "B" SAS. Heroes of the South Atlantic.* 22 books. London, 1993.
Commander "Sharky" Ward RN: *Sea Harrier over the Falklands.* Naval Institute Press, Annapolis, 1992.
Critchley, Mike (editor): *Falklands Task Force Portfolio.* Cornwall: Maritime Books, 1983. (Parts I and II)
Dabat, Alejandro and Lorenzano, Luis: *Argentina: The Malvinas and the End of Military Rule.* Verso Editions, 1984.
Dalyell, Tam: *One Man's Falklands.* Cecil Woolf, 1982.
Dalyell, Tam: *Thatcher's Torpedo: The Sinking of the Belgrano.* Cecil Woolf, 1983.
Dobson, Christopher; Miller, John and Payne, Ronald: *The Falklands Conflict.* Coronet, 1982.
English, Adrian with Watts, Anthony: *Battle for the Falklands (2) Naval Forces.* Osprey, 1982.
Express, Sunday Magazine: *War in the Falklands: The Campaign in Pictures.* Weidenfleld, 1982.
Fitz-Gibbon, Spencer: *Not mentioned in despatches.* The Lutterworth Press, Cambridge, 1995.
Fowler, William: *Battle for the Falklands (1) Land Forces.* Osprey, 1982.

Fox, Robert: *Antarctica and the South Atlantic*. BBC Publications, 1985.

Fox, Robert: *Eyewitness Falklands*. Methuen, 1982.

Franks, The Rt Hon The Lord (Chairman): *Falkland Islands Review. Report of a Committee of Privy Counsellors*. HMSO, 1983.

Frost, John: *2 Para Falklands, The Battalion at War*. Buchan & Enright, 1983.

Gamba, Virginia: *The Falklands/Malvinas War*. Allen & Unwin, Boston, 1987.

Geraghty, Tony: *This is the SAS - Who Dares Wins*. Warner Books, London 1980-1992.

Goebel, Julius: *The Struggle for the Falkland Islands* (Introduced by Metford, J. C. J.). Yale University Press, 1982.

Gordon Smith: *Battles of the Falkland War*. Ian Allan, London, 1989.

Greenberg, Susan and Smith, Graham: *Media Freedom and the Falklands*. Campaign for Press and Broadcasting Freedom, 1983.

Hands, Jeremy and McGowan, Robert: *Don't Cry for Me, Sergeant-Major*. Future/MacDonald, 1983.

Hanrahan, Brian and Fox, Robert: *I Counted Them All Out and I Counted Them All Back*. BBC Publications, 1982.

Harris, Robert: *Gotcha! The Media, The Government and the Falklands Crisis*. Faber, 1983.

Hastings, Max and Jenkins, Simon: *The Battle for the Falklands*. Michael Joseph, 1983.

Higgins, Jack: *Exocet* (a novel). Collins, 1983.

HMSO: *The Falkland Islands: The Facts*. 1982.

HMSO: *The Falklands Campaign*: a Digest of Debates in the House of Commons 2 April to 15 June, 1982. 1983.

HMSO: *The British Army in the Falklands, 1982* (Introduction by General Sir John Stanier). 1983.

HMSO: *Falkland Islands Report on the Proceedings of the Foreign Affairs Committee* (2 vols). 1984.

Ingrams, Richard and Wells, John: *My Round!* Private Eye/André Deutsch, 1983.

Jolly, Rick: *The Red and Green Life Machine: A Diary of the Falklands Field Hospital*. Century Publishing, 1982.

Kitson, Linda: *The Falklands War: A Visual Diary*. Mitchell Beazley/Imperial War Museum, 1982.

Kon, Daniel: *Los chicos de la guerra*. New English Library, 1983.

Laffin, John: *Battle for the Falklands*. Sphere Books, 1982.

Latin America Bureau: *Falklands/Malvinas: Whose Crisis?* 1982.

Latin American Newsletters: *The Falklands War: The Official History*. Official Communiqués (English and Spanish). April 1983.

Lord Franks: *Falkland Islands Review (Franks Report)*. HMSO, London, 1983

Marshall Cavendish: *The Falklands War*. (Series in 14 weekly parts). 1983.

Middlebrook, Martin: *The fight for the "Malvinas"*. Penguin Books, London, 1989.

Miller, Robert: *Liability or Asset - A policy for the Falkland Islands*. Occasional Papers 22. Inst for European Defence and Strategic Studies, London, 1986.

Minority Rights Group: *Diego García: A Contrast to the Falklands*. Report N° 54, August 1982.

Monnery, David: *Soldier "K" SAS. Mission to Argentina*. 22 books. London, 1994. New

Left Review N° 134. *Iron Britannia* (Special Issue). July-August 1982.

Peace Study Briefings N° 19. *An Assessment of Argentine Rearmament.* School of Peace Studies, University of Bradford, January 1985.

Pearce, Joan (ed.): *The Falkland Islands Dispute: International Dimensions.* Chatham House, 1982.

Perrett, Bryan: *Weapons of the Falklands Conflict.* 1982.

Ponting, Clive: *The Right to Know: The Inside Story of the Belgrano Affair.* Sphere, 1985.

Preston, Anthony: *Sea Combat off the Falklands. The Lesson That Must Be Learned.* Collins/Willow, 1982.

Report from the House of Commons Defence Committee: *The Handling of the Press and Public Information During the Falklands Conflict* (II vols) Session 1982-83. HMSO. 1983.

Rice, Desmond and Gavshon, Arthur: *The Sinking of the Belgrano.* Secker and Warburg, 1984.

Shackleton, The Rt Hon Lord (Chairman): *Falkland Islands Economic Study 1982.* HMSO. 1982.

Smith, John: *74 days: An Islander's Diary of the Falklands' Occupation.* Century. 1984.

Speed, Keith: *Sea Change: The Battle for the Falklands and the Future of Britain's Navy.* Ashgrove Press, 1982.

Sunday Times Insight Team: *The Falklands War.* André Deutsch, 1982.

Tinker, David: *A Message from the Falklands.* Junction Books, 1982.

Underwood, Geoffrey: *Our Falklands War. The Men of the Task Force Tell Their Story.* Introduction by General Sir Jeremy Moore. Cornwall: Maritime Books. 1983.

van der Byl, Nicholas & Hannon, Paul: *Argentine forces in the Falklands.* Osprey Military Men-at-Arms Series N° 250. London, 1992.

Winchester, Simon: *Prison Diary, Argentina.* Chatto and Windus, 1983.

Woolf, Cecil and Moorcroft Wilson, Jean (eds): *Authors Take Sides on the Falklands.* Cecil Woolf, 1982.

SOME USEFUL ARTICLES

Beck, Peter J.: "Research problems in studying Britain's Latin American past: the case of the Falklands dispute 1920-1950", *Bulletin of Latin American Research.* 1983.

Beck, Peter J.: "Britain's Antarctic dimension", *International Affairs* 59 (3) 1983.

Calvert, Peter: "Sovereignty and the Falkland Crisis".

Collier, Simon: "The First Falklands War? Argentine Attitudes".

Deas, Malcolm: "Falklands title deeds", *London Review of Books* 19 August 1982.

Freedman, Lawrence: "Bridgehead revisited: the literature of the Falklands", *International Affairs* 59 (3) 1983.

George, Bruce and Little, Walter: "Options in the Falklands-Malvinas dispute", *South Atlantic Council Occasional Papers, N° 1,* London, April 1985.

Menaul, Stewart: "Lessons from the Falklands Campaign", *Foreign Affairs Research Institute.* 1982.

Parsons, Anthony: "The Falklands crisis in the United Nations, 31 March-14 June 1982", *International Affairs* 59 (2) 1983.

Smith, John: *74 Days.* Century Publishing Co., London, 1984.
Spence, J. E.: "The Falklands conflict and South Atlantic policies", *Optima* 31 (3) September 1983.
Terragno, Rodolfo: "Falklands futures", *London: Commonwealth Institute.* 1983.
Ware, Richard: "The Case of Antonio Rivero and Sovereignty over the Falkland Islands." *The Historical Journal,* 27/4, (1984).
Wheatcroft, Geoffrey: "The Fighting and the writing", *Times Literary Supplement,* 13 May 1983.

THEATRE AND TELEVISION
"The Falklands War", Thames Television.
"The Falkland Factor", BBC Television, 26 April 1982.
"Malvinas: Story of Betrayals", Channel 4 Television, 5 December 1983.
"Falklands Sound/Voces de Malvinas", The Royal Court Theatre Upstairs, 3 June 1983. Max Stafford-Clark (dir.).

PUBLISHED SOURCES RELATING TO THE FALKLANDS WAR

"ACORN: Argentinian Accounts of the Landings at Port San Carlos on 21 May 1982", *BAR,* August, 1987.
Adkin, Maj (Retd) M.: *The Last Eleven?,* chapter 10 of draft of book.
Adkin, M.: *Goose Green: A battle is fought to be won.* Leo Cooper, London, 1983.
Arthur, M.: *Above All, Courage.* Sphere, London, 1986.
Bailey RA, Maj J.: "Training for War: The Falklands 1982" *BAR* 73. April, 1983.
Belgrano Enquiry: *The unnecessary war: proceedings of the Belgrano Enquiry.* Spokesman, Nottingham, 1988.
Bilton, M. and Kosminsky, P.: *Speaking Out: Untold stories from the Falklands war.* André Deutsch, London, 1989.
Bishop, P. and Witherow, J.: *The Winter War: The Falklands.* Quartet, London, 1982.
Brown, D.: *The Royal Navy and the Falklands War.* Leo Cooper, London, 1987.
Calvi Report: The official Argentinian military report of the Falklands/Malvinas war. "Calvi 1" here refers to the British MoD"s translation: "Calvi 2" refers to that part not translated by MoD but supplied to me in Spanish and translated in Manchester by Saul Belmar.
Carrizo Salvadores, Maj CE: "The Fight on Mount Longdon", an article originally in *Malvinas: relatos de soldados.* Buenos Aires, 1983; translated by the Defence Languages Centre. RAEC Centre, Beaconsfield, and published in *Pegasus,* the journal of The Parachute Regiment (late 1980s).
Defence Looks at the Falklands Conflict: a Defence Special. November 1982.
Ethell, J. and Price, A.: *Air War South Atlantic.* Sidgwick and Jackson, London, 1983
Field RHG/D, Capt RAK: "A vignette of the Falklands as a watchkeeper, infanteer and

car commander". *Guards Magazine* (date unknown).

Fitz-Gibbon PhD, Spencer: "Manoeuvre war and vital ground: A study of military structure and function in the mobile defensive battle". *BAR*. December, 1993.

Fox, R.: *Eyewitness Falklands: A Personal account of the Falklands campaign.* Methuen, London, 1982.

Frost, Maj Gen J., 2 Para Falklands: *The Battalion at War.* Sphere, London, 1983.

Fursdon, E., Maj Gen CB MBE DLit: *The Falklands Aftermath: Picking Up the Pieces.* Leo Cooper, London, 1988.

Hastings, M. and Jenkins, S.: *The Battle of the Falklands.* Pan, London, 1983.

Jones RTR, Lt Col Andrew: "British Armour in the Falklands", *Armour* (USA) vol XCII N° 2, March-April, 1983.

Laffin, J.: *Fight for the Falklands!* Sphere, London, 1982.

McManners, Hugh: *Falklands Commando.* Grafton, London, 1987.

McManners, Hugh: *The scars of war.* Harper Collins, London, 1993.

Middlebrook, M.: *Task Force: The Falklands War, 1982.* Penguin, London, 1987. (Originally published as *Operation Corporate: The Story of the Falklands War, 1982.* Viking, 1985).

Middlebrook, M.: *The Fight for the "Malvinas": The Argentine Forces in the Falklands War.* Viking, London, 1989.

Morgan RA, Maj M.J. (BC 148(Meiktila) Commando Forward Observation Battery RA during Operation Corporate): "Naval gunfire support for Operation Corporate 1982" (source of publication unknown).

Moro, R.: *The South Atlantic Conflict: The War for the Malvinas.* Praeger, New York, 1989.

Neame RA, Maj N.: "Some thoughts on out of area operations: gunner contribution and command arrangements", *Royal Artillery Journal* vol CXI N° 1, March 1984.

Price MD, US Army Medical Corps. Capt H.H.: "The Falklands: Rate of British Psychiatric Combat Casualties Compared to Recent American Wars". *Journal of the Royal Army Medical Corps* vol 130 N° 2, June 1984.

Rodríguez Mottino, Col (R) Horacio: extracts from his book *La Artillería Argentina en Malvinas*, published in *El Artillería*, Montevideo, year 1 N° 2 May 1986; translated by Col R.D.Garnett, British defence attaché in Montevideo, as "Experiences of the Argentine field artillery in the Falklands war 1982".

Secretary of State for Defence: *The Falklands Campaign: The Lessons.* HMSO, London, 1982.

Stewart, N.K.: *South Atlantic Conflict of 1982: A Case Study in Military Cohesion.* Research Report 1469, US Army Research Institute for the Behavioral and Social Sciences, 1988.

Stewart, N.K.: *Mates and Muchachos: Unit Cohesion in the Falklands/Malvinas War.* Brassey's, Washington, 1991.

Summers Jr, US Army, Col Harry G.: "Yomping to Port Stanley", *Military Review* (USA) vol LXIV N° 3, March 1984.

Thompson RM, Brig J.: *No Picnic, 3 Commando Brigade in the South Atlantic.* Pen & Sword Brooks, 1982.

Waring RA, Lt M.: "Into Action with Black Eight". *Royal Artillery Journal* (?) 1982.

Washington, L. (ed): *Ten years on the British army in the Falklands war.* National Army Museum, London, 1992.

BIBLIOGRAPHY

GENERAL AND POLITICAL

Cawkwell, Mary: *The Falkland Story 1592-1982.* Anthony Nelson, 1983.

Coll, Alberto R. and Arend, Anthony C., editors: *The Falklands War: Lessons for Strategy, Diplomacy and International Law.* George Allen and Unwin, 1985.

Daynes, John A.: *The Forces Postal History of the Falkland Islands and the Task Force.* The Forces Postal History Society, 1983.

Fox, Robert: *Antarctica and the South Atlantic: Discovery, Development and Dispute.* British Broadcasting Corporation, 1985.

Goebel, Julius: *The Struggle for the Falkland Islands: A Study in Legal and Diplomatic History.* Yale University Press, 1982.

Hastings, Max and Jenkins, Simon: *The Battle for the Falklands.* Michael Joseph, 1983.

Headland, Robert: *The Island of South Georgia.* Cambridge University Press, 1984.

HMSO: *Falkland Islands Review: Report of a Committee of Privy Counsellors* (The Franks Report), 1983.

HMSO, Foreign and Commonwealth Office: *The Disputed Islands, The Falklands Crisis: A History and Background.*

HMSO, House of Commons: *The Falklands Campaign: A Digest of Debates in the House of Commons 2 April - 15 June 1982.* 1982.

HMSO: *The Falkland Islands: The Facts.* 1982.

HMSO: *The Falklands Campaign: The Lessons.* 1982.

Middlebrook, Martin: *Task Force: The Falklands War, 1982* (Revised edition). Penguin Books, 1987.

Smith, John: *74 Days, An Islander's Diary of the Falklands Occupation.* Century Publishing, 1984.

Strange, Ian J.: *The Falkland Islands,* 3rd edition. David and Charles, 1983.

Sunday Express Magazine Team: *War in the Falklands: The Campaign in Pictures.* Weidenfeld and Nicolson, 1982.

Sunday Times Insight Team: *The Falklands War: The Full Story.* Andre Deutsch, 1982.

Way, Peter, editor: *The Falklands War in 14 parts.* Marshall Cavendish, 1983.

Whitakers Almanac, 1983.

MILITARY AND COMBINED OPERATIONS

Arthur, Max: *Above All, Courage: The Falklands Front Line: First-hand Accounts.* Sidgwick and Jackson, 1985.

Fox, Robert: *Eyewitness Falklands: A Personal Account of the Falklands Campaign.*

Methuen, 1982.

Jolly, Rick: *The Red and Green Life Machine: A Diary of the Falklands Field Hospital.* Century, 1983.

Kitson, Linda (The Official War Artist): *The Falklands War: A visual Diary.* Michael Beazley, 1982.

McGowan, Robert and Hands, Jeremy: *Don't Cry for Me Sergeant Major.* Futura, 1983.

Perrett, Bryan: *Weapons of the Falklands Conflict.* Blandford Press, 1982.

Supplement to *The London Gazette,* 8 October 1982 (British gallantry awards).

AVIATION, INCLUDING NAVAL

Braybrook, Roy: *Battle for the Falklands (3) Air Forces, Osprey "Men-at-Arms"* Series, 1982.

Braybrook, Roy: *British Aerospace: Harrier and Sea Harrier.* Osprey Publishing, 1984.

Burden, Rodney A.; Draper, Michael I.; Rough, Douglas A.; Smith, Colin R. and Wilton, David L.: *Falklands: The Air War.* British Aviation Research Group, 1986.

Ethell, Jeffrey and Price, Alfred: *Air War: South Atlantic.* Sidgwick and Jackson, 1984.

LAND FORCES, INCLUDING MARINES

Fowler, William: *Battle for the Falklands (1), Land Forces.* Osprey "Men-at-Arms" Series, 1982.

Frost, Maj-Gen John: *2 PARA, Falklands: The Battalion at War.* Buchan and Enright, 1983.

Gander, Terry: *Encyclopaedia of the Modern British Army.* Patrick Stephens, 2nd edition, 1982.

Geraghty, Tony: *This is the SAS: A Pictorial History of the Special Air Service Regiment.* Arms and Armour Press, 1982.

HMSO: *The British Army in the Falklands 1982.* 1983.

Keegan, John: *World Armies.* MacMillan, 1983.

Ladd, James D.: *SBS: The Invisible Raiders: The History of the Special Boat Squadron from World War 2 to the Present.* Arms and Armour Press, 1983.

McManners, Capt Hugh, Royal Artillery: *Falklands Commando.* William Kimber, 1984.

Strawson, John: *A History of the SAS Regiment.* Secker and Warburg, 1984.

Thompson, Julian: *No Picnic: 3 Commando Brigade in the South Atlantic: 1982.* Secker and Warburg, 1985.

Vaux, Nick: *March to the South Atlantic: 42 Commando Royal Marines in the Falklands War.* Buchan and Enright, 1986.

Weeks, Col John: *Jane's Pocket Book: Armies of the World.* Janes, 1981.

NAVAL AND MARITIME

Beaver, Paul: *Modern Combat Ships 2, "Invincible" Class.* Ian Allan, 1984.

BP Shipping Ltd: *Operation Corporate: BP Shipping Ltd's Involvement in the Falkland Island Crisis 1982.* 1982.

Brown, David: *The Royal Navy and the Falklands War.* Leo Cooper, 1987.

Director of Naval Air Warfare: *Flight Deck, The Fleet Air Arm Quarterly: Falklands Edition.*

Ministry of Defence, 1982 (Journal).

English, Adrian and Watts, Anthony: *Battle for the Falklands (2), Naval forces.* Osprey "Men-at-Arms" Series, 1982.

Hill, Rear-Adm J. R. RN: *The Royal Navy: Today and Tomorrow.* Ian Allan, 1982.

Gavshon, Arthur and Rice, Desmond: *The Sinking of the "Belgrano".* Secker and Warburg, 1984.

Jane's Fighting Ships, 1981/82.

Koburger, Jnr, Charles W.: *Sea Power in the Falklands.* Praeger, 1983.

Lockett, Andrew; Munro, Neil and Wells, David, editors: *HMS Endurance 1981-82 Deployment: A Season of Conflict.* Andrew Lockett, 1983.

Marriot, Leo: *Modern Combat Ships 3, type 42.* Ian Allan, 1985.

Meyer, Cdr C. J., OBE, RN: *Modern Combat ships 1, "Leander" Class.* Ian Allan, 1984.

P & O Steam Navigation Company: *P & O in the Falklands: A Pictorial Record, 5th April - 25th September 1982.* 1982.

Preston, Anthony: *Sea Combat off the Falklands.* Willow Books, 1982.

Ross, P. J. (editor): *HMS Invincible: The Falklands Deployment 2nd April - 17th September 1982,* privately printed. 1983.

Royal Fleet Auxiliary Service: *The RFA in the Falklands* (Journal).

Speed, Keith: *Sea Change: The Battle for the Falklands and the Future of Britain's Navy.* Ashgrove Press, 1982.

Tinker, Hugh, compiled by: *A Message from the Falklands: The Life and Gallant Death of David Tinker, Lt RN.* Junction Books, 1982.

Villar, Capt Roger: *Merchant Ships at War: The Falklands Experience.* Conway Maritime Press, 1984.

INDEX